INTERSECTIONAL FEMINIST RESEARCH METHODOLOGIES

Intersectional Feminist Research Methodologies: Applications in the Social Sciences and Humanities is a multi-disciplinary volume in which emerging and established scholars present new feminist research methods and re-evaluate existing approaches.

This collection examines how both new and established feminist methods address intersecting identities and structures of inequality, including gender, race, sexuality, and class. Each chapter provides a case study of a methodology or methodologies that have been adopted, developed, or adapted within the author's field – including sociology, criminology, political science, history, literature, and performance studies. The volume articulates the importance of knowledge production that arises from the situated and lived experiences of individuals, groups, and communities. It discusses how we survive as feminists in today's neoliberal universities, and includes research on trans and nonbinary people, Indonesian history and the #MeToo movement, world-literature from the Philippines, memory work, and crime on the London transport network. The contributors engage with intersectionality in different ways but collectively they demonstrate the pervasiveness of intersectional thinking and practice in feminist scholarship today.

Intersectional Feminist Research Methodologies will be of value to both undergraduate and graduate students conducting research, as well as doctoral researchers and more established feminist researchers.

Jennifer Cooke is Reader in Contemporary Literature and Theory at Loughborough University, UK.

Line Nyhagen is Professor of Sociology at Loughborough University, UK, and Adjunct Professor at Western Norway University of Applied Sciences, Bergen, Norway.

INTERSECTIONAL FEMINIST RESEARCH METHODOLOGIES

Applications in the Social Sciences and Humanities

Edited by Jennifer Cooke and Line Nyhagen

Designed cover image: wildpixel / Getty Images

First published 2025
by Routledge
4 Park Square, Milton Park, Abingdon, Oxon OX14 4RN

and by Routledge
605 Third Avenue, New York, NY 10158

Routledge is an imprint of the Taylor & Francis Group, an informa business

© 2025 selection and editorial matter, Jennifer Cooke and Line Nyhagen; individual chapters, the contributors

The right of Jennifer Cooke and Line Nyhagen to be identified as the authors of the editorial material, and of the authors for their individual chapters, has been asserted in accordance with sections 77 and 78 of the Copyright, Designs and Patents Act 1988.

The Open Access version of this book, available at www.taylorfrancis.com, has been made available under a Creative Commons Attribution-Non Commercial-No Derivatives (CC-BY-NC-ND) 4.0 license.

Any third party material in this book is not included in the OA Creative Commons license, unless indicated otherwise in a credit line to the material. Please direct any permissions enquiries to the original rightsholder.

Trademark notice: Product or corporate names may be trademarks or registered trademarks, and are used only for identification and explanation without intent to infringe.

British Library Cataloguing-in-Publication Data
A catalogue record for this book is available from the British Library

ISBN: 978-1-032-50770-5 (hbk)
ISBN: 978-1-032-50769-9 (pbk)
ISBN: 978-1-003-39957-5 (ebk)

DOI: 10.4324/9781003399575

Typeset in Sabon
by Deanta Global Publishing Services, Chennai, India

An electronic version of this book is freely available, thanks to the support of libraries working with Knowledge Unlatched (KU). KU is a collaborative initiative designed to make high quality books Open Access for the public good. The Open Access ISBN for this book is 978-1-003-39957-5. More information about the initiative and links to the Open Access version can be found at www.knowledgeunlatched.org.

CONTENTS

Contributors		*vii*
Acknowledgements		*x*
	Introduction *Jennifer Cooke and Line Nyhagen*	1
1	Living and researching embodied intersectionality: Heidi Safia Mirza in conversation with Line Nyhagen *Heidi Safia Mirza and Line Nyhagen*	13
2	The play's the thing: Using creative methods to place trans and queer knowledge-making centre stage *Harvey Humphrey*	29
3	Decolonising feminism and feminist decolonialism: The case of the #MeToo movement in Indonesia *Soe Tjen Marching*	47
4	Understanding sexual harassment on public transport through feminist epistemologies and intersectional rhythmanalysis *Sian Lewis*	63

vi Contents

5 On the creation of new ecological writing: Alycia
Pirmohamed in conversation with Jennifer Cooke 79
Alycia Pirmohamed and Jennifer Cooke

6 Memory work as a collaborative intersectional feminist
research method 98
Line Nyhagen and Jackie Goode

7 Ageing, care, and women's work: A world-systems
feminist approach to Filipina literature 114
Jennifer Cooke and Demi Wilton

8 Becoming a strongwoman: An auto/ethnographic study
of the pursuit of strength, power, and gender aesthetics 129
Hannah J.H. Newman

9 The archival is personal is political: Historiography,
the archive, and feminist research methods 145
Charlotte Riley

10 Conducting survey research while a feminist: Taking
intersectional and decolonial approaches 160
Shan-Jan Sarah Liu

11 Close reading: Critical feminist method and pedagogical
process 176
Sophia Kier-Byfield

12 Cultivating a 'feminist reflexive sensibility' in
social research: A re-evaluation of reflexivity and
intersectionality in the neoliberal academy 189
Karen Lumsden

13 Location, contradiction, ambivalence: Feminist
methodologies within and beyond the university 205
Olive Demar

Index 221

CONTRIBUTORS

Jennifer Cooke is Reader in Contemporary Literature and Theory at Loughborough University, UK. Her most recent books include *Contemporary Feminist Life-Writing: The New Audacity* (Cambridge University Press, 2020) and the edited collection, *The New Feminist Literary Studies* (CUP, 2020).

Olive Demar is a US-based researcher informed by feminist, Marxist, and psychoanalytic methods. She previously was the editor in chief of *Dance Chronicle*, a scholarly journal for dance research.

Jackie Goode is Visiting Fellow in Qualitative Research at Loughborough University, UK. She edited and contributed to *Clever Girls: Autoethnographies of Class, Gender and Ethnicity* (Palgrave Macmillan, 2019). Her latest book is *Crafting Autoethnography: Processes and Practices of Making Self and Culture* (Routledge, 2023), co-edited with Karen Lumsden and Jan Bradford.

Harvey Humphrey is an activist-academic and occasional poet and is a Lecturer in Social Research Methods at the University of Glasgow, UK, following previous employment at the Universities of Edinburgh, Northumbria, and Strathclyde. They focus on co-production, creative methods, creative practice, ethics, and representation. Their work cuts across queer disability and trans studies.

Sophia Kier-Byfield is a postdoctoral researcher based at the George Ewart Evans Centre for Storytelling, University of South Wales, UK. Her research

viii Contributors

interests include inclusive education, feminist pedagogies, and the wellbeing of survivors of domestic violence.

Sian Lewis is Lecturer in Criminology at the University of Plymouth, UK. Her research examines sexual harassment, gender, fear, and safety in public spaces, focusing specifically on public transport. Her current work applies sensory criminological perspectives to feminist issues.

Shan-Jan Sarah Liu is Senior Lecturer in Gender and Politics at the School of Social and Political Science at the University of Edinburgh, UK. Her research and teaching broadly focus on the way contexts – women's political representation, social movements, immigration, and COVID-19 – shape the gender gaps in public opinion and political behaviour.

Karen Lumsden is a sociologist, criminologist and qualitative researcher at the University of Aberdeen, UK. Her research focuses on policing, victims, and cyber-crime. Publications include the monographs *Boy Racer Culture* (2013) and *Reflexivity: Theory, Method and Practice* (2019) and the edited collections *Crafting Autoethnography* (2023), *Online Othering* (2019), and *Reflexivity in Criminological Research* (2014).

Soe Tjen Marching is Senior Lecturer in the department of Languages, Cultures and Linguistics at SOAS University of London, UK. She is also a creative writer and award-winning composer. She has published several academic books in English and novels in Indonesian.

Heidi Safia Mirza is Emeritus Professor of Equality Studies in Education at UCL Institute of Education, London, UK. A daughter of the Windrush generation from Trinidad, she is known for her pioneering intersectional research on race, gender, and identity in education. She is author of several best-selling books, including *Black British Feminism* (Routledge, 1997) and *Young Female and Black* (Routledge 1992). She co-edited the flagship book, *Dismantling Race in Higher Education: Racism, Whiteness and Decolonising the Academy* (Palgrave Macmillan, 2018).

Hannah J.H. Newman is a researcher in the School of Health and Social Work at the University of Hertfordshire, UK. Their research interests include participation and inclusion in sport, exercise, and physical activity, with a particular focus on LGBTQ+ inclusion and engagement.

Line Nyhagen is Professor of Sociology at Loughborough University, UK, and Adjunct Professor at Western Norway University of Applied Sciences, Bergen, Norway. She has authored the books *Religion, Gender and Citizenship:*

Women of Faith, Gender Equality and Feminism (with Beatrice Halsaa; Palgrave 2016), *Majority-Minority Relations in Contemporary Women's Movements: Strategic Sisterhood* (with Beatrice Halsaa, Palgrave 2012) and *Issues of Gender, Race and Class in the Norwegian Missionary Society in Nineteenth Century Norway and Madagascar* (Edwin Mellen Press 2003).

Alycia Pirmohamed is the author of the poetry collection *Another Way to Split Water* (Polygon, 2022). Her nonfiction debut, *A Beautiful and Vital Place*, won the Nan Shepherd Prize for nature writing in 2023 and is forthcoming with Canongate. Alycia currently teaches creative writing at the University of Cambridge. She has held postdoctoral positions at the University of Liverpool and the University of Edinburgh, where she also gained her PhD.

Charlotte Lydia Riley is Associate Professor of Twentieth-Century British History at the University of Southampton, UK. Her recent book is *Imperial Island: A History of Empire in Modern Britain* (Bodley Head, 2023). She writes more broadly on histories of the British women's movement, the Labour Party, humanitarianism, and aid.

Demi Wilton is a Lecturer in English Literature at Birmingham City University, UK. Her research is particularly concerned with representations of climate change, migration, and knowledge production in twenty-first-century world-literature. She has served as the ECR and Diversity Officer for the Association of Literature and Environment, UK and Ireland (ASLE-UKI) since June 2021.

ACKNOWLEDGEMENTS

The editors would like to note that the editorial work on this volume was collaborative and shared equally. This includes decisions about what types of research and which researchers to commission, how to structure the book, and the writing of the introduction. Jennifer led on editing the humanities contributions and Line led on editing the social science chapters, but both editors have read and commented upon all chapters and discussed how they fulfil the vision we had for the book. This has been a productive, generative, and feminist collaboration that has sustained both of us during a period when we also had considerable administrative roles, leading our respective departments. To reflect this shared labour, we have listed our names alphabetically.

The editors thank everyone who has been involved in this book since the start of commissioning. Not everyone who started this long journey with us is featured in the final publication, but we appreciate the time and efforts of everyone who was with us along the way. We would also like to thank the co-organisers of and participants in the Feminist Methodologies symposia at Loughborough University, UK, in 2018 and 2019, and acknowledge generous support towards these events from Loughborough University's Advanced Research Methods Institute, the Centre for Research in Communication and Culture, and the Doctoral College.

INTRODUCTION

Jennifer Cooke and Line Nyhagen

Feminist research today is undeniably exciting. As the first book to focus upon intersectional methodological approaches across feminist research in both the social sciences and humanities, this contribution gives a sense of the great variety, but also porousness and adaptability, of the conceptual and methodological work currently being done. Across the social sciences and humanities feminist researchers are using both new and established methodologies to forge fresh understandings of texts and experiences, of social life and the stories we tell about it. It is our contention that there are rich cross-disciplinary benefits to be had from exposing researchers who share the same foundational feminist texts and theories, but who work in different departments and disciplines, to methodologies used in other fields. In the chapters to come, we can see that disciplines are indeed borrowing methodological ideas from each other to productive and insightful ends, and it is our hope that the essays here further stimulate such transdisciplinary fertilisation and knowledge-sharing.

The seeds of this book were initially sown during two research symposia on Feminist Methodologies, the first held in 2018 and the next the following year. These were organised by the multi-disciplinary Gendered Lives Research Group at Loughborough University, UK, which ran from 2015 until 2020 and was chaired by Jennifer Cooke. The two-day symposia were organised by an interdisciplinary group of scholars and doctoral researchers and featured invited academics from a range of social science and humanities backgrounds, who were chosen to present a spectrum of approaches that would spur new thinking and the adoption and adaptation of methodologies by and for disciplines that were less used to encountering them. Then, as now, it was important to us to feature academics at different career stages,

DOI: 10.4324/9781003399575-1

This chapter has been made available under a CC-BY-NC-ND license.

2 Jennifer Cooke and Line Nyhagen

and to be as inclusive as possible, which means enacting a feminism that embraces trans, nonbinary, and intersex experiences. A similar intention underpins this collection, and it is fantastic that we can feature the work of several participants at those original symposia, which seem now, especially after the interruption of the Covid-19 pandemic, like they took place so long ago.

Methods and methodologies

This is not a textbook, even while it presents and explores different methodologies. Readers will not necessarily learn in detail how to implement a particular methodology in these pages. It is a book by researchers for researchers, whether they are professors, mid- or early-career, or working towards their doctorate. Here, those who employ feminist methods and theories present case studies of their work, discuss advantages and limitations of specific methodologies, and, in some chapters, reflect more broadly on their discipline's methodological commitments and blind spots. When we commissioned work for the book, we asked contributors to consider a series of questions which would help them to speak specifically to the concerns that are affecting the academy at this time. They were:

1. What feminist epistemologies and/or theoretical perspectives or concepts anchor your work?
2. How does your research develop and engage with feminist methodologies or adapt a methodology to feminist ends?
3. How does your feminist methodological approach and research address gender and intersecting social structures and identities (e.g. 'race', age, ethnicity, gender, sexuality, class, disability)?
4. How and what can feminist methodologies contribute to social critique that addresses contemporary forms of inequality and social justice issues? (e.g., #MeToo, Black Lives Matter, and decolonisation movements, anti-poverty campaigns, physical and mental health).

Our contributors have taken up these questions as they speak to their disciplines and individual research projects but have done so organically rather than schematically: the questions have not been used to structure chapters or inform chapter sections, for example. Instead, they have operated more like guiding principles that underpin the presentation of research and its discussion by each author. For us, one element of the richness of this volume is that each chapter both discusses a different methodology or methodologies and at the same time does so in the way most appropriate to that discussion and the discipline within which the author is working, rather than to a predetermined structure set by us as editors. Different disciplinary conventions are therefore evident throughout, which is instructive: how one discipline produces its research has much to teach another, and vice versa, and we all gain a greater perspective on the advantages and limitations of our own disciplinary norms by observing how research findings, insights, analysis, and discussions are presented in other parts of the academy.

The title of this book signals that it is about 'intersectional feminist research methodologies', yet it also discusses intersectional and feminist uses of specific research methods. Crucially, United States of America (US) sociologist Patricia Hill Collins (2019, 152) argues that '[t]here are no inherently "intersectional" methodologies or methods' and counsels that 'intersectionality's core premises [...] can influence methodological choices within intersectional scholarship' (see also Misra et al., 2021). As noted by British sociologist Caroline Ramazanoğlu (2002), 'methodology' and 'method' are often confused. A research method 'simply refers to techniques and procedures used for exploring social reality and producing evidence (such as ethnography, interviews, observations, focus groups, questionnaires, life histories, documentary analysis, laboratory experiments, analysis of texts, objects or images)' (Ramazanoğlu 2002, 11). All the chapters herein engage with one or more research method while seeking to make explicit how the method has enabled an intersectional lens and/or how an intersectional lens has enhanced the method. A methodology, on the other hand,

> comprises rules that specify how social investigation should be approached. Each methodology links a particular *ontology* (for example, a belief that gender is social rather than natural) and a particular *epistemology* (a set of procedures for establishing what counts as knowledge) in providing *rules* that specify how to produce *valid knowledge of social reality* (for example, the real nature of particular gender relations; e.g., feminist knowledge deemed as 'better' than patriarchal knowledge).
>
> *(Ramazanoğlu 2002, 11)*

All the chapters in our volume engage with methodology, including ontological and epistemological issues. Ontologically, they share the notion that social structures and identities are changeable, rather than fixed, and that power relations (including discursive and material forms of power) shape the conditions in which people are enabled to live well, thrive, and pursue their dreams. Epistemologically, the chapters articulate the importance of knowledge production that arises from the situated and lived experiences of individuals, groups, and communities in different contexts. The chapters also share a feminist commitment to activism and social justice that moves beyond gender justice to encompass justice for groups that are minoritised due to their 'race', ethnicity, indigeneity, nationality, class, religion, sexuality, disability, and age. Building on New Zealand Māori scholar Linda

Tuhiwai Smith's (2012) work, Collins (2019, 144) suggests that '[o]ne way of conceptualizing intersectionality is to see it as a methodology for decolonizing knowledge'. As such, she counsels that existing power relations within Western epistemologies must be scrutinised, deconstructed, and decolonised and that the validation of knowledge claims must be based on more inclusive and democratic practices. The ways in which the chapters in this volume engage with intersectionality differ across methodologies, methods, and forms of critical inquiry. Collectively, they demonstrate both the pervasiveness of intersectional thinking in feminist scholarship and its diverse expressions.

Careful attention to specific historical, geographical, and socio-political contexts is a key element of intersectional analyses. In our editorial practice, we have asked each author to avoid 'writing from nowhere' or from a universal perspective by providing background information about the main scholars they address. This includes making clear the geographical location, discipline, and, at times, the gender and/or racialised identities of referenced scholars. Such writing practices enable the author to demonstrate awareness of academic subject positions and hierarchies and give the reader insights into how literatures are situated, including locations of knowledge production and citation practices.

Definitions of intersectionality

Academic literature on intersectionality itself produces and reproduces histories and genealogies about the origins of intersectionality, and these are in turn contested, as Heidi Safia Mirza's and Sophia Kier-Byfield's contributions to this volume particularly highlight. Some scholarly works tend to discuss intersectionality as if it originated almost exclusively via social activism and academic scholarship in the US, thus ignoring and silencing contributions from other parts of the world. Moreover, and most notably within literature on intersectionality stemming from the US, there are contestations about who has contributed what and when to the canon of intersectionality (see, e.g., Hancock 2016; Nash 2019). For example, while one may state that Kimberlé Crenshaw 'coined' the concept of intersectionality in 1989, alternative narratives, such as those offered by Collins and Bilge (2016) and Hancock (2016), emphasise the importance of a long durée perspective that acknowledges intersectional social activism and earlier academic contributions. Important activist moments range from African American abolitionist and women's right activist Sojourner Truth's 'Ain't I A Woman' speech at the Ohio Women's Rights Convention in 1851 to the Combahee River Collective's 'A Black Feminist Statement' from 1977, which addresses 'how systemic oppressions of racism, patriarchy and capitalism interlock' (Collins and Bilge 2016, 67; see also Hancock 2016, 30, for references to earlier historical works). Momentous contributions from US academics and activists include Black feminists bell hooks's *Ain't I A Woman: Black Women and Feminism* (1982), Angela Davis's *Women, Race, and Class* (1981), Audre Lorde's *Sister Outsider* (1984), Crenshaw's articles (1989 and 1991), and Collins's *Black Feminist Thought* (1991).

In addition to pioneer activism and works by Black feminists, other US-based women of colour have also contributed significantly to the intersectionality canon from the 1970s and onwards, including Chicana and Latina, Asian-American, and indigenous Native-American women (e.g. Moraga and Anzaldúa 1983; for further examples see Collins and Bilge 2016, 71–75). Notably, Black feminist and political theorist Ange-Marie Hancock (2016) also credits activists and scholars located in different times and spaces across the world with what she calls 'intersectionality-like thought' (24), highlighting the works of Egyptian-born Nawal El Sadaawi (1980), Senegalese-born Awa Thiam (1986), and the Indian-born Gayatri Spivak (1988), Chandra Talpade Mohanty (1988), and Uma Narayan (1997). Furthermore, intersectional thinking spread globally in connection with the United Nation's (UN) Fourth World Conference on Women in Beijing, 1995, and via feminist preparations (with contributions by Crenshaw) for the UN's World Conference Against Racism in Durban, South Africa, 2001 (Collins and Bilge 2016, 89–91). The wider global history of intersectionality is yet to be written and is sure to include a multitude of marginalised and minoritised voices, including indigenous and migrant women across countries, world regions, and continents.

There is also a significant history of activist and scholarly engagement with intersectionality in Great Britain. For example, Black and Asian women united under the banner of Black feminism in the Organization of Women of Asian and African Descent (OWAAD, 1978–1983; see Bryan, Dadzie and Scafe 1985; see also Mirza with Nyhagen, this volume). They also mobilised together in Southall Black Sisters (1979-), an organisation 'for Asian and Afro-Caribbean Women' (Southall Black Sisters 1990). These and other women's organisations have worked intersectionally in different ways, advocating for the necessity of simultaneously analysing gender and 'race' and their relations to, e.g., class, religion, and/or sexuality. Pioneering scholarly writings articulating intersectional perspectives on inequalities and identities include: Amrit Wilson's *Finding a Voice: Asian Women in Britain* (1978); Hazel Carby's *White Woman Listen! Black Feminism and the Boundaries of Sisterhood* (1982); Floya Anthias and Nira Yuval-Davis's 1983 *Feminist Review* article on ethnicity, gender and class; Beverley Bryan, Stella Dadzie, and Suzanne Scafe's *The Heart of the Race: Black Women's Lives in Britain* (1985); and Mirza's *Young, Female and Black* (1992) (see also Mirza's 1997 collection of writings on Black British feminism). In her work, Carby (1982) argued that Black women's lived experiences represent a 'triple oppression' in which gender, race, and class are interconnected. In a powerful critique of the marginalisation of Black women in White feminist theory and activism, Carby discussed how concepts such as the family, patriarchy, and reproduction have different meanings for Black and White women, as Black women's experiences are deeply intertwined with histories and legacies of slavery, colonialism, and imperialism as well as with state authoritarianism and racism. Carby thus called for feminism to be transformed through the application of an intersectional lens on women's experiences.

As the editors of this volume, we are writing this introductory chapter from our location in the United Kingdom (UK), as British (Cooke) and Norwegian (Nyhagen) scholars, as privileged White employees of a British university, as feminists, as daughters, mothers, and partners, as migrants (Nyhagen), and as White allies in struggles against racism and discrimination. We owe a great debt to all the women activists and scholars who have come before us. This volume is inspired by Black feminist activists and thinkers, and we pay tribute to them. The definition of intersectionality proposed by Patricia Hill Collins and Sirma Bilge constitutes a guiding light for our editorial work:

> Intersectionality is a way of understanding and analyzing the complexity in the world, in people, and in human experiences [...]. When it comes to social inequality, people's lives and the organization of power in a given society are better understood as not being shaped by a single axis of social division, be it race or gender or class, but by many axes that work together and influence each other. Intersectionality as an analytical tool gives people better access to the complexity of the world and of themselves.
>
> *(Collins and Bilge 2016, 2)*

Collins's distinctions between 'the use of metaphoric, heuristic, and paradigmatic thinking within intersectionality' are particularly useful in assessing intersectionality's methodological and theoretical status (2019, 23). The notion of intersectionality as metaphor takes us back to feminist legal scholar Crenshaw's (1989) use of a crossroad or intersection to depict how Black women were made invisible in the American legal system. The metaphor suggested that the intersecting roads of racism, colonialism, and patriarchy combined to marginalise Black working-class women in a legal system which favoured White middle-class men. Collins (2019, 26) suggests that, while metaphors are literary devices, they 'are also important in shaping how people understand and participate in social relations' by serving as 'a foundation of thinking and action'. Furthermore, Collins argues, 'the metaphor of intersectionality as a crossroads works well as a mental map that encourages people to look toward particular intersections in order to guide their intellectual work and political practice' (28–29). The use of intersectionality as a metaphor is visible in several of the chapter contributions to this volume.

Next, Collins discusses the use of intersectionality as a heuristic device that 'offers guidance, as rule of thumb or common practises, for social action' (34). As an example, Collins refers to Crenshaw's use of a 'race/class/gender heuristic' to question the limitations of existing knowledge about violence against women and to produce new knowledge that specifically addresses the experiences of women of colour. Intersectionality as a heuristic also encompasses attention to other forms of inequality and identity categories, including sexuality and age (37). Furthermore, it applies to other fields of inquiry including 'work, family, the media, education, health, and similar fundamental social institutions' (35) and to studies of how our social identities are multi-layered and shifting (37).

Collins also discusses (and confirms) the potential for intersectionality to constitute a paradigm shift:

> When applied to intersectionality, the concept of a paradigm shift suggests that intersectionality convincingly grapples with recognized social problems concerning social inequality and the social problems it engenders; that its heuristics provide new avenues for investigation for studying social inequality; and that it has attracted a vibrant constellation of scholars and practitioners who recognize intersectionality as a form of critical inquiry and praxis.
>
> *(Collins 2019, 42)*

Setting out a list of six core constructs (relationality, power, social inequality, social context, complexity, social justice) and a set of guiding premises concerning systems of power and intersecting power relations, the production of social inequalities along 'race, class, gender, sexuality, nationality, ethnicity, ability and age', and the solving of social problems through intersectional analyses in specific contexts, Collins then argues that intersectionality is a paradigm shift that 'constitutes more a starting point for developing a critical social theory, and not the end point of intersectionality as critical theory' (Collins 2019, 44 and 50). The authors partaking in this volume thus contribute to the co-creation of a global community of scholars who engage with intersectionality as methodology, as method, and as a critical form of inquiry that aims not only to examine social inequalities but also to articulate demands for social justice.

While there is an understanding of intersectionality shared by the scholars in this volume, it is worth noting that intersectionality is taken up and enacted differently depending on the discipline and field. Broadly speaking, a divide exists in this respect between the humanities and social sciences, and this is evident in certain chapters in this volume. While it is not

8 Jennifer Cooke and Line Nyhagen

unusual to find humanities scholars quoting Crenshaw, Collins, or Davis, for example, since these foundational feminist thinkers are also central to many of the discussions that happen in humanities disciplines, there is also a less thoroughly performed originalist impetus than in the social sciences when it comes to tracing concepts to the authors who are perceived to have first proposed them. Thus, 'intersectionality' may well be used in humanities research as a commonly understood term to name how gender, class, 'race', ethnicity, disability, and age are identifiable layers of experience which interact to make discrimination multi-factored, stretch across several different areas of life, and require complex unpacking, but without a corresponding quote or reference to those seen as coining it or elaborating it first. Such acceptance of the term as part of the scaffolding of intellectual ideas in the twenty-first century to the extent that it becomes widely understood is, on the one hand, a sign of its academic usefulness and vigour, its contemporary indispensability. However, the risk of its acceptance into the language of social critique and its theoretical dispersion across various disciplines is that the contributions of Black and other marginalised feminists who gave us the term 'intersectionality' and related concepts, as well as the ideas that lie behind them, are obscured or even erased. In this volume, both Mirza and Kier-Byfield point to how intersectionality is not necessarily embedded well into research and thinking if it is *only* seen as important to quote Crenshaw to establish the term and that there are others working on and with intersectionality who are offering productive refinements and new articulations of our understanding of it.

That said, it is the case here that each of the social science chapters seeks to define intersectionality whereas not all the humanities chapters do. Instead, in some of the humanities chapters, a different approach is taken which starts from the embodiment of the researcher. For example, South Asian poet, writer, and scholar Alycia Pirmohamed writes about the complexity of being a Brown woman in the White British landscape poetry tradition. Her chapter does not mention intersectionality as a term but her analysis of the poetic context in which she operates is an example of intersectional understanding, nevertheless. There is, we believe, space for the inclusion of both types of research knowledge in a volume such as this. As editors, we have striven to ensure diversity in our commissioning. There are contributions from political science and sociology as well as interdisciplinary social science chapters, and we have humanities scholars representing the fields of Creative Writing, Education Studies, English Literature, History, Languages and Culture, and Theatre and Performance Studies. We have also striven to represent a diverse grouping of academic contributors in terms of nationality, 'race', class, gender identity, ethnicity, and academic career stage.

Are there forms of working that seem particularly feminist? Collaboration is a key attribute to many of the different research projects discussed

Introduction **9**

and presented here, whether in the form of collaborative and co-created research methods (Humphrey; Marching; Newman; Nyhagen and Goode; Pirmohamed), co-authored chapters (Cooke and Wilton; Nyhagen and Goode), or the interview form (Mirza with Nyhagen; Pirmohamed with Cooke). Creative methods are not, as one might presume, used only in the humanities. Personal experience is, perhaps unsurprisingly for feminist researchers, of key importance across many of these chapters, whether in the formal methodological commitments of autoethnography (Newman), the calls for a reflexive sensibility (Lumsden; Demar) to underpin what we do, or in the understanding that we take our whole, embodied selves into archives (Riley) and that the experience might thus be as much an affective mission as it is a factual or interpretive one. Collectively, the essays here work across disciplinary boundaries and showcase how methodologies are not simply aligned with the disciplines we might once have assumed they would be.

Chapter summaries

There is more that resonates between and across the social science and humanities chapters in this book than that divides them. We have reflected this in the decision to alternate between chapters from different fields and disciplines rather than splitting the book into two sections. We begin with Mirza's interview with Nyhagen, a wide-ranging reflection from one of sociology's leading professors, whose writing and theorising has been significantly recognised beyond her discipline too. We hear about Mirza's early life and how her experiences honed her sense of social injustice, leading to involvement in activism in the 1970s and 1980s. She discusses her work and its contributions to understandings of intersectionality, especially in how intersectionality should be seen as embodied. Lived experience is central to an understanding of intersectionality, she argues.

Harvey Humphrey's work with trans, nonbinary, and intersex research participants draws directly upon their lived experience and their activism, and employs collaborative creative methods to bring them to the public. Research participants' words were dramatised and staged in a play, which brings research findings to new audiences but also helps with anonymisation through combination – some play characters represent the experience of more than one research participant – and fictionality. In a different context, Soe Tjen Marching also shows that fiction can be a way of voicing experience that is difficult to share otherwise. Marching uses #MeToo's lack of traction in Indonesia to explore the historical and political reasons why there might be silence around sexual harassment and violence in the country. Sexual violence and harassment against women are also at the heart of Sian Lewis's work with the British Transport Police, investigating the reporting

10 Jennifer Cooke and Line Nyhagen

and experience of sexual harassment on the London Underground network. She shows that knowledge gathering needs to respect and take account of the individual's experience of sexual harassment, how this is shaped and facilitated by the rhythms of the transport system, and the institutional and formal systems of crime recording undertaken by the police. Movement is important in a different way to poet and scholar Alycia Pirmohamed, who discusses in an interview with Jennifer Cooke the centrality of collaboration in the research endeavour to her creative writing, focusing in on several examples of landscape poetry. Attentive to being in the landscape, and what that means in terms of location, post-coloniality, and racialisation, Pirmohamed showcases how creativity can be stretched and challenged through collaborative projects.

If the interview is also a form of collaboration, as Chapters 1 and 5 showcase, then Nyhagen and Jackie Goode's chapter on memory work details and performs, through its co-authorship, several other ways that co-creation and collaboration can inform research knowledge. Memory work is a methodology that uses stories of the self that are gathered from a group of participants who have agreed on a theme to then, through analysis, identify the social structures that sit beneath our quotidian and often individualised experiences to reveal more pervasive themes and preoccupations that emerge from the collective. Research material is thus co-created and collectively analysed in a methodology that clearly follows a feminist interest in intersectionality and what the personal reveals about wider social structures. In their co-authored chapter, Cooke and Demi Wilton provide a case study of short fiction by women from the Philippines to combine a feminist appraisal of gendered care with world-systems analysis, originally a theory from political science that helps understand the local as a peripheral product of the dominant global. That care work is gendered and that it is accompanied with a raft of assumptions about what women should and should not be doing continues to be the case across hugely varied contexts and geographical locations. Assumptions about gender are also part of Hannah Newman's analysis, underpinned by an auto/ethnographic study of strongwoman culture. Participants experience their involvement in the sport as requiring them to engage with gendered assumptions – their own and others – about what women should look like and what constitutes a 'feminine' appearance, even while they relish the challenge that strongwoman training and competitions entail.

The next two chapters provide reflections on feminist work in their traditionally male-centric subject areas, history and political science. Charlotte Riley reflects on how history, often seen as the discipline that provides the factual narratives of powerful men of the past, has responded to calls for intersectionality. This includes studying a wider range of historical figures and groups and affirms the need for the researcher to take her whole self into the archives: archival work is embodied and affective, Riley argues, not just neutral fact-finding. Shan-Jan Sarah Liu's chapter reflects on the perception that survey work, quantitative research with either existing or bespoke survey data, is positivist and therefore outside the scope of a feminist agenda. Instead, she argues that it is indeed possible to be a feminist political scientist working with large-scale data and simultaneously committed to intersectionality and de-colonization: there are challenges but there are also mitigations, Liu shows.

Our final three chapters reflect upon feminism itself and how it operates within the academy. Kier-Byfield's examination of and advocacy for close reading as a methodology also engages with a topic highly pertinent to this book: the debates within feminist scholarship over how important it is to continually return to 'origin' texts or whether a concept like intersectionality can develop new angles as it is used in alternative contexts and fields. Karen Lumsden reminds us of how inhospitable the neoliberal university can be to feminist methodologies and research, which often take time and require emotional labour (see Hochschild 1983). Finally, Olive Demar looks at how we can reinvigorate our research within the academy so that it is beneficial to social justice feminism beyond the university, offering practical guidance on how we can ensure that our research projects have meaning and are properly committed to enabling feminist flourishing in all the spaces we inhabit, institutional and otherwise. Collectively, these chapters provide a rich reflection of intersectionality in feminist research today.

References

Anthias, Floya and Nira Yuval-Davis. 1983. "Contextualising Feminism: Ethnic, Gender and Class Divisions." *Feminist Review* 15: 62–75. https://doi.org/10.2307/1394792

Bryan, Beverley, Stella Dadzie and Suzanne Scafe. 1985. *The Heart of the Race: Black Women's Lives in Britain*. London: Virago Press.

Carby, Hazel V. 1982. "White Woman Listen! Black Feminism and the Boundaries of Sisterhood." In *The Empire Strikes Back: Race and Racism in 70s Britain*, edited by The Centre for Contemporary Cultural Studies, 212–235. London: Hutchinson.

Collins, Patricia Hill. 1991. *Black Feminist Thought: Knowledge, Consciousness, and the Politics of Empowerment*. New York: Routledge.

Collins, Patricia Hill. 2019. *Intersectionality: A Critical Social Theory*. Durham and London: Duke University Press.

Collins, Patricia Hill and Sirma Bilge. 2016. *Intersectionality*. Cambridge: Polity Press.

Crenshaw, Kimberlé W. 1989. "Demarginalizing the Intersection of Race and Sex: A Black Feminist Critique of Anti-discrimination Doctrine, Feminist Theory and Antiracist Politics." *The University of Chicago Legal Forum* 1989, Article 8.

Crenshaw, Kimberlé W. 1991. "Mapping the Margins: Intersectionality, Identity Politics, and Violence against Women of Color." *Stanford Law Review* 43, no. 6: 1241–1299. https://doi.org/10.2307/1229039

Davis, Angela. 1981. *Women, Race and Class*. New York: Random House.

El Sadaawi, Nawal. 1980. *The Hidden Face of Eve*. London: Zed Press.

Hancock, Ange-Marie. 2016. *Intersectionality: An Intellectual History*. New York: Oxford University Press.

Hochschild, Arlie Russell. 1983. *The Managed Heart: Commercialization of Human Feeling*. Berkeley: University of California Press.

hooks, bell. 1982. *Ain't I A Woman: Black Women and Feminism*. London: Pluto Press.

Lorde, Audre. 1984. *Sister Outsider: Essays and Speeches*. Trumansbury, NY: Crossing Press.

Mirza, Heidi Safia. 1992. *Young, Female and Black*. London: Routledge.

Mirza, Heidi Safia, ed. 1997. *Black British Feminism: A Reader*. London and New York: Routledge.

Misra, Joya, Celeste Vaughan Curington, and Venus Mary Green. 2021. "Methods of Intersectional Research." *Sociological Spectrum* 41, no.1: 9–28. https://doi.org/10.1080/02732173.2020.1791772

Mohanty, Chandra Talpade. 1988. "Under Western Eyes: Feminist Scholarship and Colonial Discourses." *Feminist Review* 30: 65–88. https://doi.org/10.2307/302821

Moraga, Cherríe L. and Gloria E. Anzaldúa, eds. 1983. *This Bridge Called My Back: Writings by Radical Women of Color*. 2nd ed. New York: Kitchen Table Women of Color.

Nash, Jennifer C. 2019. *Black Feminism Reimagined: After Intersectionality*. Durham: Duke University Press.

Narayan, Uma. 1997. *Dislocating Cultures: Identities, Traditions, and Third World Feminism*. London and New York: Routledge.

Ramazanoğlu, Caroline, with Janet Holland. 2002. *Feminist Methodology: Challenges and Choices*. London: Sage.

Smith, Linda Tuhiwai. 2012. *Decolonizing Methodologies*. 2nd ed. London: Zed Books.

Southall Black Sisters. 1990. *Against the Grain. Southall Black Sisters 1979–1989*. Southall, Middlesex: Southall Black Sister.

Spivak, Gayatri Chakravorty. 1988. "Can the Subaltern Speak?" In *Marxism and the Interpretation of Culture*, edited by C. Nelson and L. Grossberg, 271–313. Basingstoke: Macmillan Education.

Thiam, Awa. 1986. *Black Sisters, Speak Out! Feminism and Oppression in Black Africa*. Translated by Dorothy S. Blair. London: Pluto.

Wilson, Amrit. 1978. *Finding a Voice: Asian Women in Britain*. London: Virago Press.

1

LIVING AND RESEARCHING EMBODIED INTERSECTIONALITY

Heidi Safia Mirza in conversation with Line Nyhagen

Heidi Safia Mirza and Line Nyhagen

The conversation between Heidi Safia Mirza and Line Nyhagen took place in London at St Pancras International train station on 18 December 2023. To find a quiet space, they chose a table with two chairs located in the hallway adjacent to the toilets of the main restaurant and bar on the upper concourse of the station. The conversation was wide-ranging and covered personal and political issues as well as academic research, with a focus on intersecting identities and inequalities. The conversation has been edited by Nyhagen into the following five sections: quilting a feminist life; Black feminist activism in a post-colonial racist order; intersectionality: from buzzword to embodied intersectionality; Muslim women's agency and resistance through the lens of embodied intersectionality; and intersectional feminist methodologies and methods and the importance of history.

Quilting a feminist life

Nyhagen: It was fascinating to read your chapter on 'Race, gender and educational desire' in your book *Race, Gender and Educational Desire: Why Black Women Succeed and Fail* (Routledge, 2009). In the chapter, you use the example of a quilt you bought in India, which was 'made of fragments of women's bridal dresses' (137) to make the point that, while women might be unseen or marginalised, through the making of the quilt they are remaking their own story by stitching together individual pieces of cloth. The finished quilt becomes a coherent story. You then link the quilt to your book *Black British Feminism*, a collection of writings by Black British feminist women whose stories have also been unseen by

DOI: 10.4324/9781003399575-2
This chapter has been made available under a CC-BY-NC-ND license.

14 Heidi Safia Mirza and Line Nyhagen

others, including by White women. What are the main pieces of cloth that form your own feminist academic quilting, or life story and journey?

Mirza: That is a very nice and emotional way to start. Growing up in Trinidad as I did, I had a perspective of being a little girl in what was quite a masculine world. When I say masculine, I mean patriarchal, and yet women were very visible. I didn't know my grandmother but my aunts and other women – they were all strong women – and I was aware from a very young age of the power of women. But their voices were not heard in a public arena, they didn't have powerful jobs like you could see men were having. There are many men in the Caribbean that don't have powerful jobs, but I could see there was a class divide, I could see there was a Race divide and a gender divide in everyday life. And I was very influenced by the women in my life, my mother and my grandmother, especially by the stories of my grandmother. So, I would say one of the big pieces of the quilt is the intergenerational stories passed down through our feminist ancestral oral traditions.

Isn't it interesting that quilting is a women's craft and that is what really struck me on this trip in India. I saw these tapestries of the women's bridal dresses and I thought each person's dress has a story behind it of anguish, of pain, of happiness, of sadness, of trials and tribulations, and we don't hear their voices. And what really struck me with the Palestinian Nakba catastrophe and with the ethnic cleansing and genocide that is going on, the children are writing their names on their hands. Small children, three, four, five years old. Ten years old. They are writing their name because they say, 'at least when they find my body you will know who I am'. And so, this thing of making the quilt, it is like knowing that you existed, knowing that you were somebody. It is about finding a voice however you do, in desperate situations, whether with the massacre of children in Palestine or even the everydayness of being silenced, with nobody ever listening to you. And that is what struck me about the quilt, finding a voice. The British feminist Amrit Wilson wrote a book called *Finding a Voice* (1985). It is a powerful concept, who gets to speak, when you get to speak, who defines what you can speak about.

Nyhagen: And you have been quilting your own story, even though you might not have done it literally with the pieces of cloth, but you have done it with writing?

Mirza: With using my life and my experiences and talking about them and different parts of my life, yes. I hadn't thought about it, thank

Embodied Intersectionality **15**

you so much for telling me that I quilted my life. You know I don't think it is exceptional in any way, I think that everybody wants to make sense of their lives. And when it is racialised and gendered and classed as mine was, because after struggling with racism in England, my father went back to Trinidad and got a good job in the oil industry and we had privileges. My mother was White, we had privileges, and I could see that I could walk through the world in a different way than my Black African and Indian Caribbean friends. I had privileges and I felt I needed to explore that.

Nyhagen: Does your sociological mind have its roots from when you were a young woman growing up?

Mirza: The other day we had a conference with the first women of colour to be professors in Britain and we were discussing what had inspired us.[1] I was always angry; I was very angry at injustice, and I told a story at the conference. I was born in Britain. Actually, my father was from the Windrush generation, he came on the boat called the Colombi and he married my mother. My brother and I were born here, we went to school here until the ages of five and four, then we went back to Trinidad. I am telling you this because I went to school here in Britain. It was at a combined primary and nursery school in Tooting in South London. This would have been in the early 1960s, when the treatment of Black, Gypsy, and Roma Traveller children was horrendous, and I still have that scar on my mind of when the teacher stripped an Irish Traveller girl naked. The little girl, I remember her hugging her arms in a protective mode and she was shivering. I have the memory of how unfair this was and how wrong it was to humiliate someone because they are poor and I knew that at that time, and I was four years old. And I remember being told to get out of the way in the playground and being thrown over and being laughed at, and I remember the dinner ladies making me eat the custard that I had vomited in. There was a cruelty; there was a power game, it was so unfair. And I think that just triggered me into this journey. I was always fighting for the underdog, fighting for the right to be heard. It was feeling like no one listens, no one listened to that little girl who was being stripped of her dignity.

Nyhagen: How did that play out when you became a teenager?

Mirza: My mother was Austrian, and my father, Indo-Caribbean, and I noticed from a very young age at secondary school, for example, that if my Mum came to pick me up, I was seen as more special than if my Dad did. And I always wanted my Mum to come because it meant that I got status. Whiteness automatically meant privileges, and this was in the Caribbean; it was very colonial, there was a White elite, like in South Africa. There was a gradation of fairness of the skin. Fairness has a kudos that being dark skinned does not. It is a very hierarchical, colour coded place. And again, that injustice really riled me because I could not understand why people would be treated differently just because of their background, their culture, their Race, their gender. It seemed wrong and I could not accept it. When I go back to Trinidad, I find that it is still a very hierarchical place and there are still certain enclaves of people that have a lot of income and privilege and wealth and there isn't the redistribution and social justice you would hope – which is a key issue for me.

Black feminist activism in a post-colonial racist order

Nyhagen: To what extent are Black women's stories and experiences still unseen in Britain? Thinking back to when you were at university in the 1980s, and then looking forward to today. Has anything changed, and if so, what?

Mirza: It's interesting that you have been to see the Women in Revolt! exhibition at Tate Britain today.[2] You should look at some of the posters from the 1970s. I was on the streets in the 1970s against the National Front and I was part of OWAAD [Organisation for Women of African and Asian Descent, 1978–1983; see Bryan, Dadzie, and Scafe 1985] in the 1980s. There was a lot of activism at that time. Now we have Black Lives Matter, Say Her Name, and many other similar outpourings of injustice. And the thing that struck me about the posters from the 1970s and 1980s was the rawness of them. You can see the anger, you can see the streets filled with people, there were things like the New Cross Massacre of 13 young Black people and the Brixton Riots in 1981, marches against the National Front and the Notting Hill Carnival clashes with the police. There were so many incidents and Black Lives Matter is on a continuum of all those things. There is a saying that the more things change, the more they stay the same. And what struck me about the pictures you just showed me from the Women in Revolt! exhibition was that they seemed static, they are in a museum gallery, they make it seem like it is history and I feel almost angry about that because domestic violence and abuse is as bad as ever, Black women's pay, migrant women's pay is as bad as ever. I have just done a big study for the Institute of Fiscal Studies (IFS) as part of the ISF Deaton Review (Mirza and Warwick 2022), looking at Race and ethnic inequalities. The health inequalities of Black groups, especially of people of

African Caribbean descent and from Pakistan and Bangladesh, and particularly with the advent of the Covid-19 pandemic, it is off the scale. The statistics are undeniable, and the inequalities have grown and become entrenched. So, this idea of seeing static pictures of the past, I just feel angry again. We live in a racialised economic social order that needs Black and Brown and migrant bodies to support a standard of living and a standard of wealth for the White majority population. It is a racialised social order. So why are we celebrating something to say, 'look we recognise and see Black women', but you're not actually seeing them. You are now ossifying them and putting them in a cabinet and going, like, 'oh aren't they wonderful?'. We now have people of colour in top political positions, and they are even more outrageous than any other right-wing White person. This is an example of what Homi Bhabha (1984) calls 'mimic men'. It is like in the colonial project where you get the local elites to do your bidding, to do your dirty work. The idea that we are in a post-racial moment, where Race does not matter because we have got top people of colour in the job, is an illusion. It is worse than ever for the masses and the working classes.

Nyhagen: You have chosen to identify as a Black British feminist. Can you talk a bit about why and how you use this term?

Mirza: I was really influenced by the African American feminist Angela Davis. I saw her on TV in Trinidad when I was 10 years old, giving the Black Power salute after her release from prison. She was beautiful and strong and had an afro and fair skin, a mixed-race woman of colour, and I immediately identified as a mixed-race young woman with her. She exuded power and confidence, which I didn't see around me. I did get to meet her many times with my wonderful Kill Joy feminist sister Sara Ahmed who is friends with Angela. It has been a wonderful experience to meet your icon, we even went to the loo together, and look at us, we are here now just outside the loos too! There is something about loos and revolutionary movements for women meeting in the toilets! Angela Davis was part of the Black Panther movement, and Black Power defined post-colonial movements in Africa and America in the 1960s and 1970s. Then, the only collective word available for racial revolution was Black. It stood for power, for fighting injustice as a woman of colour; it became an umbrella term under which I and other post-colonial activists in Britain sheltered. But it has not been an easy path and rightly so – I have described it as a rollercoaster ride with the highest highs and lowest lows (Mirza and Gunaratnam 2014). At university, on my course, most of the revolutionary people I knew were from places like the Caribbean, Pakistan, and Tonga. There were many freedom fighters from South Africa and Zimbabwe and so on, and there was the sense in which it was about comrades and camaraderie, that we were together in our post-colonial struggle against apartheid and for independence. I ended up going to university in England. It was 1977 and a moment in time when our countries were fighting for liberation and self-determination, and I was at the University of East Anglia doing Development Studies. It was a momentous time that was so crucial to me as a young woman. I was inspired by the anti-western Iranian revolution and converted to Islam. It was the 1970s and the White feminist movement had just started but it did not speak to me. Nearly everybody on my course was a man, there were not many women, we did not have professors that were women and the only few female tutors we had were the White wives of male lecturers.

Nyhagen: We were talking about you identifying as a Black feminist. This was also a unifying banner in the 1970s and 1980s for women in the Organisation for Women of African and Asian Descent – OWAAD.

Mirza: Yes, there was a solidarity, that we're all in this together. In those days we were very much a minority. I remember going to the OWAAD meetings in Brixton. There were fall outs, there were arguments, between women of African Caribbean and women of Asian descent, but we were all in the same room having these heated debates. There were LGBT issues too that were really thrashed out. There was a sense that we were creating and doing something together and that even if we were having these very strong arguments between us, we were still a sisterhood. We had a bigger purpose. We might have had different identities and needed to have these discussions, but at the same time our political purpose overshot that.

Nyhagen: In the 1970s and 1980s, four national conferences were organised by OWAAD, the umbrella organisation for many Black and Asian women's groups in the UK. With a goal to fight both racism and sexism, its conferences focused on issues such as immigration and deportation, domestic violence, exclusion of children from school, industrial action by Black women, police violence, health, and reproductive rights. Sexuality and lesbianism were also discussed as part of the fight against homophobia in the Black community. Looking back at that time, are there specific issues and events that stand out in your memory?

Mirza: The reason for our focus on intersectionality was the fact that Black and Asian women are not treated the same. Take the police, for example. When Black women make a complaint about domestic violence or a complaint against the police, they are not believed in the same way White women are. And I remember reading a study in the 1980s, very early on in my career, that in America White women could get abortions, they were middle class, they had access to money. They could get abortions, but Black women couldn't. There was this sense in which you had access to a lot of services automatically through class, through your Race, that you wouldn't have as an African American woman or an African Caribbean woman or an Indian woman. And when I came to England in the 1970s there was the scandal of virginity testing of Asian women at Heathrow Airport.

It was an actual immigration policy at that time to test the hymen of Indian, Bangladeshi, and Pakistani women when they came to the UK, to make sure that they were here for the legitimate reason of marriage. The violation of our bodies in the 1970s and 1980s was palpable. At the time, I had my daughter and my treatment was shocking, nobody believed me when I said I wasn't well. They talked to me as if I couldn't speak English using chalk on a board to explain things even though I had my degree. You were stereotyped, you were seen as not intelligent. And then there was the issue of the Depo-Provera and forced sterilisation of migrant women. I had done my thesis as an undergraduate student on Depo-Provera and I knew what was going on. When I was in hospital with my daughter and after I had her, they offered it to me, without telling me about the potential consequences. They said, 'we're going to give you a little prick, it will help you not to get more children?'. I thought of the irony. If I didn't know what I knew, they would have given me an injection of Depo-Provera. This happened to me, and I was a university graduate. Imagine if I couldn't speak English? These were the ways we were being treated, exposed by activists like Southall Black Sisters. I am sure such things are still going on today with Black, Muslim, and White working-class women, and with Gypsy, Roma, and Traveller women. I have no doubt about the continued health inequalities for these women, especially in pregnancy and childbirth. I think sometimes we are too rigid about the politics of identity. Because White working-class women and White middle-class women are in different worlds, but White privilege allows you to move between classes, to move between privileges in a way that is not available for Black and Asian women in White post-colonial

Intersectionality: from buzzword to embodied intersectionality

Nyhagen: In your recent chapter 'A Vindication of the Rights of Black Women: Black British Feminism Then and Now' (*The Palgrave Handbook of Critical Race and Gender*, 2022), you talk about how '[t]he concept of "intersectionality" has enabled Black feminists to interrogate the ways in which power, ideology and the state intersect with subjectivity, identity and agency to maintain social injustice and universal patterns of gendered and racialized economic inequality' (10). What is your assessment of the power and influence of the concept of intersectionality within and beyond a Black feminist analysis?

Mirza: I want to go back a little bit around intersectionality because it has become this huge buzz word, and everyone talks about intersectionality as if it is a simple thing like just declaring 'we are all intersectional', like, 'I'm a young gay man' or 'I'm a Muslim woman' or I'm an intersectional being', as if that's enough. It is being reduced to the new EDI term [equity, diversity, and inclusion – EDI] and the notion that if we could just grasp this idea of intersectionality then we would have solved all our problems. We are complex beings and my Race matters, my gender matters, everything matters, but my question is, *how* does it matter? And what difference does it make if we know how it matters and how can we change the world once we have this understanding of how important it is? That we are multiple beings with complex lives? As we talked about, there is Race, gender, class, disability, sexuality, etc. in my life and in your life too. And while the term 'intersectional' is being used too simply and in too trite a way, it still holds the key to understanding how we structure social relations in the racial order that we live in.

Nyhagen: You suggested that 'intersectionality' has become a buzzword. Do we need to go back to the roots of the concept?

Mirza: Yes, I do think so. One thing is that it is a very old concept. The first articulation of intersectionality that we have is in the words of Sojourner Truth at the 1851 Ohio Women's Rights Convention in Ohio, the United States, where she, an African woman and former slave, asked of White America 'Ain't I a woman?'. We also have the foundational work of the Combahee River Women's Collective in 1977, Angela Davis's book *Women, Race and Class* from 1981

Embodied Intersectionality **21**

and the work of Valerie Amos, Gail Lewis, Amina Mama, and others who wrote about Race, class, and gender for the special issue of *Feminist Review* (1984) called 'Many Voices, One Chant: Black Feminist Perspectives'. There is also my own book *Young, Female and Black* from 1992. We used to call it the triple subordination of gender, Race, and class or the additive model of multiple inequalities, and the popular double or triple whammy, and we used to call it intersecting, not intersectionality. All of that was a long time ago. I went to a talk the other day where a White woman was talking about the concept of intersectionality to some health workers, and she was saying that African American feminist and legal scholar Kimberlé Crenshaw coined the concept. I value Crenshaw's work greatly; her writings are pivotal in shaping the debate but at the same time it didn't begin and end there. For as much as we like an origin story the concept has been in use a very long time. Everything that happens to women of colour from time immemorial has been about Race, class, and gender, and about religion, disability, sexuality, and all of the myriad layered ways that we are constructed and unseen. The concept of intersectionality might make it more accessible to White feminists, but at its root it is about Whiteness, power, brutality, cruelty, and exclusion, it is about all of the horrible things that we are seeing at the moment unfolding in Palestine, it is about all of that negation and invisibility. Intersectionality is about understanding that multiple layers of politics and economics affect your life and about who gets to decide whose lives matter. Intersectionality is a very powerful concept, and it is a Black feminist concept.

Nyhagen: Building on and expanding the work of other Black feminists, you have coined the concept of 'embodied intersectionality' (Mirza 2009). Can you give an example of how you use 'embodied intersectionality'?

Mirza: The other day I met a nurse, she is an intensive care nurse. I gave a talk, and she came up to me afterwards. She was a White woman, she was in tears, and she said, 'I have two Black sons, and I fear for their life'. And she said, 'I can't cope, can you help me?' I thought, how do I help her? She said her sons have no father, their father has abandoned them, and she thought that her mothering was not enough for these boys. They need a role model; they need their Black father. She seemed exhausted from being a White woman bringing up these Black children who are seen in and by the system as mixed-race children. Mixed-race children with White mothers are doing particularly badly in the system, they are excluded from school, they are more likely to be criminalised, they are more likely to be in care. Our Institute of Fiscal Studies report on racial inequality shows how this group is not faring well and in fact are going under the radar because they are largely the children of White mothers. Intersectionality as a sociological tool enables us to see the way in which these children embody and experience difference.

Embodied intersectionality takes it one stage further and allows us to place the body at the centre of the analysis so that we can begin to see how the way we look, the places we live, the perceptions of our Race, the perceptions of our class all play a role in how the structural systems that we live in reinforce the identities and social locations that we have and make them real. The idea of embodied intersectionality is the extent to which your Race, class, and gender become sedimented as a structural issue; how difference is interpreted by the systems in which we live. The social world exists in relation to us as Raced, minoritised, classed, gendered, and religious bodies. To give you an example, if you walk into a doctor's room to be seen as a patient, before you even enter that room, there is an understanding of what an Asian woman is. If I walk into the doctor's room and they see me, a short and small Brown woman, they will have a lot of preconceived ideas about who I am. They would not know who I am, they would not know that I have degrees and I am a professor, and I am this and that; to them I am just a little Asian woman. And all these ideas flood in, 'well maybe she lives in a small house, maybe she's got a husband that beats her up. Maybe she isn't eating very well and getting enough sunshine, so she has vitamin D deficiency', because I always get asked that. There is a lot of assumed information about me that exists in that room and no matter how I think about myself, the system has already decided who I am.

If a young Black man walks into the room, a lot of things follow him into that room. It is like a social identity baggage that comes with you. When the police see a young Black kid on the street, the baggage is in his body whether he likes it or not and he will be treated in a particular way. And when you are treated in a particular way because you embody that difference then you are criminalised, and that reinforces the idea that Black guys are criminals. So, you become a criminal. The notion of embodied intersectionality allows us a way in to understand that the external social structures mesh with our understandings of our identity, the racialised, sexualised, and normative ideas about who you should be. And if you exist outside the White norm then you are criminalised, misrecognised, and devalued. You are seen as a difficult case; it can happen with age, it can happen with Race, it can happen with your gender and sexuality. It is the way in which differences become solidified into social structures and they become real. The world does not have to be the way it is, though. One of my favourite books is Toni Morrison's *A Mercy*, and Mercy is a little girl, she is an African American child in the 16th/17th century, before the slave trade was fully established. She is living in America and Toni Morrison talks so beautifully about how this was a time before the racial order was as we know it now. For me, embodied intersectionality allows me a window into seeing how the world could be different because everything ultimately is a social construct. Embodied intersectionality is giving me a voice. Maybe at last I found my voice.

Muslim women's agency and resistance through the lens of embodied intersectionality

Nyhagen: In your work on Muslim women in Britain, you explore women's agency and resistance, and you argue that '[t]he notion of embodied intersectionality thus enables us to see how, through the articulation of their identities, Muslim women continually resist and rename the regulatory effects of hegemonic gendered, Raced, and classed discourses of inequity and subjugation in their daily lives. Such resistance is played out in the subjecthood of racialised Muslim women, whose agency ultimately challenges and transcends such dominance' (Mirza 2013, 7). I am intrigued that the concept of embodied intersectionality can be used to analyse oppression, in the form of racism, misogyny, and other inequalities, while at the same time it can be used to examine agency and resistance.

Mirza: I worked for a few years on the School Standards Taskforce in London. When policy is honed through and through, it has the power to change lives. This was in the early 1990s under Tony Blair's Labour Government. There was a policy called the City Challenge which set up very good schools in the inner city. One of those places was Tower Hamlets, where many people of Bangladeshi heritage live. Now the parents of these young women in the 1990s possibly did not speak English, many of them worked in very tough jobs in restaurants and the rag trade and most mothers would not be literate. These girls went to the schools established by the City Challenge programme – schools that were identified as key institutions, got the best teachers, and had money pumped into them. I did some research in those schools. For context, Tower Hamlets is on the cusp of the City of London, there are lawyers, banks, insurance companies, and all kinds of businesses. It is interesting to note that the poorest and the richest communities are living side by side in Tower Hamlets.

Some of the existing research on Muslim women was damning in those areas, but these schoolgirls became nuclear scientists within one generation. They are going to the moon and back, they are going to Oxford and Cambridge, they are doing engineering, they have their doctorates. They are not some little Asian women being virginity tested. And they are changing their families, they are changing everything, but they are Muslim women first and foremost. They wear their hijabs, they are proud of that, they don't see it as a mark of oppression, they see it as a mark of strength and their faith keeps them going. And this idea that your faith is oppressive and patriarchal, well, their fathers back them even more than their mothers do, and it has been an incredible privilege for me to do research in their community. These women don't need White feminists to save them. These women are saving themselves through educational opportunities that they have seized, and they are changing their families. [...] It is not all hunky dory because you have to negotiate things such as sexism on your journey. But within one generation they have just turned it around. Their problem is not their culture, and it is not their religion either – it is poverty and the racism that they face in the White institutions in which they study or work. The idea of embodied intersectionality refers here to Muslim women's embodied reality as Raced and gendered and classed Muslim women in Britain. Also, their embodied modesty is articulated through their religious agency and the wearing of the hijab, which they see as non-negotiable. Embodied intersectionality allowed me to explore this idea of the epidermalisation of the veil as a second skin. The Muslim women participants in my research said their veil defines them – it is who they are, it is as tangible as the skin. The concept of embodied intersectionality allows us to methodologically reveal the internal identity of the women and link it to the external processes of racialisation and Islamisation of Muslim women in the West. The mainstream negative connotations of the veil, like the negative connotations of Black skin, show how discrimination comes to being and solidifies in the corridors of the school or workplace aided by unfettered media hatred, misinformation, and historical racism. Similarly, I am a well-educated woman, a Professor of Sociology, and yet all people see when I enter a room is my gender, my skin, my age, and they are surprised when I open my mouth to speak – it is a constant battle to be seen as more than the tropes that exist of me outside of myself – I am so much more than the 'coffee lady' that I am so often mistaken for in the corridors of power.

Nyhagen: The Runnymede Trust justly defines Islamophobia as a form of racism.

Mirza: Yes, racism changes its form in many ways in different times and in different locations. Islamophobia is the notion that all Muslims are a possible terror, a threat; you are to be feared, we have got to be afraid of you just because of your name or your clothes or your place of birth. We see it in the UK government's securitisation agenda, and it is institutionalised in programmes such as PREVENT in schools and universities. There is this sense that you can't escape your religion, you can't escape the body when you are being 'known' from outside of yourself. It is a form of racism as you are fixed and pre-judged. The whole idea of embodied intersectionality is about how we know ourselves from within, in opposition to how we are 'known' or seen by others from without who only see and fear our religion from their dominant perspective.

Intersectional feminist methodologies and methods and the importance of history

Nyhagen: Intersectionality is such a ground-breaking sociological concept, yet it seems that it is far easier to talk about the concept than to implement it in one's research. Feminist scholars continue to grapple with how intersectionality can be operationalised methodologically. Critiques have for example been raised about an additive approach to intersectionality. In your book *Race, Gender and Educational Desire* (2009, 3), you write about how additive models are inadequate. You go on to suggest that 'A black feminist epistemology is contextual and contingent and examines the differentiated and variable organising logics of Race, class and gender, and other social divisions such as sexuality, age, disability, culture, religion and belief that structure women's lives in different historical times (Yuval-Davis 2006) and geographic places (McKittrick 2006)'. Why do you think it is so difficult for feminist scholars to operationalise intersectionality in their research?

Mirza: I don't find it difficult, I really don't. It seems natural to me and I have been doing it instinctively for over 45 years from when I did my undergraduate dissertation on Pakistani young people in schools and later my PhD on Caribbean young women. It was like telling my own story – using ethnography to peel back the layers of meaning to reveal the hidden world of Raced and gendered subjects. But I haven't seen a lot of evidence of good intersectional research because it's quite hard to do it well. Everyone says they are doing it, but they are not really doing it. I just completed a study looking at Race and inequality in Britain for the Institute for Fiscal Studies, funded by the Nuffield Foundation. It gathered senior scholars, academic experts in different fields including health, education, employment, and so on, to look at inequalities. It was a huge project and they asked me to look at Race inequality. To look at Race inequality is not the same as looking at either health, education, or any of the substantive areas in isolation. It took three years to complete because it is a cross cutting intersectional study. If you are looking at Race inequality, you have to look at education and health and employment and pay and all of the elements of your life, and you also have to look at Race, class, and gender and the ways in which they intersect with each of these areas. It is hard work, but it is very illuminating because you can begin to see who does well and who does not across different regions of the country, looking at factors such as gender, age, ethnicity, and class. For example, the Muslim women who are living in Tower Hamlets have a very different trajectory than the Muslim women living in Bradford. Region matters. Geography, like nationality and citizenship, is an important intersectional layer or avenue of advantage and disadvantage to explain inequalities.

Nyhagen: It seems important that statistical and qualitative research evidence is brought together?

Mirza: That's crucial; you must use both. In explaining why there are so many female-headed households in the Caribbean community as opposed to in the Bangladeshi and Pakistani Muslim communities, you have to look at historical and empirical evidence together. The reasons that Black women are disproportionately heads of households is a topic that I explored in *Young, Female and Black* (1992) and Angela Davis talks about in *Women, Race and Class* (1981). White enslavers in America and the Caribbean actually set out to destroy the Black family structure as a means to control labour and reproduction and insurrection among them. And that destruction plays out today in the denigration and criminalisation of Black men and the sexualisation and exploitation of Black women. And this destruction of social fabric also happened in indigenous First Nation communities, like Aboriginal and Native American communities. The purposeful destruction of those communities and the stripping of their wealth, the stripping of their own cultural knowledges through Christianity and residential schools has left these communities devastated, and now they are criminalised too, like Gypsy, Roma, and Traveller people are. Any community – including the Palestinian people – where the land defines them, the ancestral homeland of people – when White settlers move in and strip them of that birthright or steal and dislocate whole nations and communities of people, you leave them in a state of trauma. And that trauma lives on through generations. We need to understand that history and we can't do intersectionality without understanding history and the interlocking systems of power that preserve those social systems of domination. Without understanding geography, without understanding culture and religion and colonial histories of exploitation and devastation that happened in the name of what the late great Black feminist bell hooks calls 'imperialist white supremacist capitalist patriarchy' (as cited in Kawesa 2022, 161) we cannot heal and make ourselves whole. For me, healing needs to be the final patch in my quilt.

Notes

1 The conference, entitled 'In her wake', was held at the School of Advanced Study, University of London, UK, on 14 December 2023. See https://www.sas.ac.uk/events/in-her-wake.
2 Women in Revolt! Art and Activism in the UK, 1970–1990. See https://www.tate.org.uk/whats-on/tate-britain/women-in-revolt.

References

Bhabha, Homi. 1984. "Of Mimicry and Man: The Ambivalence of Colonial Discourse." *October* 28: 125–133. https://doi.org/10.2307/778467
Bryan, Beverley, Stella Dadzie and Suzanne Scafe. 1985. *The Heart of the Race: Black Women's Lives in Britain.* London: Virago Press.
Davis, Angela. 1981. *Women, Race & Class.* London: Women's Press.
Feminist Review 17, no. 1, November 1984. Special issue "Many Voices, One Chant: Black Feminist Perspectives."
Kawesa, Victoria. 2022. "And Then We Wept – an Academic Obituary of Bell Hooks 1952–2021." *NORA - Nordic Journal of Feminist and Gender Research* 30, no. 2: 161–166. https://doi.org/10.1080/08038740.2022.2071989
McKittrick, Katherine. 2006. *Demonic Grounds: Black women and the Cartography of Struggle.* Minneapolis: University of Minnesota Press.
Mirza, Heidi S. 2022. "A Vindication of the Rights of Black Women: Black British Feminism Then and Now." In *The Palgrave Handbook of Critical Race and Gender*, edited by Shirley Anne Tate and Encarnación Gutiérrez Rodriguez, 189–207. London: Palgrave Macmillan.

Mirza, Heidi Safia and Yasmin Gunaratnam. 2014. '"The Branch On Which I Sit'. Reflections on Black British Feminism." Heidi Safia Mirza in conversation with Yasmin Gunaratnam. *Feminist Review* 108: 125–133.

Mirza, Heidi Safia and Ross Warwick. 2022. "Race and Ethnicity." In *IFS Deaton Review of Inequalities*. Institute of Fiscal Studies, UK. Available at: https://ifs.org.uk/inequality/race-and-ethnicity-chapter/

Mirza, Heidi S. 2013. "'A Second Skin': Embodied Intersectionality, Transnationalism and Narratives of Identity and Belonging Among Muslim Women in Britain." *Women's Studies International Forum* 36: 5–15. https://doi.org/10.1016/j.wsif.2012.10.012

Mirza, Heidi S. 2009. *Race, Gender and Educational Desire: Why Black Women Succeed and Fail.* London: Routledge.

Mirza, Heidi S., ed. 1997. *Black British Feminism. A Reader.* London: Routledge.

Mirza, Heidi S. 1992. *Young, Female and Black.* London: Routledge.

Morrison, Toni. 2008. *A Mercy.* London: Chatto & Windus.

Wilson, Amrit. 1985. *Finding A Voice: Asian Women in Britain.* London: Virago

Yuval-Davis, Nira. 2006. "Intersectionality and Feminist Politics." *European Journal of Women's Studies* 13, no. 3: 193–209. https://doi.org/10.1177/1350506806065752

2

THE PLAY'S THE THING

Using creative methods to place trans and queer knowledge-making centre stage

Harvey Humphrey

This chapter considers the relevance of creative methods for representation, with a particular focus on representing queer, trans, and intersex lived experiences.[1] The chapter offers an example of ethnodrama, a playscript written from research, and discusses the experience of producing that ethnodrama as a piece of ethnotheatre staged in a theatre with a queer cast and crew and a live audience. The long-standing feminist concerns of representing others (Alcoff 1991) underpin the contemporary decisions that were made within this project to share research considering trans and intersex activism at a time of vulnerability and contestation for these communities. Ethnodrama is discussed as a creative approach to deal with the unique ethical challenges within intersectional feminist, queer, and trans research. The chapter introduces the context of trans and intersex activism across the United Kingdom (UK), Malta, and Australia (the research settings) at the time of the initial interviews and discusses the specific UK and Scottish legal and media context in 2022 – the time of the performance of the ethnotheatre, the *As Is* play. The chapter considers the representative work in creating characters from real participant interviews and the complexities of protecting participants' anonymity. This involved remaining faithful to their accounts and reproducing the nuances of their identities and their stories. This representative work in the creation of the ethnodrama's script was further developed by the work of the cast and crew in bringing the ethnodrama to the stage. The chapter addresses the further complexities of representation, with actors playing characters created from multiple real participants, and their consideration for their fellow trans and queer cast and our imagined audience. This chapter considers the challenges of intersectional methodologies and

DOI: 10.4324/9781003399575-3

This chapter has been made available under a CC-BY-NC-ND license.

the representative work of the researcher and the cast. It discusses producing this play drawn from research as an example of intersectional feminist, queer, and trans methodologies to challenge dominant narratives that are cisnormative, heteronormative, and heteropatriarchal.

Acting up: the queer methodological approach

The methodology for this research draws on feminist and queer epistemologies and methodologies. Ramazanoğlu and Holland (2002), British sociologists and advocates of feminist methodologies, argue that challenging power relations and centring knowledge-making in women's experiences unites feminist research despite differing methodological decisions. Adapting Ramazanoğlu and Holland for a queer lens, Catherine Nash, a Canadian human geographer, suggests that queer methods have a political approach to 'epistemology and ontology that enables critical explorations of disciplined normative truths about gender, sexuality and sex' that seek to bring about social change (Nash 2010, 131). The extent to which methods are or can be queer in their outlook is a contested topic (Browne and Nash 2010; Compton, Meadow, and Schilt 2018; Seidman 1996) but adopting an intersectional epistemological and ontological framework that works to challenge cisnormative and heteronormative assumptions is important for this research project that worked with individuals who experience societal marginalisation as a result of those normative sex and gendered assumptions.

This project adopts Kimberlé Crenshaw's approach to intersectionality in an attempt to understand and represent the contestations within the activist groups within the research project. As Crenshaw offers, '[t]hrough an awareness of intersectionality, we can better acknowledge and ground the differences among us and negotiate the means by which these differences will find expression in constructing group politics' (Crenshaw 1991, 1299). However, despite attempts to consider the intersections of participants' identities and experiences across the research project, the final piece of ethnotheatre failed to fully represent those intersectional experiences on stage. Some complex intersectional experiences were represented such as those of non-binary trans and non-binary intersex participants. There was also a deliberate visual engagement with disability on stage reflecting the many disabled participants who discussed the way those experiences shaped their trans and intersex activism. This reflects emerging work within queer disability studies which has prioritised trans inclusion despite significant backlash (Slater and Liddiard 2018; Humphrey et al. 2023). However, the all White cast let an assumed Whiteness cast a shadow over the research project and failed to represent the non-White participants in the study. Katrina Roen's work with indigenous New Zealand trans people 'critique[d] the way perspectives of whiteness echo, largely unacknowledged, through transgender (and queer) theorising' (Roen 2001, 262). More recently scholars have adopted a Black/Trans* Studies approach to develop black trans theory to counter these historic and ongoing failings (Ellison et al. 2017; Nicolazzo 2016). This remains ongoing work of research participation, engagement, and citational practice.

I use queer creative methods as a political tool to centre queer, trans, and intersex knowledge-making and to attempt to bring about social change. This chapter offers an example of that queer creative methodological approach with a research project on trans, intersex, and LGBTI[2] activist relationships. Principles of queer knowledge-making and authentically representing these trans and intersex stories underpin every stage of this work from research design to participant interviews and the dissemination work in staging a play for a contemporary audience. The audience of this work is a public one and an academic one, although academic spaces have become hostile to trans research and researchers in recent years (Slater and Liddiard 2018; Phipps 2020; Pearce 2020). In the face of this backlash, it is important to hear queer, trans, and intersex voices in research, as participants and researchers.

Setting the scene

The original research project interviewed 36 trans, intersex, and LGBTI activists across the UK, Malta, and Australia from 2016 to 2018 at a time of increased media coverage and political consideration of trans and intersex rights (Pearce, Erikainen, and Vincent 2020). All of the research sites had faced recent legislative engagement with trans and intersex legal recognition, although not all bills discussed by activists were passed into law (see reference list). These real laws and bills discussed in interviews formed the basis of a fictionalised Acquired Sex and Intersex Status [ASIS] bill discussed by characters in the play text. The performance of *As Is*, the ethnodrama drawn from these interviews, was staged in Glasgow, Scotland, in 2022, at a time when the Scottish Government and other media and political actors across the UK were discussing the *Gender Recognition Reform (Scotland) Bill* [GRR] (Humphrey 2023a). This bill would have reformed the process of trans legal recognition in the UK but did not consider intersex legal recognition. This Scottish reform of the UK-wide *Gender Recognition Act 2004* [GRA] had become a particular focus of hostile media coverage and political scrutiny (Cowan et al. 2021). This hostility towards trans people and media coverage advocating against trans legal recognition had also emerged across the UK following a since-abandoned decision by the UK government to reform the GRA (Hines 2020). This UK and Scottish context created a potential performance space that could include actors and audience members who had been made vulnerable by these intimidating and unwelcoming transphobic conditions.

Ethnodrama and ethics

As a brief introduction to the methodological approach, ethnodrama offers a method of 'dramatising the data' (Saldaña 2005, 2). Johnny Saldaña, American qualitative methods and theatre scholar, contrasts ethnodrama with ethnotheatre, explaining that ethnotheatre is 'a live performance event of research participants' experiences and/or the researcher's interpretations of data', whereas ethnodrama is 'the written script, [which] consists of dramatized, significant selections of narrative collected through interviews, participant observation field notes, journal entries, and/or print and media artifacts' (Saldaña 2005, 1). There are a range of examples of ethnodrama across sociological research, including Lisbeth Berbary's analysis of gender in sororities (2011, 2012); Jim Mienczakowski's analysis of service users and workers in drug and alcohol rehabilitation contexts (1995); and Saldaña's work on autoethnodrama about experiences of marginalisation (2008). There is a theme of using this approach to discuss complex ideas and offer nuanced analysis. The example of ethnodrama in this chapter prioritises sharing the lived experience of trans, intersex, and LGBTI activists in their own words and the ethnotheatre provided a format for those words to be spoken as much as possible by a cast of actors who shared those lived experiences and identities.

The example of ethnodrama discussed in this chapter, the *As Is* play (Figure 2.1), was drawn from the above-mentioned 36 semi-structured interviews with trans, intersex, and LGBTI activists across the UK, Malta, and Australia (Humphrey 2022). Many of these participants knew each other and this form of ethnodrama as ethical fictionalisation intends to minimise the harm of sharing these stories and their complex relationships outside of their real-world contexts, which could risk damaging ongoing relationships. The ethnodrama consists of six small scenes with ten composite characters representing my participants and one entirely fictional narrator. These six scenes address key themes relating to language, identities, and representation, as well as exploring relationships between trans and intersex activists and activisms.

The props and set design featured in the play were drawn from the real settings of interviews in participants' offices or other locations of their activist work. The settings, including any organisational names, have been fictionalised to anonymise the real locations while offering a sense of the different locations in which activists work, enabling further analysis of these relationships. For instance, Kate and Sandy (Figure 2.2), the characters from the fictitious trans organisation Real Health Experience [RHE], sit together in an office surrounded by trans campaigning materials, including a trans flag, which they make reference to in the script. Alternatively, one intersex activist, Georgiann, from the organisation Orchids XOXO, works from her

FIGURE 2.1   The full *As Is* cast, L-R: Narrator (Hev Clift); Kate (Gina Gwenffrewi); Sandy (Jacqueline Jay Wilde); Leslie (Leni Daly); Bo (Syd Hymanson); Jack (Mathew Wilkie); Georgiann (Poppy Lironi); Katrina (Jackie Sands); Iain (Odhran Thomson); Stephen (Len Lukowski); and Dean (Erden Göktepe).

home with a kettle, cups, television remote, and healthcare-related literature resting on a coffee table (Figure 2.3). Lavender's office is full of older lesbian and gay activist material going back decades, with posters and props referring to work in the 1980s and 1990s. There is a line in the script that refers to a toaster with US comedian and actor Ellen DeGeneres's face on it.[3] These props and set design offer an analysis that highlights broader relationships of funding bodies, healthcare settings, and activist histories that also feed into personal relationships.

As noted, fictional organisations are used to further protect participants' identities. Names were chosen that reflected real organisations such as references to healthcare activism for some trans and intersex exclusive organisations. Across the research sites, LGBTI organisations that had historically been gay or lesbian-and-gay organisations often retained their older names for a sense of continuity and history, but those names made reference to sexuality or specific gay/lesbian activist contexts and campaigns. For example, see the fictional name of Lavender discussed further below. In the *As Is* play, the fictional name chosen for the broad trans activist organisation is Real Health Experience [RHE]. This is a fictional name but a play on words that references the concept 'Real Life Experience' [RLE], which is the

FIGURE 2.2 Kate (Gina Gwenffrewi) and Sandy (Jacqueline Jay Wilde).

FIGURE 2.3 Georgiann (Poppy Lironi) and Narrator (Hev Clift).

requirement of a minimum of twelve months of living in one's preferred gender role in order to access genital surgery, according to the World Professional Association for Transgender Health's [WPATH] Standards of Care for the Health of Transsexual, Transgender, and Gender-Nonconforming People guidelines (Bockting 2008; Coleman et al. 2012). Thus, the name RLE reflects the experiences of gatekeeping within healthcare access faced by trans individuals in all the research sites and which influenced activism in these locations. The replacement of the word 'life' with the word 'health' highlights that these requirements do not necessarily reflect real life as it is lived but reflect the expectations healthcare professionals have of 'real life', which can include an individual's occupation and their suitability to passing as cisgender (Barrett 2007). The wordplay in the name to accommodate health experiences highlights that this group acknowledges a more diverse range of trans and non-binary gendered lives than the medical literature acknowledges. In the play, Sandy and Kate's trans activist group, RHE, now focuses on issues outside of healthcare but the name reflects the importance of healthcare activism in previous work.

Similarly, the fictitious organisation Orchids XOXO takes its name from the orchid plant, which is associated with the intersex variation Androgen Insensitivity Syndrome [AIS] and often features on AIS groups' logos. Furthermore, orchidectomy and orchiectomy are the terms for removing internal testes, which many individuals with AIS may choose to undergo or even be subjected to without consent (Callahan 2009). The 'XOXO' in the group's name is a reference to XO chromosomes associated with the intersex variations Turner Syndrome and mixed gonadal dysgenesis (Harper 2007). Several real groups for specific conditions also include references to chromosomes in their names, thus the fictional group name retains similarities to real group names through references to orchids and chromosomes while preserving anonymity for participants.

The use of fictional names allows for some of the participants' real stories of their organisation's activism and history to be revealed while preserving anonymity. This highlights the potential of creative methods to tell stories of queer, trans, and intersex lives without causing harm. The playscript itself told some of these complex histories. For instance, Dean, the character who is a cisgender gay man and who represents the voices of the six cisgender LGB participants, reveals some of the reasons behind those LGBTI activist groups across the research sites choosing to retain their historical names despite changing their membership and activities:

DEAN

The Lav and Lavender are the same thing. It's from the early days. Some homophobes started to call us The Lav in a derogatory way. Some tabloid started it. Us using it was a way of reclaiming these terms people were trying to use to hurt us.

(Humphrey, 2022)

The suggestion that the organisation was nicknamed The Lav as a shorthand for lavatory, and then how this nickname was deliberately adopted by Lavender to reclaim a word used against them as a slur, is a reference to the disputed reclamation of the term queer to 'negate the term's power to wound' (Epstein 1994, 195). This is something that can speak to an international cross-generational queer audience and original participants, who discussed a range of slurs aimed at members of their groups. The name Lavender is a fictional name. Its shorthand title is similarly fictitious, and these terms have replaced a real organisation's name in a participant's discussion. Lavender's name makes reference to the 'Lavender Scare' (Johnson 2004) which led to the expulsion of gay men from the US government, and to the 'Lavender Menace' (Jay 1999), a lesbian group that formed following the exclusion of lesbians from feminist activist groups in the USA. This history of lesbian and gay activism through experiences of exclusion offers a sense of dramatic irony in the name Lavender with many of those real groups experiencing criticism from trans and intersex activists due to their exclusion of trans and intersex members and the difficult journey to adding the letters T and I.

Several cisgender LGB participants discussed how their LGBTI (formerly lesbian-and-gay or gay) groups had been subject to media criticism and unfavourable comments about their groups' names, or their groups' aims and activities, going back several decades. This history of media criticism and standing up to those attacks provides further context to the real groups Lavender fictitiously represents that chose to keep their historically gay, lesbian, or LGB names. These choices were made despite adding the letters T and I to their representative activist groups and work, which led to them facing critique from those trans and intersex members for not updating their group names. These naming choices are also seen with other groups and organisations in countries not included in the study. For example, GLAAD is an American organisation that protests homophobic, biphobic, and transphobic media reporting. GLAAD's acronym originally stood for Gay and Lesbian Alliance Against Defamation. Since 2013, GLAAD has dropped this wording to reflect the bi and trans inclusion within its work but retained its acronym (LGBTQNation 2013; GLAAD 2015). In a similar move, in 2014, the American organisation PFLAG, which previously stood for Parents, Families and Friends of Lesbians and Gays, following an earlier iteration of POG Parents of Gays, dropped this wording to reflect greater LGBTQ+ inclusion but retained PFLAG as a name (PFLAG 2024).

The ethnodrama is set in a non-specific location in order to take participants' discussions from all research sites to construct it. This also helps to preserve anonymity. Therefore, composite characters discuss issues that were faced by participants across different fieldwork sites, further complicating this form of representation. The lines spoken by the characters in the ethnodrama are taken directly from the words spoken by my participants, with the exception of the character The Narrator, a fictionalised inclusion who allows for questions to be asked of characters to explain key terms and issues for an imagined audience. The Narrator begins the play sitting in the front row with the audience and interrupts at the end of Scene Three, asking:

NARRATOR

Do you guys know what's happening here? This law do you know what that's about? I'm a bit confused so I've been messaging this trans youth activist Iain (points out IAIN on the stage) and a few others to see what's going on. Iain's invited me to help set up some campaigning materials so I'm going to go say hi.

(Humphrey, 2022)

The Narrator allows for some of the more complex ideas, identities, and legal issues to be explained by the characters in ways in which they would have no need to explain themselves to each other or a more informed audience.

Composite characters

The decision to create composite characters for the ethnodrama was influenced by the desire to preserve participant anonymity. I was conscious of the fact that many of my participants knew each other and that they were often expressing dissatisfaction with other queer, trans, and intersex activists who they worked with and would continue to work with long after the interview had ended, and I had left the field. I was concerned participants could read the research publications and seek themselves and others they know out within the findings. Therefore, I was conscious that while strategies used to anonymise data, such as the removal of names, locations, and personal details, may anonymise these participants to those not familiar with the community, it would not be sufficient to hide their identities from those who work with them in their activist groups. I was also concerned that the shifting political context for trans and intersex activism across the research sites created a further complexity to the dangers of insufficient anonymity for participants.

However, the use of composite characters to protect participants' ongoing relationships with each other is an imperfect solution to this problem. The characters created have been drawn together to construct trans and intersex men, women, and non-binary people in order to reflect on the ways in which participants discussed those identities and their inclusion in the law – the setting for the *As Is* play. This constructs these characters solely in relation to those identities from a diverse participant cohort with a range of other identities. For example, the eight non-binary trans participants' identities differed across age, class, ethnicity, and disability. This is a failure within this work to include and adequately represent the intersectional experiences of participants across multiple identity categories and group memberships. These differences amongst participants were echoed across the sample. Unfortunately, there is an implied homogenous non-binary trans identity and experience when those participants' stories are subsumed from eight non-binary trans people into the one non-binary trans character of Leslie. This ignores the diversity of these real participants. This is made further complex by the diverse locations of participants in Australia, Malta, and the UK.

The work of one character representing the views of multiple participants implies that there was a set of uniform identities and experiences, or agreements and understandings across these experiences. However, the reality is more complicated. The ethnodrama itself, *As Is*, focuses on the complex relationships within communities of activists. Those complexities are also present within the participants that make up each composite character. A different ethnodrama from the same data may have focused on experiences in relation to types of activist work and created different composite characters as a result. While all the words from the text of the ethnodrama script come from these participants, choices have been made, and the rich diversity of participants that disagreed with each other or individuals who offered conflicting accounts within their own interviews is lost within the construction of each composite character. The fictionalisation of the composite character to tell a story works in this context but it comes at a representational cost of depth and diversity within the composites created. This complexity of representation and authenticity is further complicated by the staging of the ethnodrama as a piece of ethnotheatre with a cast of actors.

Casting

This queer methodological approach to ethnodrama prioritised the work of finding a queer cast and crew and actors who defined the same way as characters as much as possible. I was conscious that the original participants in this research project had spoken to me and trusted me with their stories because of my own connection to their communities as a queer non-binary trans man who had been involved in queer and trans activism for many years. Many of those participants wanted to know more about my queer and trans identities and experiences prior to interview and some searched for me on social media or asked other community members about me. Several participants also asked for my opinions on recent activist campaigns or wanted to know more about my own activist work before agreeing to an interview. This is important work of queer research, and researcher disclosures about shared identities and experiences can be an important component to enable participants to feel safe to talk to researchers (Humphrey 2023b). However, other scholars have noted the ways in which researcher disclosures can make the researcher vulnerable (Hughes 2018) or the researcher may find that participants interpret or read researchers' bodies in ways they cannot control (Harris 2015).

Acknowledging the importance of shared identities and understanding to many of my participants shaped my approach to finding a theatre space and the hiring decisions taken for directors, cast, and crew. This was also inspired by the work of UK-based Emma Frankland, a trans theatre practitioner, who has been critical of 'the trans representation that we do see' which 'is also filtered through a cisgender lens – directed by, written by, commissioned by cisgender people' (Frankland 2019, 801). This work of queer and trans representation on stage is further complicated in the context of the ethnodrama because the fictional characters on stage and lines they speak are taken directly from interviews with the real research participants.

I recruited a Director, Assistant Director, and a Stage Manager all of whom were non-binary trans and all of whom had experience working with diverse casts including trans actors, inexperienced actors, and disabled actors. They all had experience using theatre to tell difficult and personal stories and they had a personal connection to the play's focus on trans and intersex legal recognition. This made them uniquely qualified to tell the stories of this research through theatre. Together we selected a local theatre which had previously held trans and queer productions. I also recruited a queer filming company and a queer photographer and ensured all the cast and crew would be comfortable being filmed and photographed. All of the cast had a connection to the LGBTI community, with all but one being queer or trans. The one cast member who was not queer or trans themselves was the cisgender mother of a trans young person and she played the character Katrina, who is a cisgender mother of a trans young person (representing the four 'Mum' participants who saw their role as 'Mum' as essential to their identity and activism in this sphere). Her trans daughter joined us in the audience of the play.

The majority of the cast played characters with identities they shared – all trans characters were played by trans actors and all non-binary characters were played by non-binary actors. Finding actors who understood these characters and shared identities with them as much as possible was more important than previous acting experience. For some cast members this was their first acting experience whereas others who had been acting for many years had never had the opportunity to play their own genders before.[4]

However, despite securing funding to pay actors, and recruiting based on identities and experiences rather than acting experience, I was unable to find any intersex actors willing to play the intersex characters. This was made visible during the play with all three actors wearing t-shirts that read 'I am not an intersex actor' (Figures 2.3 and 2.4). This failure of representation was also discussed in the programme given to the audience. This included the words 'we would have preferred if the lines of intersex characters drawn from the interviews with intersex participants could have been spoken by intersex people'. The programme also stated that 'we have worked hard to find a cast and production team who all have a connection to the LGBTI community' and we chose to include pronouns next to names in the cast list to make this visible (Figure 2.5). I also failed to recruit any non-White actors. This incorrectly suggests that all of my research participants were White, which they were not. This constitutes another failure of representation of the diversity of my participants. During this project, I tried to prioritise the queer representation of my participants' voices, but I failed to represent their diversity in other ways. I was able to recruit several disabled actors, and this does reflect that many of my participants were disabled. However, in reflecting on the possibilities of ethnodrama for representation there are risks that the intersectional identities of original participants are lost in the performance of ethnotheatre. I do think there is potential in this

FIGURE 2.4 Cast, L-R: Jack (Mathew Wilkie); Leslie (Leni Daly); Bo (Syd Hymanson); Georgiann (Poppy Lironi); Narrator (Hev Clift); and Stephen (Len Lukowski).

FIGURE 2.5 The inside of the programme given to the audience with the cast list including their pronouns.

approach to tell important stories of research to diverse and non-academic audiences, but it is an imperfect method.

Ethnodrama as prefigurative acts

Scholars such as Gouweloos (2021) in Canadian contexts and Lohman and Pearce (2021) in UK contexts have discussed the prefigurative potential of queer performance spaces to imagine and enact alternative futures. For example, Lohman and Pearce highlight that '[c]ommunity arts may be prefigurative in that the act of creation is linked not only to imagining different futures, but also to the process of enacting social change through art' (Lohman and Pearce 2021, 114). The performance of the *As Is* play offered

42 Harvey Humphrey

an opportunity to co-create a prefigurative space of imagined social change through research dissemination.

In our first in-person rehearsal, the entire cast, including the Director and Producer/Researcher, sat on the stage with the full script, taking turns to read each line aloud. We did not take on specific characters and each read the next line, one after another. We paused frequently to discuss what words meant or how they might be understood by our imagined audience. We collectively agreed on our understanding of words and ideas, creating a piece of ethnodrama for our current contexts. We were aware of the ongoing discussion of the GRR bill in Scotland and the wider UK and its importance to ourselves and our audience. This led to a slight change in the script from 'I feel let down by the government' to 'I feel let down by this government'. We were aware that some audience members might be filling out consultations or contacting politicians in relation to the GRR bill, the text of which had been released but parliamentary discussion had not yet started. Therefore, we felt an urgency to include references to our current situation, thinking about the potential to influence such audience members. The same *As Is* play performed at a different time or in a different location may have produced a different prefigurative space with a focus on different possibilities of social change.

The possibilities of ethnodrama allow for space to be created to explore current contexts of audiences and cast members as well as the original research participants. However, there is still a duty to accurately and faithfully tell research participants' stories. The time period of initial data collection included ongoing UK-wide discussion of GRA reform and discussion of similar legislation in Australia, including the states and territories of Victoria and the Australian Capital Territory. This meant the reflection on the GRR bill felt in keeping with the original research as well as the wishes of the cast and crew. Other scholars producing ethnodrama from other research projects may not find such an easy relationship between the previous contexts of collecting data and the contemporary contexts of dissemination.

Conclusion

This chapter has considered one example of using ethnodrama and ethical fictionalisation to share queer, trans, and intersex research. It offers consideration of some of the ethical concerns that are uniquely shaped by contemporary contexts facing those working in queer research spaces. Creative methods and ethnodrama have been shown to provide an ethical solution to the long-standing issues of preserving anonymity amongst participants. However, the possibilities of failing to authentically represent participants with this approach have been highlighted. Composite characters cannot retain the entirety of the real complexity of the intersectional identities of participants from whom they originated. Furthermore, using actors to represent these composite characters creates a further layer of complicated representational work in this environment. Prioritising queer and trans voices on stage was highlighted as important to this work, and this has been reflected by others working in queer performance spaces (Frankland 2019), but in this example, some of the intersectional diversity of the original participants was lost. This form of representation was imperfect. I hope others working in these spaces and sharing work in this way continue to seek creative solutions to these complex problems of research representation. Although this work was imperfect, it was important. Despite rising hostility towards trans people in the UK, and specific hostility towards trans research and trans researchers in UK universities, this project produced a play in a city centre theatre that shared trans, intersex, and LGBTI research using participants' words, spoken aloud by a queer and trans cast without causing harm.

For many queer and feminist scholars our research is personal and political. There is a contemporary urgency and potential hostility for trans researchers and those engaged in trans research in the UK. This is not unique to trans research and many feminist researchers across a range of disciplines face similar hostile environments. This chapter does not offer easy solutions to our contemporary dilemmas. It offers one example of creative ways to share participants' stories and do justice to them. I hope that as an example it also offers hope. Research that is personal and political has the power to bring about social change. While laws may not pass, and media coverage may become more sensationalist, we can reach new audiences for our research. We can tell important stories that matter to our participants on our own terms. That is a powerful act.

Notes

1 This work was supported by ESRC grant number ES/W005689/1.
2 This research project interviewed participants across the UK, Malta, and Australia who engaged with trans, intersex, and/or LGBTI activism. The methodological approach within this project was queer but it is important to note that not every participant would use the term queer to describe themselves or this activism, with LGBTI being more appropriate in some contexts. For instance, queer and intersex have a complex history as discussed by Iain Morland in a UK context (Morland 2009). Furthermore, queer is not a term typically used by Maltese LGBTI activists or community groups.
3 The toaster with Ellen DeGeneres's face on it is a reference to the two-part coming out episode of the American television comedy show Ellen that celebrated Ellen the character and Ellen DeGeneres the actor coming out as a lesbian (Junger 1997a, 1997b). The toaster alludes to a joke in this episode about toaster ovens offered to successful lesbian recruiters. The toaster in this scene illustrates the ways in which popular culture and artefacts can be coded as queer, but these can be dependent on a temporal and geographical context that may not be understood over 20 years later.

44 Harvey Humphrey

4 Several actors shared their experiences as 'Production Notes' offered alongside the film of the play, which offers a greater understanding of their experience for those involved (Humphrey et al. forthcoming). The film of the play will also be available within this forthcoming online publication.

References

Equal Opportunity Act (VIC) 2010. Australia. https://www.legislation.vic.gov.au/in-force/acts/equal-opportunity-act-2010/020

Equality Act 2010. United Kingdom. https://www.legislation.gov.uk/ukpga/2010/15/contents

Gender Identity, Gender Expression and Sex Characteristics Act 2015. Malta. https://humanrights.gov.mt/en/Documents/GenderIdentity,GenderExpressionandSexCharacteristicsAct.pdf

Gender Recognition Act 2004. United Kingdom. https://www.legislation.gov.uk/ukpga/2004/7/contents

Gender Recognition Reform (Scotland) Bill 2022. Scotland. https://www.parliament.scot/bills-and-laws/bills/gender-recognition-reform-scotland-bill

Hate Crime and Public Order (Scotland) Act 2021. Scotland. https://www.legislation.gov.uk/asp/2021/14/introduction/enacted

Offences (Aggravation by Prejudice) (Scotland) Act 2009. Scotland. https://www.legislation.gov.uk/asp/2009/8/contents

Parentage Act (ACT) 2004. Australia. https://www.legislation.act.gov.au/a/2004-1/

Sex Discrimination Amendment (Sexual Orientation, Gender Identity and Intersex Status) Act 2013. Australia. https://www.legislation.gov.au/C2013A00098/asmade/text

Alcoff, Linda. 1991. "The problem of speaking for others." Cultural Critique 20, 5–32.

Barrett, James. 2007. Transsexual and other disorders of gender identity: A practical guide to management. Oxford, New York: Radcliffe Publishing.

Berbary, Lisbeth A. 2011. "Poststructural writerly representation: Screenplay as creative analytic practice." Qualitative Inquiry 17, no. 2, 186–196. https://doi.org/10.1177/1077800410393887

Berbary, Lisbeth A. 2012. "'Don't be a whore, that's not ladylike' discursive discipline and sorority women's gendered subjectivity." Qualitative Inquiry 18, no. 7, 606–625. https://doi.org/10.1177/1077800412450150

Bockting, Walter O. 2008. "Psychotherapy and the real-life experience: From gender dichotomy to gender diversity." Sexologies 17, no. 4, 211–224. https://doi.org/10.1016/j.sexol.2008.08.001

Browne, Kath, and Catherine Nash. 2010. "Queer Methods and Methodologies: An Introduction." In Queer Methods and Methodologies, edited by Kath Browne and Catherine Nash, 1–23. London: Ashgate.

Callahan, Gerald. 2009. Between XX and XY: Intersexuality and the Myth of Two Sexes. Chicago, IL: Chicago Review Press.

Coleman, Eli, Walter Bockting, Marsha Botzer, Peggy Cohen-Kettenis, Griet DeCuypere, Jamie Feldman, Lin Fraser, Jamison Green, Gail Knudson, and Walter J Meyer. 2012. "Standards of care for the health of transsexual, transgender, and gender-nonconforming people, version 7." International Journal of Transgenderism 13, no. 4, 165–232. https://doi.org/10.1080/15532739.2011.700873

Compton, D'Lane, Tey Meadow, and Kristen Schilt. 2018. Other, Please Specify: Queer Methods in Sociology. Oakland, CA: University of California Press.

Cowan, Sharon, Harry Josephine Giles, Rebecca Hewer, Becky Kaufmann, Meryl Kenny, Sean Morris, and Katie Nicoll Baines. 2021. "Sex and gender equality law and policy: A response to Murray, Hunter Blackburn and Mackenzie." Scottish Affairs 30, no.1, 74–95. https://doi.org/10.3366/scot.2020.0347

Crenshaw, Kimberlé Williams. 1991. "Mapping the margins: Intersectionality, identity politics, and violence against women of color." Stanford Law Review 43, no. 6, 1241–1299. https://doi.org/10.2307/1229039

Ellison, Treva, Kai M Green, Matt Richardson, and C Riley Snorton. 2017. "We got issues: Toward a black trans*/studies." Transgender Studies Quarterly 4, no. 2, 162–169. https://doi.org/10.1215/23289252-3814949

Epstein, Steven. 1994. "A queer encounter: Sociology and the study of sexuality." Sociological Theory 12, no. 2, 188–202.

Frankland, Emma. 2019. "Trans Women on Stage: Erasure, Resurgence and #notadebate." In The Palgrave Handbook of the History of Women on Stage, edited by Jan Sewell and Clare Smout, 775–805. London: Palgrave Macmillan.

GLAAD. 2015. "GLAAD observes second annual Bisexual Awareness Week." accessed 04/03/2024. https://glaad.org/releases/glaad-observes-second-annual-bisexual-awareness-week/

Gouweloos, Julie. 2021. "Intersectional prefigurative politics: Queer cabaret as radical resistance." Mobilization: An International Quarterly 26, no. 2, 239–255. https://doi.org/10.17813/1086-671X-26-2-239

Harper, Catherine. 2007. Intersex. Oxford: Berg Publisher.

Harris, Magdalena. 2015. ""Three in the room" embodiment, disclosure, and vulnerability in qualitative research." Qualitative Health Research 25, no. 12, 1689–1699. https://doi.org/10.1177/1049732314566324

Hines, Sally. 2020. "Sex wars and (trans) gender panics: Identity and body politics in contemporary UK feminism." The Sociological Review 68, no. 4, 699–717. https://doi.org/10.1177/0038026120934684

Hughes, Cayce C. 2018. "Not Out in the Field: Studying Privacy and Disclosure as an Invisible (Trans) Man." In Other, Please Specify: Queer Methods in Sociology, edited by D'Lane Compton, Tey Meadow and Kristen Schilt, 111–125. Oakland, CA: University of California Press.

Humphrey, Harvey, writer. 2022. As Is. Directed by Slater Cain. 2 July 2022. Glasgow, UK: Scottish Youth Theatre.

Humphrey, Harvey. 2023a. "Gender Recognition Reform (Scotland) Bill: GRA reform tries to rights a wrong." Feminist Legal Studies 31, no. 2, 265–272. https://doi.org/10.1007/s10691-022-09503-8

Humphrey, Harvey. 2023b. "Making meanings out of me: Reading researchers' and participants' bodies through poetry." Open Scholarship of Teaching and Learning 2, no. 2, 70–89. https://doi.org/10.56230/osotl.58

Humphrey, Harvey, Tig Slater, Edmund Coleman-Fountain, and Charlotte Jones. 2023. "Building a Community for Queer Disability Studies: Lessons from the Snail." Canadian Journal of Disability Studies 12, no. 1, 1–28.

Humphrey, Harvey, Slater Cain, Gina Gwenffrewi, Leni Daly, Odhran Thomson, and Mathew Wilkie. forthcoming. "The play's the thing: As Is and co-creating theatre from research to stage." Sociological Research Online.

Jay, Karla. 1999. Tales of the Lavender Menace: A Memoir of Liberation. New York: Basic Books.

Johnson, David K. 2004. The Lavender Scare: The Cold War Persecution of Gays and Lesbians in the Federal Government. Chicago: University of Chicago Press.

Junger, Gil. 1997a. Ellen. In The Puppy Edpisode, part 1, edited by Gil Junger: American Broadcasting Company [ABC].

Junger, Gil. 1997b. Ellen. In The Puppy Episode, part 2, edited by Gil Junger: American Broadcasting Company [ABC].

LGBTQNation. 2013. "GLAAD 'no longer an acronym,' alters name as part of broadened mission." accessed 04/03/2024. https://www.lgbtqnation.com/2013/03/glaad-no-longer-an-acronym-altering-mission-to-better-embrace-bisexual-transgender-people/

Lohman, Kirsty, and Ruth Pearce. 2021. "Queering community development in DIY punk spaces." In Arts, Culture and Community Development, edited by Rosie Meade and Mae Shaw, 111–128. Bristol: Policy Press.

Mienczakowski, Jim. 1995. "The theater of ethnography: The reconstruction of ethnography into theater with emancipatory potential." Qualitative Inquiry 1, no. 3, 360–375. https://doi.org/10.1177/107780049500100306

Morland, Iain. 2009. "What can queer theory do for intersex?" GLQ: A Journal of Gay and Lesbian Studies 15, no. 2, 285–312. https://doi.org/10.1215/10642684-2008-139

Nash, Catherine. 2010. "Queer Conversations: Old-time Lesbians, Transmen and the Politics of Queer Research." In Queer Methods and Methodologies, edited by Kath Browne and Catherine Nash, 129–142. London: Ashgate.

Nicolazzo, Z. 2016. "'It's a hard line to walk': Black non-binary trans* collegians' perspectives on passing, realness, and trans*-normativity." International Journal of Qualitative Studies in Education 29, no. 9, 1173–1188. https://doi.org/10.1080/09518398.2016.1201612

Pearce, Ruth. 2020. "A methodology for the marginalised: Surviving oppression and traumatic fieldwork in the neoliberal academy." Sociology 54, no. 4, 806–824. https://doi.org/10.1177/0038038520904918

Pearce, Ruth, Sonja Erikainen, and Ben Vincent. 2020. "TERF wars: An introduction." The Sociological Review 68, no. 4, 677–698. https://doi.org/10.1177/0038026120934713

PFLAG. 2024. "PFLAG: Evolution of a name." accessed 04/03/2024. https://pflag.org/pflag-evolution-of-a-name/

Phipps, Alison. 2020. Me, Not You: The Trouble with Mainstream Feminism. Manchester: Manchester University Press.

Ramazanoglu, Caroline, and Janet Holland. 2002. Feminist Methodology: Challenges and Choices. London: Sage.

Roen, Katrina. 2001. "Transgender theory and embodiment: The risk of racial marginalisation." Journal of Gender Studies 10, no. 3, 253–263. https://doi.org/10.1080/09589230120086467

Saldaña, Johnny. 2005. Ethnodrama: An Anthology of Reality Theatre. Walnut Creek, CA: AltaMira Press.

Saldaña, Johnny. 2008. "Second chair: An autoethnodrama." Research Studies in Music Education 30, no. 2, 177–191. https://doi.org/10.1177/1321103X08097506

Seidman, Steven. 1996. Queer Theory/Sociology. New York: Blackwell.

Slater, Tig, and Kirsty Liddiard. 2018. "Why disability studies scholars must challenge transmisogyny and transphobia." Canadian Journal of Disability Studies 7, no. 2, 83–93. https://doi.org/10.15353/cjds.v7i2.424

3

DECOLONISING FEMINISM AND FEMINIST DECOLONIALISM

The case of the #MeToo movement in Indonesia

Soe Tjen Marching

Indonesia's postcolonial history – combined with its cultural, ethnic, and religious diversities – requires a multifocal lens that can link oppressions that seem unrelated. Intersectional feminist approaches help in identifying different problems that can potentially intensify one another. Such approaches encourage different groups of women not to see their problems as separated from those of other groups and thus can motivate coalition-building amongst feminists in a place like Indonesia.

Nevertheless, these approaches have been criticised by several decolonial feminists because they believe that intersectional feminism does not sufficiently address the colonial dimensions of women's issues in the Global South, nor does it help to build a coalition amongst women of colour who are working towards equality (Lugones 2020; Velez 2019). My chapter demonstrates that although deep coalitions with other women of colour are crucial for progress towards women's equality, such coalitions are not always possible. This is because one oppressed group can in turn also become an oppressor of other more disadvantaged groups, so that what we witness can become a situation of oppressions within oppressions. Accordingly, we need a coalition of feminist approaches that can identify the complexities of oppressions without stigmatising women of colour in the Global South. In this chapter, I argue how an intersectional lens is necessary in discussions about the #MeToo movement in Indonesia.

The #MeToo movement has changed the environment around reporting sexual harassment and violence (Cobb 2020; Erickon 2018). Many mass media outlets have mentioned the importance of global solidarity and empathy in this movement (Sayej 2017; Pflum 2018). The hashtag has spread in various languages, and while many applauded the collective and global

DOI: 10.4324/9781003399575-4

This chapter has been made available under a CC-BY-NC-ND license.

48 Soe Tjen Marching

dimensions of this movement, some language-specific hashtags have gained less traction among social media users than others. The Indonesian feminist Tunggal Pawestri coined #sayajuga (the Indonesian translation of #MeToo), but did not receive abundant responses (Cobb 2020). US-based bullying and harassment expert Ellen Pinkos Cob blames this on the Indonesian legal system: 'Indonesia currently has no law to protect women from such uncomfortable and sometimes even violent cases' (Cobb 2020, 144). This has sustained the silence in relation to sexual harassment and violence in Indonesia despite the popularity of #MeToo worldwide. Like Cobb, several other writers and critics blame this on the patriarchal society, mass media, and justice system in Indonesia, which endorse victim-blaming (Kartika 2019; Erickon 2018).

In this chapter, I explore other reasons for the failure of #MeToo, besides the judicial system in Indonesia, by relating it to the discourses of several women who were raped during the 1965–66 genocide of communists in Indonesia. The historical tensions between secular and religious groups in Indonesia that still persist today have played a big part in stigmatising these female victims and in silencing them. I also discuss the importance of a combined decolonial and intersectional scholarly lens, focusing on sexual harassment and violence via the cases of secular feminist Indonesian women victims abused in the aftermath of Indonesia's independence from its colonial oppressor. In such oppressive circumstances, fiction became a medium for some women who were too intimidated to reveal their identities. Among the Indonesian rape victims I have met and talked with, one of them was willing to have her story narrated in fiction only. A version of her story is published in my 2015 novel entitled *Dari Dalam Kubur (From Inside the Grave)*. Fiction can be an alternative channel for revealing women's stories, including their past experiences of sexual abuse: considered controversial, these phenomena are often suppressed in texts considered to be more factual. Because of the multi-layered oppressions that come not only from colonial contexts but also from within societies themselves, a combination of feminist approaches – namely the decolonial feminist and intersectional feminist approaches – will enable a deeper and more thorough understanding of the disadvantages suffered by women in the Global South.

Between decolonialism and intersectional feminist approaches

As the #MeToo movement was generally considered to be born in the US in 2017 and the news regarding the movement was dominated by the faces of bourgeois White women for the remainder of that year, the name Tarana Burke, initiator of the US MeToo movement in 2006, way before Alyssa Milano's tweet in 2017, was largely not mentioned. The mass media seemed to be more interested in famous actresses (mostly White), instead of a Black

Decolonising feminism, feminist decolonialism **49**

female activist. Eventually Burke was acknowledged as the originator of MeToo and became one of *Time Magazine's* People of 2018. For this very reason, decolonial feminist movements are crucial in approaching minoritised women's experience. Decolonial feminists emphasise the importance of inclusion and of challenging dominant White discourses. Nevertheless, women of less privilege also have different degrees and complex layers of oppression: certain groups can be more dominant than others and claim to be representative of culturally disadvantaged parts of society. For this reason, besides a decolonial feminist approach, we also need an intersectional lens to focus on various minoritised women's experiences of inequality and exclusion, because intersectional feminism aims to see the possibility of how various forms of discrimination and oppression can intensify each other beyond identity politics. As Kimberlé Crenshaw argues: 'The problem with identity politics is not that it fails to transcend difference, as some critics charge, but rather the opposite – that it frequently conflates or ignores intragroup differences' (Crenshaw 1994, 1242). Indeed, a new 'universal' can also risk being created amongst different disadvantaged groups which may silence the most stigmatised. Failing to recognise intra-group diversities risks toppling the existing hegemony only to make certain oppressed groups into a new hegemony.

However, scrutinising internal problems experienced by women in the Global South also carries the risk of portraying them through what amounts to a 'colonial discourse'; that is, typecasting them as living in a chaotic society, unable to determine who they are and thus needing to be saved. A coalition of feminist theories in this matter is very important so that while we acknowledge the problems within different minoritised societies, we do not further stigmatise less privileged groups of women.

#MeToo and the publicity boost of White celebrities

As the phrase 'me too' implies, this movement is a matter of reaction and response; it demonstrates solidarity and support towards those who are in the same boat and aims to defy the stigma surrounding victims of sexual violence and rape. One of the important messages of this movement is that hitherto clandestine sexual abuse, harassment, and rape carried out by powerful men can now be voiced and made public without shaming the victims. As quoted in *The Guardian*, Tarana Burke states that the #MeToo movement is not just about Harvey Weinstein, but about 'elevating the stories of women who are perpetually unheard – their Black and brownness often rendering them invisible' (Morris 2020).

Burke does not have any issue with the fact that 'it was only when white Hollywood celebrities joined in that the #MeToo movement reached millions' because she sees the advantage of this: 'it was the only way for it to gain international attention' (Morris 2020). For Burke, it is more important to promote the struggle for women's rights and issues instead of scrutinising the possibility that these White celebrities may have overshadowed her contributions or may have shifted her original agenda as a Black woman. As she continues: 'Prior to #MeToo going viral, it was a real challenge to get folks who believed in social justice, who were progressive thinkers, to hold sexual violence in the same regard as they did other issues' (Morris 2020).

Thus, Burke intends the movement to be for women in general and for this reason the gaining of international attention somehow takes priority over the cultural particularity of this movement. Viewed from a different perspective, Burke may also be seen to have implied that the globality of this movement has helped to gain attention to its cultural particularity. Burke does not seem to worry about the necessity of seeing these 'dominant' White celebrities in decolonising perspectives. Nevertheless, she often emphasises the importance of Blackness in her movement and activism. In an interview, she states that 'We are socialized to respond to the vulnerability of white women, and it's a truth that is hard for some people to look in the face, and they feel uncomfortable when I say things like that' (Mosley 2023). She is not oblivious and does not want people to ignore that there is a 'stark difference in what it takes to get attention around Black women and girls' (Mosley 2023). However, rather than claiming that White celebrities have taken over her agenda, Burke views them as its positive drivers. Burke does not consider White celebrities to have overshadowed her movement as a Black activist. She acknowledges that in a world in which White celebrities are still dominant, this is 'the only way' to gain attention and advance her work (Morris 2020).

The #MeToo movement: too White for Indonesia?

While many White #MeToo celebrities are also well-known in Indonesia, why have members of the Indonesian public not reacted much to the #MeToo movement? Pawestri speculated on Twitter (now X) about the reason why this movement has not received much response in Indonesia: 'Takut kena UU ITE? Malah dikriminalisasi pelaku' ('Fear of the law on Electronic Information and Transactions? This can decriminalise the perpetrator') (@tunggalp, 26 January 2023). Under the Indonesian law on Electronic Information and Transactions (the ITE Law), spreading defamation online can be considered a crime punishable by up to six years imprisonment. This law has recently been used to prosecute Baiq Nuril Maknun, who worked as a bookkeeper at a school on the island of Lombok and whose name has been mentioned by several mass media outlets when discussing the #MeToo movement in Indonesia. Nuril's problem started when the school principal, Haji Muslim, started harassing her in 2012. Eventually she decided to record the sexual comments made by the school principal. The recording, according to Nuril, was forwarded by a colleague to the local Department of Education. Shortly after, Haji Muslim reported Nuril and sued her for defamation. She spent 15 days in police custody and 15 days in prison before facing trial in the Mataram District Court on 26 July 2017.

Initially, the District Court cleared Nuril, but the prosecutors appealed to the Supreme Court, which found her guilty in September 2018. Supported by various human rights activists and feminists, Nuril asked Indonesian President Jokowi for a pardon, and finally in July 2019, the President granted an amnesty to her. Nuril has been named by several reporters as the icon of Indonesia's #MeToo movement (Bisara 2019; Haryadi 2019), which may indicate the mass media's desperation to extend this popular movement to countries beyond Europe and North America. Nuril herself has actually never indicated that she was aware of #MeToo. She may be considered a kind of accidental hero. However, another possibility is that making her the icon of Indonesia's #MeToo movement is a misinterpretation or misjudgement, as Nuril has never publicly expressed any intention of sharing with other women or relating her experience to theirs. According to her, she only recorded the conversation with the school principal and played the recording to a male colleague. Her main aim was to halt the rumour that she was having an affair with the principal rather than to report his crime. Nevertheless, Nuril was still punished for this. How can someone like Nuril relate to those White celebrities and respond to #MeToo if her circumstances are very different?

Writing about #MeToo in Indonesia, Eva Nisa, a religious studies anthropologist at Victoria University in Wellington, New Zealand, argues that this movement 'has been criticised by some feminists, particularly due to its exclusivity and accessibility' because the movement has been predominantly linked to 'middle or upper-class white women' (Nisa 2019). Nisa further refers to Muslim women as a disadvantaged group by relating this to Nuril's case (Nisa 2019). Suggesting that there is a need for more opportunities for minoritised women like Nuril to speak up, Nisa mentions the importance of Muslim-specific versions of the #MeToo movement, such as #MosqueMeToo, introduced by the Egyptian-American feminist author Mona Elthaway in early 2018 (Nisa 2019). Nisa continues: 'Eltahawy encourages Muslim women to voice their concerns regarding sexual assault and to share their experiences of being sexually harassed even within sacred places' (Nisa 2019). Nisa emphasises how women can be targeted in places considered as safe havens: 'While Eltahawy's movement emphasises that sexual harassment and assault can occur even in the most sacred of spaces, Nuril's experience has added to the long list of sexual abuse experienced in academic learning environments' (Nisa 2019).

Nisa argues that because of Nuril's struggle for justice, she has been considered as 'the icon of Indonesia's #MeToo movement' (Nisa 2019). By making Nuril the face of the Indonesian #MeToo movement and relating her identity to her religion (Islam) vis-à-vis the White celebrities, Nisa reminds us of the existing tension between secular Western feminists and Muslim women. Several feminists have indeed criticised Western feminism for its emphasis on secularism, and its ignorance of the struggle of religious and, especially, Muslim women (Scott 2018; Abu-Lughod 2002).

As the Netherlands-based feminist philosopher Rosi Braidotti argues, in most Western feminist circles, thinkers who embrace spirituality and/or religion rather than secularism are generally considered as backward, irrational, or even oppressive and archaic (Braidotti 2008, 4–5). Similarly, scholar of Islamic feminism Miriam Cooke asserts that this division has consciously or unconsciously been influenced by postcolonial history:

> For way too long, Muslim women have been used as competing political and economical tools. This has caused a divide between those that are secular and those that identify as Islamic feminists and can be traced back to modernization and colonization.
>
> *(Abu-Lughod 2002, 228)*

Cooke argues that such binary oppositions have repeated the discourse of White people as saviours who fix, educate, and, if necessary, enforce certain values in societies in the Global South. The 'rhetoric of empire', Cooke continues, perceives these Brown women to be in need of rescue not because 'they are more "ours" than "theirs", but rather because they will have become more "ours" through the rescue mission' (2002, 228). Thus, it is not equality that encourages White people to want to save these women, but the desire to transform these women to suit their purposes. At the heart of their action is a superiority complex instead of a will to promote equality. Cooke further explains how women in the Muslim world have been powerful in challenging their own oppression and increasingly refuse to submit to patriarchal measures that threaten their rights (2002, 229).

However, several Western feminists have disagreed with this binary perspective in relation to secular versus non-secular women. A sociologist at Loughborough University, Line Nyhagen, and the Norwegian feminist Beatrice Halsaa argue that Braidotti is 'complicit in a reproduction of the dichotomy between the secular and the sacred' because of her framing of secular feminists as 'the hegemonic norm and religious or spiritual feminists as the exception' (2016, 47). Nyhagen and Halsaa state that Braidotti has overlooked 'important historical activism by European and other Christian, Muslim and Jewish religious feminists in national and international contexts' (2016, 47). Nyhagen and Halsaa point out that differences between

Decolonising feminism, feminist decolonialism **53**

the 'secular' and the 'religious' are not static and can even be ambiguous. Indeed, diverse practices can also make definitions of the 'secular' and the 'religious' overlap. The sociologist of religion Grace Davie, for instance, brings awareness of how some Christians continue to believe in God but do not attend church services. On the other hand, there are people who have continued to attend church services without believing in God (Davie 2002, 2007). Thus, Davie believes that people's habits, cultures, and practices can intertwine the religious with the secular.

In Indonesia, however, the distinction between those who are religious and those who are not has historically been made sharper by the state. While Indonesia has the largest Muslim population in the world, the country also contains layers of hegemonies, as well as social and cultural complexities to do with it being a multilingual and multicultural archipelago. Despite these cultural diversities, people who identify as or are considered to be non-religious can be easily stigmatised because of the requirement for citizens to embrace religion and due to historic as well as recent persecution of those considered atheist. Rendering Baiq Nuril the face of the Indonesian #MeToo movement risks forgetting that secular Indonesian women have also suffered sexual discrimination and abuse, and that secularism in Indonesia does not have to be related to the West.

Secularism versus Islam in Indonesia

The history of conflicts between secular and Islamic groups since the early days of Indonesia allows for a better understanding of the #MeToo movement in Indonesia and the silence of many rape victims. However, the tensions between Islam and secularism in Indonesia existed long before the country's independence on 17 August 1945 (Hadler 2008; Madinier 2015; Anderson 2009). At the end of the colonial period, Muslims were split into the so-called *santri* (observant Muslims) and *abangan* (Muslims who follow a syncretic tradition and are generally more secular). For many *santri* Islamic leaders, to oppose Western imperialism, Islam had to become the basis of the national struggle. For the more secular groups, nationalism had to be the basis of the national struggle, and several secular leaders even viewed Islam as incompatible with the modernisation of Indonesia (Madinier 2015). Thus, secularism in Indonesia was not particularly influenced by the West: the secularism of most *abangan* Muslims emanated instead from local wisdom and philosophies.

During the preparatory phases of Indonesian independence, the first Indonesian President, Sukarno, tried to find a middle way which pleased both secularist and Islamic groups. After long discussions, Sukarno eventually agreed with the alteration of Indonesia's philosophical principles (known as *Pancasila)* by including the phrase 'the belief in One God' to appease the Islamic groups. After independence, the tension between Islamists and secularists intensified, especially because the Indonesian Communist Party (PKI), which was largely secular, became more popular during the mid-1950s (Ricklefs 2012, 90). Amongst women's organisations that were active after Indonesian independence, the left-wing group Gerwani was one of the largest. Many members were religious Muslims but they largely kept their religion private. Gerwani women were known to be politically active and educated their members about socialism and left-wing ideologies (Martyn 2005, 84–85). Besides Gerwani, there were also women's organisations that proceeded from different political and religious ideologies (many were Islamic), and these differences often created disunity amongst them (Martyn 2005, 111).

The propaganda against communists who were accused of attempting a coup as well as of brutally murdering six top army generals and one aide on 1 October 1965 spread widely and became a pretext for the mass murder and imprisonment of millions of communists and left-wing sympathisers in Indonesia (Marching 2017, 18–19). The destruction of the Communist Party from October 1965 until early 1966 was supported by several Western countries because the first Indonesian President, Sukarno, was considered to be too close to the Communist Party of Indonesia (PKI). As the Cold War reached its peak, one of the missions of the West was to remove Sukarno (Kolko 1988, 173). The support of the West, especially the US, was crucial to the success of the genocide against Indonesian communists in 1965–66 (Robinson 2018, 84–95). The American government used journalists as well as academics to spread the stigma about the danger of communists (Johnson 1962, 222–3). Malicious rumours about Gerwani were disseminated, portraying them as evil atheist women who brutally raped, castrated, and murdered several generals while dancing seductively. This gave excuses for the army and paramilitary forces to detain, torture, rape, and/or murder these women (Fealy and Gregor 2010).

During the genocide in Indonesia, several Western countries, especially the US, were supportive of the use of religion in eradicating Communist Party members, who were often considered atheists (Fealy and Gregor 2010). The success of the American government in overthrowing the left-wing President Sukarno (who governed from 1945 to 1967) threw Indonesia into the grip of a new regime, led by Soeharto, for the next 32 years (until 1998). To ensure that communism did not resurface, Soeharto made it mandatory for Indonesians to adhere to one of the five state-recognised religions (Hinduism, Buddhism, Catholicism, Anglicanism/Protestantism, and Islam). Soeharto's regime, known as the New Order, also created a special column on the identity card which required citizens to register their religion. those who failed to do so would by default be considered as communists and atheists, and the consequences could be severe. Women who were identified as

Decolonising feminism, feminist decolonialism **55**

or alleged to be communists were considered morally and sexually debased, and were heavily stigmatised (Wieringa 2020, 103–10).

Eradication of the communists and their supporters was considered to be a religious duty and a purification of the nation. In this case, Gerwani women were doubly victimised because they were politically active and considered atheist. Sexual slanders against such women had spread widely in Indonesia, as the Gerwani women were often portrayed as aggressive and immoral, as opposed to the ideal submissive and pious Indonesian women (Wieringa 2020). The US-based Islamic Studies scholar Nelly van Doorn-Harder states that, in Indonesia, women considered non-religious were more susceptible to stigmatisation because their lack of religion was 'related to their sexuality and allegations of impurity' (Doorn-Harder 2019, 306).

Having destroyed progressive women's movements, the second Indonesian President, Soeharto, depoliticised other women's organisations and replaced them with government-controlled entities, such as *Dharma Wanita* (Women's Duty), whose main activities focused on women becoming wives and mothers, and wives supporting their husbands, as well as family-orientated government programmes. The ideal image of women was that of homemakers or self-sacrificing nurturers of their families (Brenner 1996, 678). Politically active women were not viewed favourably. While cautious of the growth of Islamic fundamentalism that might turn against the government, the Soeharto regime had also allowed Muslim leaders to preach that communists 'were rendering Indonesia impure because they were against religion' (Doorn-Harder 2019, 306).

Many of the films produced in Indonesia during the Soeharto period (1966–98) describe the immorality of communist and atheist women. The 'documentary' film sponsored by the Soeharto government, *Pengkhianatan G30S/PKI [The Treason of G30S/PKI]*, released in September 1984, depicts fabricated scenes of communists killing Muslims in the midst of their prayers, murdering generals in front of their families, and Gerwani women slicing the generals' bodies with razor blades. School children were required to watch this film, and it was broadcast on television every year on 30 September until the end of the reign of President Soeharto in May 1998. The dichotomy between secular and religious belief was emphasised by Indonesian law and propaganda since the beginning of Soeharto's long-lasting rule in 1966.

Stigmatisation of Indonesian communists was also condoned by the propaganda of several Western countries from the late 1950s until the 1960s: the US, the UK, and Australia were complicit in anti-communism in Indonesia as well as in the resultant genocide (Wieringa and Katjasungkana 2019, 11). Thus, the differences between secular Western feminism and Muslim feminism can be oversimplified when viewing the problems in regions with a Muslim majority, such as Indonesia, because the West has directly or indirectly taken part in discrimination against non-religious people through their attacks against communists in Indonesia. As non-religious women were dehumanised in this propaganda, sexual violence was consequently perceived as legitimate punishment during the 1965 genocide (Wieringa and Katjasungkana 2019, 11). Several books have been published documenting the sexual violence against Gerwani women (Fealy and Gregor 2010; Marching 2017; Wieringa and Katjasungkana 2019; Wieringa 2020; Doorn-Harder 2019). However, discussions of how this violence has specifically impacted non-religious and/or atheist women are very few and far between, most probably because of the silencing of these women's views. Although the current Indonesian President, Joko Widodo (Jokowi), acknowledged in January 2023 that there were gross human rights violations in 1965–66, he has not specified who the victims were or who were the perpetrators. By using ambiguous language, he avoids mentioning that widespread sexual abuse and rape happened during that period. This has undoubtedly discouraged the victims from speaking up and from openly sharing their sexual abuse or the violence they experienced as part of a public campaign such as #MeToo. Such huge atrocities still haunt the country, and discussing Indonesian women's struggles today without mentioning the destruction of secular women's organisations in 1965–66 can lead one to misleading conclusions. The Indonesian humanities scholar Ariel Heryanto observes that present-day Indonesian society cannot be understood without reference to the impact of the 1965 genocide, because these events continue to have a hold on many people's minds and society at large (Heryanto 2006, 9). This is still true today as the spectre of communism continues to be used to stigmatise certain groups of people and even prominent politicians. Obviously, this consolidates the intimidation felt by the 1965 female survivors because of their gender as well as their disenfranchised political position.

The struggles of Indonesian women survivors before #MeToo

Many survivors of the 1965 genocide still keep quiet about what happened to them, but there have been several women who have spoken up publicly via various channels. On 5 July 2015, I met five of them in Yogyakarta, Central Java. We gathered at the home of Christina Sumarmiyati on her 69th birthday. She invited four other women survivors. While we celebrated the day together, we were also talking about the various sorrows they experienced in prison, including the sexual abuse and rape they suffered. These women encouraged each other to open up about their experiences. They have narrated their stories on YouTube, on the BBC, and in magazines (amongst others, *Bhinneka* and *Tempo*) (Channel 2021; Trisnanti 2013; Marching 2015).

They set up regular meetings to help each other financially and emotionally, and to find other former female political prisoners too. Thus, these women have done much more than just responding 'me too' alongside other survivors: they actively approached their comrades and have offered in-person solidarity and support. Similarly, several other former women prisoners did not give up on seeking justice, despite the danger they were risking. One example is Sulami Djoyoprawiro, the former third secretary of Gerwani, who was imprisoned from 1967–84. Not long after her release from prison, Sulami took part in establishing the Foundation for the Research into Victims of the 1965-66 Killings (YPKP '65). Although she received many threats from Soeharto's regime, she persisted in searching for other former women political prisoners. She also published her autobiography, *Perempuan – Kebenaran dan Penjara (Woman – Truth and Prison)* (Sulami 1999). As Ariel Heryanto maintains, 'socialist and Communist-phobic rhetoric [in Indonesia] outlived the Cold War which had created the original circumstances that brought it into existence and it also outlived the New Order which had been its main author and custodian' (Heryanto 2006, 24). Trying to encourage other women to speak up by breaking her own silence, Sulami narrated the sexual abuse she experienced in a short YouTube film: there she tells of how she was stripped naked, then ordered to stand against a wall while daggers were repeatedly thrown at her (Trisnanti 2013). Not all the women survivors I spoke to experienced rape, but they were very supportive of the different experiences and traumas each other had undergone. Thus, in a similar way to the #MeToo activists, these Indonesian women publicise their experience, encouraging their comrades to speak up and thus empowering them, but they were doing this before the #MeToo movement started and without attracting its huge global attention, most probably because no glamorous celebrities were involved.

An account of an atheist woman: the coalition of approaches

Besides the five women mentioned above, I met three other female rape survivors. These three women told me their stories but asked me not to publish them. Two of them identified themselves as atheists and stated that they did not want to publicly reveal this fact for fear of stigma. Many women, especially the non-religious ones, still conceal their pain because of the possible repercussions affecting not only themselves, but also their families. The fact that they were willing to tell me their stories demonstrates their desire to be recognised, and for their pain to be known. One of these women's stories finally found a voice in fiction, as she is represented by one of the protagonists in my novel about the 1965 genocide, *Dari Dalam Kubur (From Inside the Grave)*. With her consent, I gave her a fictional name, age, birthplace, and so on. However, even in fiction, her story encountered many problems: the biggest publisher in Indonesia, Gramedia, was only willing to publish the novel if I toned down what they considered to be strong criticisms against religion. Finally, I decided to go with a much smaller publisher to get the

58 Soe Tjen Marching

novel out without any censorship. This indicates that strong frictions persist between secularism and religion, at the expense of secularism. Therefore, women who identify themselves as atheists still find it very difficult to find a safe space for their stories to be told, even in fiction. This woman did tell me her wish that one day it could be safe for her to open up and to reveal that she had inspired me to write the novel. However, her wish will never come true. She passed away a few weeks before my novel was published in September 2020.

The stories of the above women demonstrate that while we need to decolonise feminism, we must also ensure that decolonialism is feminist. In other words, whilst we must be aware that women from different regions and ethnicities can be disadvantaged by mainstream and/or White feminism, we should take into account how different regions and ethnicities disadvantage certain groups of women, even amongst victims of rape and sexual abuse. In this case, decolonial feminism and intersectional feminism can form a coalition of approaches, so that women in the Global South are not dragged back to a version of feminism that compromises decolonialist efforts.

While generally Indonesian women have been disadvantaged by the dominant discourse of White Western feminism, there are further hidden voices of women within Indonesian society who have been desperate to be seen and/ or recognised. To decolonise feminism by aligning Indonesian women with Muslim identities and/or Western feminism through a neglect of Indonesian secularism assumes that certain 'prominent' groups can represent the whole region. This risks dismissing the stigmatisation against secular women in Indonesia. In this case, while we decolonise feminism, we must be careful that acts of decolonialism do not disadvantage women whose voices are yet to be heard.

Epilogue

The discussion of the ineffectiveness of the #MeToo movement in Indonesia demonstrates that decolonial perspectives are important in feminism, but feminist perspectives are also important in decolonialism. While Indonesia has the largest Muslim population in the world, there is considerable ideological diversity within Indonesian Islam, with some believers being more devout than others. Secularism in majority non-White countries such as Indonesia does not have to be instigated by the West. Similarly, discriminatory religiosity can be tolerated and even supported by Western countries if it serves their geopolitical interests, as demonstrated during the period known as the 1965 genocide in Indonesia. In this case, while it is necessary to acknowledge that there are problems with forming coalitions amongst women in the Global South, this does not necessarily negate the potential for feminist community because such an acknowledgement can also help to reveal the deeper impacts of colonialism. For this reason, decolonialism and intersectional feminism must always go hand in hand, rather than one superseding the other. The coalition of these approaches will help feminism to be more inclusive so that under-privileged women are not left out or silenced.

References

Abu-Lughod, Lila. 2002. "Do Muslim Women Really Need Saving? Anthropological Reflections on Cultural Relativism and Its Others." *American Anthropologist* 104 (3): 783–790. https://doi.org/10.1525/aa.2002.104.3.783

Anderson, Benedict. 2009. *Some Aspects of Indonesian Politics Under the Japanese Occupation: 1944–1945.* Sheffield: Equinox Publishing.

Becker, Amy B. 2013. "Star Power? Advocacy, Receptivity, and Viewpoints on Celebrity Involvement in Issue Politics." *Atlantic Journal of Communication* 21 (1): 1–16. https://doi.org/10.1080/15456870.2013.743310

Bisara, Dion. 2019. "Jokowi's Amnesty Last Hope for Indonesia's #MeToo Icon." *The Jakarta Globe*, July 5, 2019.

Braidotti, Rosi. 2008. "In Spite of the Times: The Postsecular Turn in Feminism." *Theory, Culture & Society* 26 (6): 1–24. https://doi.org/10.1177/0263276415590235

Brenner, Suzanne A. 1996. "Reconstructing Self and Society: Javanese Muslim Women and 'the Veil.'" *American Ethnologist* 23 (4): 673–697. https://doi.org/10.1525/ae.1996.23.4.02a00010

Butler, Judith. 2008. *Gender Trouble: Feminism and the Subversion of Identity.* New York: Routledge.

Byrne, Deirdre. 2020. "Decolonial African Feminism for White Allies." *Journal of International Women's Studies* 21 (7): 37–46.

Carby, Hazel V. 2007. "White Woman Listen! Black Feminism and the Boundaries of Sisterhood." In *CCCS Selected Working Papers*, edited by Ann Gray, Jan Campbell, Mark Erickson, Stuart Hanson and Helen Wood, 737–758. London: Routledge.

Casanova, Jose. 2011. "The Secular, Secularizations, Secularisms." In *Rethinking Secularism*, edited by Craig Calhoun, Mark Juergensmeyer, and Jonathan Vanantwerpen, 54–74. New York: Oxford University Press.

Channel, Roudhoh. 2021. "Kisah Christina Sumarmiyati." YouTube. June 29, 2021. https://www.youtube.com/watch?v=n3wgJG6BRuM

Cobb, Ellen Pinkos. 2020. *International Workplace Sexual Harassment Laws and Developments for the Multinational Employer.* London: Routledge.

Cooke, Miriam. 2002. "Islamic Feminism Before and After September 11th." *Journal of Gender Law & Policy* 9 (2): 227–235. https://doi.org/10.2979/meridians.13.2.09

Crenshaw, Kimberlé. 1994. *Mapping the Margins: Intersectionality, Identity, and Violence Against Women of Color.* New York: Routledge.

Crouch, Melissa. 2012. "Law and Religion in Indonesia: The Constitutional Court and the Blasphemy Law." *Asian Journal of Comparative Law* 12 (1): 1–46. https://doi.org/10.1017/S2194607800000582

Davie, Grace. 2002. *Europe: The Exceptional Case. Parameters of Faith in the Modern World.* London: Darton, Longman and Todd.

Davie, Grace. 2007. *The Sociology of Religion.* London: Sage.

Doorn-Harder, Nelly. 2019. "Purifying Indonesia, Purifying Women: The National Commission for Women's Rights and the 1965–1968 Anti-Communist Violence." *Crosscurrent* 69 (3): 231–342. https://doi.org/10.1111/cros.12380

Erickon, Amanda. 2018. "#MeToo — and Its Backlash — Went Global." *The Washington Post*, December 14, 2018. https://www.washingtonpost.com/world/2018/12/14/metoo-its-backlash-went-global/

Fealy, Greg and K. McGregor. 2010. "Nahdlatul Ulama and the Killings of 1965–66: Religion, Politics, and Remembrance." *Indonesia* 89: 37–60. http://hdl.handle.net/1885/51105

Goodyear, Dana. 2022. "The Harvey Weinstein Trial and the Myth of the Perfect Perpetrator." *The New Yorker*, December 7, 2022. https://www.newyorker.com/news/letter-from-los-angeles/harvey-weinstein-the-monster-of-metoo-trial-los-angeles

Grimshaw, Mike. 2011. "Encountering Religion: *Encounter*, Religion, and the Cultural Cold War, 1953–1967." *History of Religions* 51 (1): 31–58. https://doi.org/10.1086/659608

Hadler, Jeffrey. 2008. "A Historiography of Violence and the Secular State in Indonesia: Tuanku Imam Bondjol and the Uses of History." *The Journal of Asian Studies* 67 (3): 971–1010. https://doi.org/10.1017/S0021911808001228

Haryadi, Matthias. 2019. "Victim of Harassment, Female Teacher Convicted of Defamation Asks Widodo for a Pardon." *Asia News*, July 9, 2019. https://www.asianews.it/news-en/Victim-of-harassment,-female-teacher-convicted-of-defamation-asks-Widodo-for-a-pardon-47495.html

Heryanto, Ariel. 2006. *State Terrorism and Political Identity in Indonesia: Fatally Belonging*. London: Routledge.

Indrayana, Denny. 2008. *Indonesian Constitutional Reform, 1999–2002: An Evaluation of Constitution-Making in Transition*. Jakarta: Penerbit Buku Kompas.

Johnson, John Asher, ed. 1962. *The Role of the Military in Underdeveloped Countries*. Princeton, New Jersey: Princeton University Press.

Kartika, Dyah Ayu. 2019. "#MeToo has Skipped Indonesia – Here's Why." *The Conversation*, March 8, 2019. https://theconversation.com/metoo-has-skipped-indonesia-heres-why-112530

Kolko, Gabriel. 1988. *Confronting the Third World: United States Foreign Policy, 1945–1980*. New York: Pantheon Books.

Lugones, María. 2020. "Colonialidade e Gênero." In *Pensamento Feminista Hoje: Perspectivas Decoloniais*, edited by Heloisa Buarque de Hollanda, 50–60. Rio de Janeiro: Bazar do Tempo.

MacKinnon, Catherine A. 2020. "Global #MeToo." In *The Global #MeToo Movement*, edited by Ann M. Noel and David B. Oppenheimer, 1–15. Washington, DC: Full Court Press.

Madinier, Remy. 2015. *Islam and Politics in Indonesia*. Singapore: National University of Singapore Press.

Marching, Soe Tjen. 2015. "Pengakuan Empat Perempuan." *Majalah Bhinneka*. Surabaya: Lembaga Bhinneka.

Marching, Soe Tjen. 2017. *The End of Silence: Accounts of the 1965 Genocide in Indonesia*. Amsterdam: Amterdam University Press.

Martyn, Elizabeth. 2005. *The Women's Movement in Post-Colonial Indonesia: Gender and Nation in a New Democracy*. New York: Routledge.

Mohanty, Chandra. 1984. "Under Western Eyes: Feminist Scholarship and Colonial Discourses." *Boundary 2* 12 (3) (Spring – Autumn): 333–358. https://doi.org/10.2307/302821

Morris, Kadish. 2020. "Tarana Burke: 'If It Weren't for Black Women, I Would Not Have Made It'." *The Guardian*, November 15, 2020. https://www.theguardian.com/us-news/2020/nov/15/tarana-burke-if-it-werent-for-black-women-i-would-not-have-made-it

Mosley, Tonya. 2023. "'Me Too' Founder Tarana Burke Says Black Girls' Trauma Shouldn't Be Ignored". VAWNet. September 29, 2021. https://vawnet.org/news/me-too-founder-tarana-burke-says-black-girls-trauma-shouldnt-be-ignored

Nisa, Eva. 2019. "Baiq Nuril Maknun, the Face of Indonesia's #MeToo Movement." *Asia Media Centre*, August 26, 2019. https://www.asiamediacentre.org.nz/opinion-and-analysis/indonesias-metoo-movement/

Nyhagen, Line and Beatrice Halsaa. 2016. *Religion, Gender and Citizenship; Women of Faith, Gender Equality and Feminism.* Basingstoke: Palgrave Macmillan.

Pawestri, Tunggal (@tunggalp). 2023. "Takut kena UU ITE? Malah dikriminalisasi pelaku." Twitter. January 26, 2023. https://twitter.com/tunggalp/status/1618611578852737026.

Pflum, Mary. 2018. "A Year Ago, Alyssa Milano Started a Conversation About #MeToo. These Women Replied." *NBC News*, October 15, 2018. https://www.nbcnews.com/news/us-news/year-ago-alyssa-milano-started-conversation-about-metoo-these-women-n920246

Pohlman, Annie. 2012. "Spectacular Atrocities: Making Enemies during the 1965–1966 Massacres in Indonesia." In *Theatres of Violence: Massacre, Mass Killing and Atrocity throughout History,* edited by Philip G. Dwyer and Lyndall Ryan, 199–212. New York: Berghahn Books.

Ricklefs, M. C. 2008. *A History of Modern Indonesia Since c.1300.* 4th ed. London: MacMillan.

Ricklef, M. C. 2012. *Islamisation and Its Opponents in Java: A Political, Social, Cultural and Religious History, c. 1930 to the Present.* Singapore: National University of Singapore Press.

Ristianto, Christoforus. 2019. "Tujuh Tahun Baiq Nuril, Berawal dari Pelecehan, Tersangka UU ITE, hingga Terima Amnesti." Kompas.com. July 30, 2019. https://nasional.kompas.com/read/2019/07/30/09564421/7-tahun-baiq-nuril-berawal-dari-pelecehan-tersangka-uu-ite-hingga-terima

Robinson, Geoffrey B. 2018. *The Killing Season: A History of the Indonesian Massacres, 1965–66.* Princeton, NJ: Princeton University Press.

Robinson, Kathryn. 2006. "Islamic Influences on Indonesian Feminism." *Social Analysis: The International Journal of Anthropology* 50 (1) (Spring): 171–177. https://doi.org/10.3167/015597706780886012

Rodriguez, Leah and Pia Gralki. 2020. "Harvey Weinstein Verdict Is #MeToo Milestone But Changes Little for World's Sexual Assault Survivors." *Global Citizen.* March 10, 2020. https://www.globalcitizen.org/en/content/harvey-weinstein-verdict-global-implications/

Sayej, Nadja. 2017. "Alyssa Milano on the #MeToo Movement: 'We're Not Going To Stand For It Any more'." *The Guardian*, December 1, 2017.

Scott, Joan Wallach. 2018. *Sex and Secularism.* Princeton, NJ: Princeton University Press.

Smith-Hefner, Nancy J. 2007. "Javanese Women and the Veil in Post-Soeharto Indonesia." *Journal of Asian Studies* 66 (2): 389–420. https://doi.org/10.1017/S0021911807000575

Sulami. 1999. *Perempuan – Kebenaran dan Penjara* [*Woman – Truth and Prison*]. Jakarta: Cipta Lestari.

Trisnanti, Dian. 2013. "Saya Rasa Itu Sulit Untuk Dilupakan." YouTube. February 4, 2013. https://www.youtube.com/watch?v=cI2Nuq8rtKk

Tuck, Eve and K. Wayne Yang. 2012. "Decolonization is not a Metaphor." *Decolonization: Indigeneity, Education & Society* 1 (1): 1–40. https://doi.org/10.25058/20112742

Velez, Emma D. 2019. "Decolonial Feminism at the Intersection: A Critical Reflection on the Relationship Between Decolonial Feminism and Intersectionality." *Journal of Speculative Philosophy* 33 (3): 390–406. https://doi.org/10.5325/jspecphil.33.3.0390

Wieringa, Saskia. 2020. "The Women and the Generals: Unraveling a Myth of Sexual Perversion." *Archipel* 99: 23–27. https://doi.org/10.4000/archipel.1642

Wieringa, Saskia and Nursyahbani Katjasungkana. 2019. *Propaganda and the Genocide in Indonesia: Imagined Evil.* London and New York: Routledge.

4

UNDERSTANDING SEXUAL HARASSMENT ON PUBLIC TRANSPORT THROUGH FEMINIST EPISTEMOLOGIES AND INTERSECTIONAL RHYTHMANALYSIS

Sian Lewis

This chapter proposes a feminist epistemological grounding of theoretical approaches that are used to understand incidents of sexual harassment on the London Underground transport network in the United Kingdom (UK). Feminist epistemologies (standpoint and situated knowledges) influence and guide the way this research is conducted, analysed, and presented. They also intertwine with the less inherently feminist conceptual framework of 'rhythmanalysis', formulated by the French philosopher and sociologist Henri Lefebvre, and provide a lens through which to understand women's experiences of sexual harassment in transport environments. Taking a hermeneutic sociological perspective, and being informed by the feminist epistemologies outlined below, this chapter demonstrates how such an approach permits the foregrounding of women's experiences within the traditionally androcentric discipline of criminology. It also shows that we can critically engage with, rather than eradicate, the institutional voices of the police without essentialising them as objective or expert. This approach enables us to identify what constitutes both victim and police knowledge of sexual harassment on the London Underground and recognises them as situated and partial. I reflect on the way these modes of knowing intertwine with women's experiential and often subjugated knowledges to offer an in-depth understanding of the occurrence of sexual harassment within the space of public transport.

First, this chapter outlines standpoint theory and situated knowledges and describes the data set that constitutes the research on which this chapter builds. Next, the chapter critically reflects on the operationalisation of standpoint theory and situated knowledges and how these feed into the implementation of a rhythmanalysis framework, that subsequently permits an intersectional lens through which to comprehend and do justice

DOI: 10.4324/9781003399575-5

This chapter has been made available under a CC-BY-NC-ND license.

to the nuanced and complex occurrences of sexual harassment in a transitory space. The goal here is to demonstrate the value of an intersectional rhythmanalyis. Intersectionality is understood as the converging of multiple social identities that create a different or unique experience of oppression and knowledge (Crenshaw 1989). Though intersectionality and rhythmanalysis are concepts from different intellectual traditions, in this chapter, I show how they can be connected. In short, rhythmanalysis focuses on how the rhythms of everyday life shape our experiences and perceptions of the world, whilst intersectionality allows us to see the multidimensionality of women's experiences. Combined, they offer critical new avenues for understanding the situatedness and nuance of knowledge of sexual harassment on the London Underground, and of other forms of gender-based violence.

Feminist epistemologies: standpoint and situated knowledges

Some feminist epistemologies take interpretivist methodologies to challenge positivist notions and reject realist approaches that claim to represent an independent social reality (Hammersley 1992). Suggesting that knowledge is subject to critique and negotiation helps to recognise that 'realities' are often derived from a privileged, patriarchal, and partial perspective. As such, feminist scholars have long endeavoured to conduct research that recognises and destabilises patriarchal ideologies and power relations. They have sought to find ways to capture and represent women's experiences to uncover and examine the social oppression of women.

A key epistemology to recognise is feminist standpoint theory. Emerging from Marxist arguments around access to oppressed knowledge, American feminist thinkers including sociologists Dorothy Smith (1987) and Patricia Hill Collins (1990) and political scientist Nancy Hartsock (1983), introduced feminist standpoint epistemologies which acknowledge power relations and the value of marginalised standpoints (particularly those of women) (Nielsen 1990; Longino 1999). Feminist standpoint theorists often focused on researching women's lives as points of enquiry. As noted by American philosopher Sandra Harding, 'starting off research from women's lives will generate less partial and distorted accounts not only of women's lives but also of men's lives and of the whole social order' (Harding 1993, 56). Moreover, as British sociologist Sylvia Walby (2001, 486) considers: 'Standpoint epistemology makes a claim to authoritative knowledge not through the procedures of science but through the status of the oppressed as the bearer of true knowledge'. This highlights how standpoint epistemologies claim that marginalised groups (in this case, women) hold a particular and more 'truthful' claim to knowing (Douchet and Mauthner 2007). Here, standpoint and intersectionality meet in their critiques of a singular, universal perspective, and their emphasis on understanding the role of varying social identities in the formation of knowledge through experience. In my own study of sexual harassment on the London Underground, I operationalised standpoint theory throughout the data collection, analysis, and writing up process of the research. Standpoint theory acts as an epistemological guide in the attempt to reduce the hierarchical nature that is often present in sociological research (Oakley 1981), and to give weight and focus to the diversity and complexity of women's experiences and narratives of sexual harassment.

American feminist scholar Donna Haraway locates herself in relation to standpoint theory in her essay *Situated Knowledges* (1988, 590), stating: 'There is no single feminist standpoint because our maps require too many dimensions for that metaphor to ground our visions'. Rather than claiming that one (oppressed) group of people hold an objective vision or truth of reality, the notion of situated knowledges suggests that all knowledge is partial, and therefore must be critiqued. As highlighted above, both women and police officers know about sexual harassment from a particular and situated perspective. The theory of situated knowledges, then, is useful to avoid perceiving the 'authoritative' voice of the police as objective and allows consideration of women's individual and corporeal experiences of harassment.

When discussing situated and subjugated knowledges, it is paramount to be explicit as to whose 'knowledges' are being discussed. Stanley (2013, 21) discusses how, whilst feminist work has focused on showing women's 'experiences of oppression', it is important to recognise that 'women' do not share an ontological existence or material reality, and their experiences are not unified. It is here that an intersectional approach demands the consideration of women's diverse experiences and knowledge based on other intersecting elements of identity, rather than focusing solely on gender. That is, the acknowledgement that women are not a monolithic group (as critics of standpoint suggest that the theory can imply). This has been particularly highlighted by Black feminists who emphasise the need for feminist research to recognise difference in their analyses of women's experiences (Collins 1986; Lorde 1984). Welsh et al. (2006) consider this in their research on diverse groups of women in Canada, noting that women's racialised bodies and citizenship status impact how they define their experiences of harassment. Mason-Bish and Zempi (2019) examine veiled British Muslim women's experiences of street harassment and show how these can sit at the intersection of religion, gender, and other aspects of identity. Loukaitou-Sideris et al. (2020) explore this in the context of US public transport. Their research shows that students' experiences and reporting of sexual harassment are impacted by both the environment and individual characteristics such as gender, sexual orientation, and ethnicity. In summary, it is necessary to take an intersectional approach and consider how gendered experiences interrelate with class, 'race', and sexuality and with other systems of oppression and privilege (Collins 1986; Bilge 2010; hooks 1981). This draws attention to the importance of being transparent with regards to who is speaking in this research: whose experiences are being represented, and whose are not. Even within research that centres women's voices, some knowledges remain subjugated.

Research context and method

The data set for this research was primarily formed from semi-structured, qualitative interviews with 29 women who had experienced sexual harassment on the London Underground. Participants were between the ages of 22 and 45. Twenty-four of the women were White, 3 were of Asian descent, and 2 defined themselves as Mixed Race; 23 were British while 6 identified as non-British nationals; 3 identified as gay, 2 as bisexual, and 23 as heterosexual. Whilst the study called for anyone who identified as a woman, all participants were cis women. The possibility of bias when using a convenience sample such as this means that the study is not generalisable and should not be taken as representative of 'all' women's experiences. The class and age structure is also recognised as a limitation of this study. The research sample mirrors Transport for London (TfL – the governing body of the London Underground) data regarding the demographic of those who report experiencing sexual harassment on London public transport (TfL 2016). The 2016 TfL Safety and Security report showed that women aged 16–34 were most likely to experience unwanted sexual behaviour on public transport. Similarly, in police interviews when I asked about the 'demographic' of victims, they responded with a focus on age – specifically that they perceived the majority of victims to be women between 20 and 40 years of age. However, there is literature that suggests that the underreporting of sexual violence more broadly is exacerbated amongst particular groups, including the elderly (Bows and Westmarland 2017), Black, Asian, and minority ethnic women, migrant and asylum-seeking women (particularly those with limited or no English) (Rahmanipour et al. 2019; Tan and Kuschminder 2022), disabled women (Willott et al. 2020), Gypsy, Roma, and Traveller women, and LGBTQ+ women (Tillewein et al. 2020). Hence, these 'hard to reach populations' become underrepresented in data and statistics. Notably, while my research sample mirrors that of TfL and British Transport Police (BTP) data as to who is most likely to *report or speak out* about sexual harassment on the London Underground, this should not be misconstrued as being the most likely to *experience* sexual harassment.

This research is also based on 15 semi-structured interviews with employees from the BTP, the policing body under whose remit the London Underground network falls. I conducted these interviews to explore how a key stakeholder and authoritative body formulate knowledge about sexual harassment on the network and how it is used in practice. Five of the interviewed employees were women and ten were men. Fourteen were White-British, and one was Asian-British. All participants were considered 'experts' or 'specialists' in the policing of sexual offences.

Rhythmanalysis, the London Underground, and sexual harassment

The prevalence of sexually harassing behaviour within transport spaces across the globe demonstrates that these environments are structured in a way (spatially and socially) that permits these behaviours to be perpetrated. It is beyond the aim and scope of this chapter to delve into the motivations and impact of such pervasive behaviour, and this has been covered in depth elsewhere (see Valan 2020; Ceccato and Loukaitou-Sideris 2022; Chowdbury 2022). Similarly, I have also previously explored how transport environments facilitate sexual harassment to manifest in a particular way that differs from street harassment, due to the rhythmic nature of the space (Lewis et al. 2021). Henri Lefebvre's concept of rhythmanalysis has a focus on the taking place of the everyday, stating that 'everywhere where there is interaction between a place, a time and an expenditure of energy, there is rhythm' (2004, 15). These rhythms are present in a multiplicity of forms: they can be biological, psychological, social and mechanical, corporeal, natural, institutional, and collective. These collections of rhythms essentially constitute the ambiance and feel of a place, which in turn impacts on the sociabilities that occur within it. As Highmore (2002) considers, rhythmanalysis has the ability to reveal the politics of pace, as rhythms are a 'deeply political and social phenomena' (Reid-Musson 2018, 894).

Lefebvre's framework continues to be applied to contemporary societal issues and its Marxist underpinnings remain easy to locate (Horton 2005). Rhythmanalysis reveals varied experiences of life under capitalist spatio-temporal dynamics. It can unveil modes of power and oppression and has been used to expose how the rhythms of capitalism benefit some and oppress others (Farrington 2021; Lockley 2022). Yet despite this, Buckley and Strauss (2016) have critiqued Lefebvre's work as failing to acknowledge gendered subjectivities and inequalities, while Kipfer et al. (2013) critique his work for projecting an essentialist view of gender difference. Reid-Musson (2018) draws on these critiques and argues for the importance of intersectional rhythmanalysis. She considers that whilst Lefebvre addressed elements of women's 'everyday' lives, he did not critically theorise gendered exploitation, nor did he acknowledge how gender could intersect with class and racial oppressions. In recent years, more work has emerged that demonstrates an explicit feminist engagement with rhythmanalysis. For example, Thorpe et al. (2023) use a rhythmanalysis framework to explore women's experiences of the COVID-19 pandemic. They show how the pandemic posed a disruption to women's usual daily rhythms, causing a 'gendered arrhythmia' of work and family routines, a disruption that was felt and experienced through the body. This sort of feminist engagement with rhythm can extend understandings of the gendered politics of everyday life. In another example, Tamboukou (2020) uses feminist theory and narrative rhythmanalysis to focus on corporeal voices and listening practices within her work with migrant and refugee women and experiences of forced displacement. She suggests that focusing on the rhythms of oral narratives can contribute to decolonising ways of knowing.

My own contribution to this growing feminist engagement with rhythmanalysis explicitly connects it with a) gender-based violence, b) policing, and c) situated knowledges. Applying a rhythmanalysis framework in conjunction with feminist epistemologies provides insights into sexual harassment on public transport. It connects space and mobilities and explains their role in shaping such behaviours, understanding how they are experienced by women, and how they are understood by the police. Viewing this through an intersectional lens enables an understanding of how women experience sexual harassment differently. It provides a new angle for understanding perpetrations, experiences, and policing of sexual harassment on transport by revealing the situatedness and affective nature of rhythms, and importantly, how the significance of and interactions with these rhythms varies depending on an individual's background and experiences.

When considering dominant rhythms regulating everyday city life, public transport schedules are an example of institutionally inscribed urban cyclical time (Mulicek et al. 2015; Schwanen et al. 2012). As an essential part of the urban fabric of any city, transport systems act as systems of mobility and are an integral component of the infrastructure of social life. Simultaneously replicating and facilitating the (institutional) time-conscious rhythms of the city above, the Underground is a rapid, regular transport network. It is often seen as being dominated by the fast-paced circadian beat of commuters, with an impersonality and insolence that imposes itself (Bissell 2010). The rhythms of the London Underground are dominated by attributes of rationalisation: punctuality and calculability. These regular and repetitive rhythms of the Underground allow a sense of predictability that is highly valued by commuters and creates a sense of certainty or, as Edensor (2010, 8) states, it allows for an everyday 'ontological predictability and security'. Yet this rationalism exists in tension with the corporeal rhythms of individuals who move through the system, with an ever-present risk of disjuncture.

Lefebvre puts great emphasis on corporeality, claiming that understanding rhythm is always done through the body. He emphasises the necessity to always locate the body as a first point of reference and 'the tool for subsequent investigations' (2004, 12). While Lefebvre himself does not critically engage with the significance of *gendered* bodies and how they may varyingly experience rhythms, locating my research within Lefebvre's rhythmanalysis brings into focus the tension between individual bodily rhythms, shared social rhythms (habits), mechanical rhythms, and rhythms of the city that are collectively active within the space of the London Underground. Paying attention to these rhythms offers a new angle on understanding incidences of sexual harassment on the London Underground. Locating them within the spatio-temporal environment, it becomes clear that the rhythmic characteristics impact how people interact within the space. The London Underground has observable effects on the behaviour of those moving through the network. These rhythms and how they are interpreted and experienced through the situated perspectives of the individual body (and the victim of sexual harassment) and by an organisational 'body' (the police) are necessary to consider. It allows us to discern how sexual harassment is understood and negotiated by victims, as well as how the police understand and use these rhythms to target offenders. It reveals how these rhythms are known and experienced from partial perspectives, and how in turn, this underwrites what constitutes a 'situated' knowledge of sexual harassment on public transport. It is important to acknowledge that women's own corporeal and social rhythms (which vary depending on, e.g., age, biography, religion, class, ethnicity) collide and coalesce with the broader rhythms of the space of the Underground, and impact experiences and perceptions of sexual harassment.

Women's situatedness and rhythms

Feminist standpoint theory (Hartsock 1983; Smith 1987; Collins 1990) proposes that women's oppressed and unique standpoint means that their truth claims expose reality, whilst Haraway (1988) states that it is not possible for one group of people to possess objective vision. Rather, Haraway claims, all knowledge is partial and situated and therefore must be critiqued. I hope it is clear, then, that the aim here is not to critique women's knowledge of their own experiences of sexual harassment, but rather to locate them in their situated position. In my study, women's experiences of sexual harassment on the London Underground are situated within the broader context of gendered mobilities in urban space, as well as being located within a catalogue of experiences of sexism and (fear of, or actual) gendered violence. These incidents are also experienced intersectionally, individually, intimately, and corporeally, whilst on a journey, situated within a very specific social space. These factors constitute women's standpoints from which they experience sexual harassment on the London Underground. As explored below, this is often in contrast to the situatedness of police knowledge and understanding of the 'same' phenomena.

The London Underground's unique spatio-temporal and social nature means that sexual harassment occurring in transit is perpetrated and

70 Sian Lewis

experienced in a specific way, facilitated and constricted by the environment. Being static within a moving space is particularly pertinent, as this feature allows sexual harassment to be perpetrated in a way that would not be possible, or experienced in the same way, in the streets or the workplace. The sociabilities on the network, shaped by rhythms, mean that when experiencing sexual harassment, women are often uncertain about the intention of the offence due to the ambiguous nature of physical touching within the space. The rhythms of the city permeate the Underground and are used by perpetrators to facilitate and conceal sexual harassment in various ways, at different times of day. Spaces where strangers are confined create particular sites of sociability (Urry 2007) and, as Bissel (2009) considers, travelling by train is often characterised by the density of people being transported in close proximity. This is particularly observable in morning and evening rush hours, when passengers are confined and pressed up against one another on platforms and in the rail carriage, demonstrating a deceleration or friction of rhythms in contrast to the desire of commuters to be moving quickly (Urry 2007). The density of bodies permits particular types of sexual harassment to be perpetrated (groping, frotteurism) whilst the offender moves with the choreographies of the crowd and synchronises with the rhythmic motion of the carriage, often without visibly transgressing from the dominant and acceptable way of behaving. Here, the normative physical friction that occurs between passengers is exploited to perpetrate and conceal a particular type of harassment. The ambiguous and often ephemeral nature of these experiences lead to a sense of ontological uncertainty as to whether harassment 'actually' happened, whether it was real or purposeful, due to the subtle nature of how the rhythms of the space are used and abused by perpetrators. This uncertainty often acts to silence women (both at the time of the incident and when considering reporting) and encourages them to question their corporeal and experiential knowledge.

When experiencing sexual harassment on the London Underground, women were often anxious about 'making a scene' in an enclosed public space and not wanting to disrupt their own urban rhythms and codes of comportment. The rhythmic flow of movement through the London Underground network shows regulated bodies coming together to move as a 'polyrhythmic' (Lefebvre 2004) collective. Hornsey (2012, 686) describes how the Underground is designed to function with 'the logic of a factory assembly line'. Consequently, disorder that creates a disruption to people's journeys is often treated with disdain (Edensor 2010). Women's accounts described an unwillingness to overtly react to incidents of sexual harassment for fear of embarrassment, and the apprehension that their fellow passengers will react with ambivalence or condescension. This is exacerbated for women whose nexus of identities render them more likely to be dismissed, blamed, or revictimized (for example, veiled Muslim women are at risk of gendered Islamophobia (Zempi 2019)). Conversely, one participant in my research described how, when a man started chatting to her on the night Underground train, she only interacted because she thought he had recognised her as a 'fellow gay person and wanted to have a drunk chat'. When he propositioned her and turned verbally aggressive as she rejected him, he said, 'Well then why did you talk to me?'. She described to me how she felt foolish, and that as an autistic woman, she 'misread' his intentions, assuming that as 'some approaching middle aged, not stunning young woman' he was not flirting with her. In response, she stood up and physically pushed him away, but then realised that because of the nature of the London Underground, there was no place for her to go. Here, multiple intersections of her identity (gender, sexuality, disability, age) and the rhythms of the space converge to mediate her interaction and experience of sexual harassment. The example shows how a rhythmanalysis informed by feminist standpoint epistemology enables an intersectional analysis of sexual harassment.

Police's situatedness and rhythms

There is scarce research that applies either situated knowledges or rhythmanalysis to police knowledge, both with regards to sexual offences and more generally in relation to operational policing. As an authoritative body, it is easy to perceive the police as having a holistic oversight of sexual offences, yet the way sexual harassment is known by the transport police is partial and subjective, acquired through a consolidation of technologies and contextually learnt tacit knowledge. This is important, as what the police know of sexual harassment is collectively formed and then operationalised into policing protocol for managing sexual offences on the Underground. Feminist scholars have given attention to knowledge production and how certain knowledges are privileged and reproduced as authoritative truths (Collins 1990; Smith 1987; Haraway 1988). Using this epistemological foundation assisted in deconstructing police understandings of sexual harassment on the London Underground. Considering how police knowledge of sexual harassment is developed, several 'ways of knowing' should be considered. This includes how knowledge is developed and situated within a particular (police) culture; hierarchies of knowledge production; the subjective knowledge of space or 'mental maps'; and the role of technologies in producing 'objective' knowledge. I have explored this in further detail elsewhere (Lewis 2022), but for this chapter, the context of organisational (crime-fighting police) culture as the lens through which knowledge is collated and filtered is important.

Knowledge is created within particular contexts or cultures (Sackmann 1991) and the nature of police culture has long been a focus of academic attention (Reiner 1985; Westmarland 2001; Workman-Stark 2017), with 'machismo', cynicism, and in-group solidarity being identified as some of its most pervasive traits (Banton 1964; Silvestri 2017). It is within this culture that knowledges are collectively produced and reproduced. It is worth noting that the policing of sexual offences has previously been described as 'feminised policing' (Walklate 2001) or 'gendered work' (Westmarland 2001; Workman-Stark 2017). However, in this study, the majority of officers interviewed were men, and at no time was it explicitly or implicitly stated that the policing of sexual offences was not 'real police work' (Reiner 1985). Yet gendered ways of knowing still play a role here. Several of the male BTP officers expressed the sentiment that they would never tacitly 'know' how it felt to be victimised in such a way. This was summarised well by one participant who, when reflecting on a victim's response to her assault said: 'That's not, I think, what I'd do in that situation. But also, what do I know, I'm a bloke, and a cop so really who am I to say that's the right or wrong way to respond. I'm coming at it from a totally different frame of reference'.

Within the policing context there are numerous forms of knowledge production, often acting in a hierarchy, with certain ways of knowing being privileged over others. Wood et al. (2017, 176) highlight the important relationship between police culture and police knowledge, stating how officers form their knowledge basis 'on the job', from learnt and practical experience (see also Fielding 1984). Another important form of knowledge production that impacts on policing practices is evidence-based policing (EBP), an approach that is based on producing scientific evidence to guide principles and practice (Sherman 1998; Lumsden and Goode 2016). However, as a form of knowing, EBP is often critiqued as it is said to privilege positivist methods due to the perception of a lack of bias (Hope 2009), giving the impression that this knowledge is definitive and abstracted (Wood et al. 2017). This is compounded by the use of technologies to collate and map sexual offences on the network, creating a 'numbers perspective' that draws on reports that is then used to discern trends and spatio-temporal hotspots. It is this accumulation of vicariously produced knowledge (in comparison to women's individual, perceived but isolated experience) that constitutes police understandings of sexual offences on the underground train network. Once hotspots have been created, they are the focus of rhythmic policing practices. The rhythms of offending have received little to no attention. Yet this is implicitly how sexual offences are being proactively policed on the Underground. The tactics used by plain-clothed BTP officers, who patrol the network during rush hour times, are highly space-specific, based on the rhythmic attributes and concurrent social behaviours that are expected within that space. They 'blend into the crowd' and look for those who 'stand out' or act in contrast to the normal commuting rhythms. Both managing visibility and perceiving suspicious behaviour in this highly mobile space require an intimate knowledge of its spatial norms and rhythms.

The policing of sexual offences by BTP is guided by the knowledge that is available to them, and the culturally learnt, tacitly experienced rhythms of the Underground. It is a situated perspective located within and guided by a police culture of 'crime prevention'. The desire for arrests and prosecutions creates certain trajectories that are followed once a report of an offence has been made. The course of investigations and the analysis of information available is undertaken by situated agents and therefore the route taken, and the desired outcome, are often formulated by the investigator. The experiences of women are mapped by the police and reconstructed into an event that, due to the disjuncture that often occurs between police perspectives and victim perspectives, are often experienced as limiting and problematic by both the police and the women themselves. This shows that within a particular context and culture there are different ways in which knowledge is produced and privileged. With regards to sexual harassment, this is important to consider, as what officers know (which in turn shapes how they police sexual offences) is culturally and contextually situated. It is considerably impacted by the affective nature of spatio-temporal elements of the Underground network and beyond, and, moulded by these rhythms, intersects with offending patterns, victim experiences, police work, and organisational agendas. The concept of situated knowledges allows an insight and critique as to how sexual harassment is known to the police and consequently managed and investigated. Adopting the mentality that knowledge is shaped by rhythms, always situated, relational, and engaged, demonstrates the continued value of these feminist epistemologies in deconstructing authoritative 'objective' knowledge claims.

Conclusion: connecting situated knowledges, intersectionality, and rhythmanalysis

The London Underground network is a place of abundant mobility, with sexual harassment commonly occurring on the move and across space and time. The rhythmic ensemble of the space permits sexual offences to be perpetrated in a specific, often subtle way, and also implicates how these offences are experienced and managed by victims, and how the BTP police the network. Significantly, it constitutes how these crimes are 'known' and experienced from a particular standpoint.

Victims of sexual harassment primarily have access only to knowledge of their own individual experience. This has implications for the high rates of underreporting, as many women see their experiences as isolated, random, 'one-offs' and therefore do not report to the authorities as they think the nature of the incident and the rhythmic attributes of the space will make it impossible to identify or locate the offender. Yet, with a knowledge base of previous offences and repeat offenders, if a report is logged, the police immediately situate the incident within an already existing 'map' of prior offences. This allows them to connect incidents and establish patterns of offending, which they acknowledge is meaningfully impacted by urban rhythms. Therefore, offences are viewed collectively as well as individually, which permits the police a different perspective of the situation of sexual offences on the Underground and develops their knowledge base and how they police and manage sexual offences. This pertains to discussions around power and access to knowledge that feeds into crime prevention and victimology. Police interpretation of events often becomes authoritative in nature, yet employing a framework of standpoint theory and situated knowledges reveals that they remain partial and situated. That is not to say that they are 'false' or lacking in validity, rather it is a call for the recognition that authoritative knowledge is partial because it is situated, shaped by rhythms, and mediated through specific technologies, tacit understandings, and mental maps that are located within a policing culture.

This chapter has aimed to examine the production of situated knowledges about sexual harassment on the London Underground. It does so via interviews with victims and the police and using a feminist standpoint methodology and rhythmanalysis. The chapter demonstrates how uniting feminist epistemologies with creative conceptual frameworks (in this case, rhythmanalysis) can make space for a critical engagement with institutional voices without essentialising them as objective or expert. Rather, such an approach exposes what constitutes such knowledge, and recognises them as situated and partial. Acknowledging how these modes of knowing intertwine with women's experiential knowledges can progress understandings of the occurrence of sexual harassment within the space of public transport and contribute towards the combatting of sexual harassment within these spaces. Furthermore, approaching this through the lens of intersectional rhythmanalysis, I have explored how the spatio-temporal elements of these experiences are compounded, mitigated, or understood through the intersections of different social identities. This framework can be extrapolated to the study of other areas of women's everyday lives and expose both the intersectional nuance of rhythms *and* reveal the spatial and temporal (rhythmic) nature of intersectionality.

References

Banton, Michael. 1964. *The Policeman in the Community*. New York: Basic Books.
Bilge, Sirma. 2010. "Recent Feminist Outlooks on Intersectionality". *Diogenes* 57, no. 1, 58–72. https://doi.org/10.1177/0392192110374245
Bissell, David. (2009). Travelling vulnerabilities:mobile timespaces of quiescence. *Cultural Geographies*, 16 (4): 427–445. https://doi.org/10.1177/14744740093 40086

Bissell, David. (2010). Passenger mobilities: affective atmospheres and the sociality of public transport. *Environment and Planning D: Society and Space*, 28 (2): 270–289. https://doi.org/10.1068/d3909

Bows, Hannah and Nicole Westmarland. 2017. "Rape of Older People in the United Kingdom: Challenging the 'Real-Rape' Stereotype". *The British Journal of Criminology* 57, no. 1, 1–17. https://doi.org/10.1093/bjc/azv116

Buckley, Michelle and Kendra Strauss. 2016. "With, Against and Beyond Lefevre: Planetary Urbanization and Epistemic Plurality." *Environment and Planning D: Society and Space* 34, no. 4: 617–636. https://doi.org/10.1177/0263775816628872

Ceccato, Vania and Anastasia Loukaitou-Sideris. 2022. "Fear of Sexual Harassment and Its Impact on Safety Perceptions in Transit Environments: A Global Perspective." *Violence Against Women* 28, no. 1, 26–48. https://doi.org/10.1177/1077801221992874

Chowdbury, Romit. 2022. "Sexual Assault on Public Transport: Crowds, Nation, and Violence in the Urban Commons". *Social and Cultural Geography* 24, no. 7, 1087–1103. https://doi.org/10.1080/14649365.2022.2052170

Collins, Patricia Hill. 1986. "Learning from the Outsider Within: The Sociological Significance of Black Feminist Thought". *Social Problems* 33, no. 6, 14–32. https://doi.org/10.2307/800672

Collins, Patricia Hill. 1990. "Black Feminist Epistemology". In *Contemporary Sociological Theory*, edited by Craig J. Calhoun, 327. Cambridge: Blackwell.

Crenshaw, Kimberlé W. 1989. *Demarginalizing the Intersection of Race and Sex: A Black Feminist Critique of Antidiscrimination Doctrine, Feminist Theory and Antiracist Politics*. University of Chicago Legal Forum 139. Available at: https://scholarship.law.columbia.edu/faculty_scholarship/3007

Douchet, Andrea and Natasha Mauthner. 2007. "Feminist Methodologies and Epistemologies." In *21st Century Sociology: A Reference Handbook*, Vol. 2, edited by Clifton D. Bryant and Dennis L. Peck, 36–42. Thousand Oaks: Sage Publications.

Edensor, Tim, ed. 2010. *Geographies of Rhythm: Nature, Place, Mobilities and Bodies*. Burlington: Ashgate.

Farrington, Alex. 2021. "Reorienting the Production of Space: Rhythmanalysis, Desire, and "The Siege of the Third Precinct." *Environment and Planning C: Politics and Space* 39, no. 5, 938–954. https://doi.org/10.1177/2399654420970948

Fielding, Nigel. 1984. "Police Socialization and Police Competence." *The British Journal of Sociology* 35, no. 4, 568–590. https://doi.org/10.2307/590435

Gekoski, Anna, Jacqueline M. Gray, Miranda A. H. Horvath, Sarah Edwards, Aliye Emirali and Joanna R. Adler. 2015. *'What Works' in Reducing Sexual Harassment and Sexual Offences on Public Transport Nationally and Internationally: A Rapid Evidence Assessment*. London: British Transport Police and Department for Transport.

Goode, Jackie and Karen Lumsden. 2016. "The McDonaldisation of Police-Academic Partnerships: Organisational and Cultural Barriers Encountered in Moving from Research on Police to Research with the Police." *Policing and Society* 28, no. 1, 75–89. https://doi.org/10.1080/10439463.2016.1147039

Harding, Sandra. 1993. "Rethinking Standpoint Epistemology: What is 'Strong Objectivity?'" In *Feminist Epistemologies*, edited by Linda Alcoff and Elizabeth Potter. New York: Routledge.

Hargreaves, David H. 1999. "The Kowledge-Creating School." *British Journal of Educational Studies* 47, no. 2, 122–144. https://doi.org/10.1111/1467-8527.00107

Hartsock, Nancy. 1983. "The Feminist Standpoint: Developing the Ground for a Specifically Feminist Historical Materialism." In *Feminism and Methodology:*

Social Science Issues, edited by Sandra Harding. Bloomington: Indiana University Press.

Hammersley, Martyn. 1992. *What's Wrong with Ethnography? Methodological Explorations.* New York: Psychology Press. https://doi.org/10.4324/9781351038027

Haraway, Donna. 1988. "Situated Knowledges: The Science Question in Feminism and the Privilege of Partial Perspective." *Feminist Studies* 14, no. 3, 575–599. https://doi.org/10.2307/3178066

Highmore, Ben. 2002. "Street Life in London: Towards a Rhythmanalysis of London in the Late Nineteenth Century". *New Formations* 47, 171–193.

hooks, bell. 1981. *Ain't I a Woman: Black Women and Feminism.* London: Pluto Press.

Hope, Tim. 2009. "The Illusion of Control: A Response to Professor Sherman." *Criminology & Criminal Justice* 9, no. 2, 125–134. https://doi.org/10.1177/174889580910254

Horton, Dave. 2005. "Henri Lefebvre: Rhythmanalysis: Space, Time and Everyday Life." *Time and Society* 14, no. 1, 157–159. https://doi.org/10.1177/0961463X0501400105

Kipfer, Stefan., Saberi,Parastou., and Wieditz, Thorben. (2013). Henri Lefebvre: Debates and controversies. *Progress in Human Geography*, 37(1), 115–134. https://doi.org/10.1177/0309132512446718

Lefebvre, Henri. 2004. *Rhythmanalysis, Space, Time and Everyday Life.* London: Bloomsbury Publishing.

Lewis, Sian. (2022). 'We Call it Getting Your Eye In':Policing Sexual Harassment on the London Underground Through the Lens of Haraway's Situated Knowledges and Cyborgs, *The British Journal of Criminology* 63(5), 1129–1145. https://doi.org/10.1093/bjc/azac080

Lewis, Sian, Paula Saukko and Karen Lumsden. 2021. "Rhythms, Sociabilities and Transience of Sexual Harassment in Transport: Mobilities Perspectives of the London Underground." *Gender, Place & Culture* 28, no 2, 277–298. https://doi.org/10.1080/0966369X.2020.1734540

Lockley, Rhiannon Faith. 2022. "Making and Breaking Chains: A Rhythmanalysis of Labour, Education, and the Home." *Philosophy and Theory in Higher Education* 4, no. 2, 143–165. https://doi.org/10.3726/PTIHE.022022.0010

Longino, Helen E. 1999. "Feminist Epistemology." In *The Blackwell Guide to Epistemology,* edited by John Greco and Ernest Sosa. Malden, MA: Wiley-Blackwell.

Lorde, Audre. 1984. *Sister Outsider: Essays and Speeches.* Berkeley: Ten Speed Press.

Loukaitou-Sideris, Anastaia, Madeline Brozen, Miriam Pinski and Hao Ding. 2020. "Documenting #MeToo in Public Transportation: Sexual Harassment Experiences of University Students in Los Angeles." *Journal of Planning Education and Research* 44, no. 1, 210–224. https://doi.org/10.1177/0739456X20960778

Lumsden, Karen and Jackie Goode. 2016. "Policing Research and the Rise of the 'Evidence-Base': Police Officer and Staff Understandings of Research, Its Implementation and 'What Works." *Sociology* 52, no. 4, 813–829. https://doi.org/10.1177/0038038516664684

Mason-Bish, Hannah and Irene Zempi. 2019. "Misogyny, Racism, and Islamophobia: Street Harassment at the Intersections." *Feminist Criminology* 14, no. 5, 540–559. https://doi.org/10.1177/1557085118772088

Mulicek, Ondrej, Robert Osman and Daniel Seidenglanz. 2015. "Time-Space Rhythms of the City- The Industrial and Post-Industrial Brno." *Environment and Planning A: Economy and Space* 48, no. 1, 115–131. https://doi.org/10.1177/0308518X155948

Nielsen, Joyce. M. 1990. *Feminist Research Methods*. Boulder: Westview Press.

Oakley, Ann. 1981. Interviewing Women: A Contradiction in Terms? In *Doing Feminist Research*, edited by Helen Roberts. London: Routledge.

O'Donnell, Mike. 2003. "Radically Reconstituting the Subject: Social Theory and Human Nature." *Sociology* 37, no. 4, 753–770. https://doi.org/10.1177/0038038503037400

Prior, Nick. 2011. "Speed, Rhythm, and Time-Space: Museums and Cities." *Space and Culture* 14, no. 2, 197–213. https://doi.org/10.1177/1206331210392701

Rahmanipour, Setayesh, Shannon Kumar and Rachel Simon-Kumar. 2019. "Underreporting Sexual Violence Among 'Ethnic' Migrant Women: Perspectives from Aotearoa/New Zealand." *Culture, Health and Sexuality* 21, no. 7, 837–852. https://doi.org/10.1080/13691058.2018.1519120

Reid-Musson, Emily. 2018. "Intersectional Rhythmanalysis: Power, Rhythm, and Everyday Life." *Progress in Human Geography* 42, no. 6, 881–897. https://doi.org/10.1177/0309132517725069

Reiner, Robert. 1985. *The Politics of the Police*. Oxford: Oxford University Press.

Sackmann, Sonja A. 1991. *Cultural Knowledge in Organizations: Exploring the Collective Mind*. Newbury Park: Sage Publications.

Schon, Donald A. 1983. *The Reflective Practitioner- How Professionals Think in Action*. New York: Basic Books.

Schwanen, Tim, Irina van Aalst, Jelle Brands and Tjerk Timan. 2012. "Rhythms of the Night; Spatiotemporal Inequalities in the Nighttime Economy." *Environment and Planning A: Economy and Space* 44, no. 9, 2064–2085. https://doi.org/10.1068/a44494

Sherman, Lawrence W. 1998. Evidence-Based Policing. *Ideas in American Policing Lecture Series*. Washington, DC: Police Foundation.

Silvestri, Marisa. 2017. "Police Culture and Gender: Revisiting the 'Cult of Masculinity'." *Policing* 11, no. 3, 289–300. https://doi.org/10.1093/police/paw052

Smith, Dorothy. 1987. *The Everyday World as Problematic: A Feminist Sociology*. New England: Northeastern University Press.

Stanley, Liz. 2013. *Feminist Praxis: Research, Theory and Epistemology in Feminist Sociology*. London: Sage Publications.

Tamboukou, Maria. 2020. "Narrative Rhythmanalysis: The Art and Politics of Listening to Women's Narratives of Forced Displacement." *International Journal of Social Sciences Research Methodology* 24, no. 2, 149–162. https://doi.org/10.1080/13645579.2020.1769271

Tan, Sze Eng and Katie Kuschminder. 2022. "Migrant Experiences of Sexual and Gender Based Violence: A Critical Interpretative Synthesis." *Global Health* 18, no. 68. https://doi.org/10.1186/s12992-022-00860-2

Thorpe, Holly, Brice Julie, Soltani Anoosh, Nemani Mihi, O'Leary Grace and Barrett Nikki. (2023). The pandemic as gender arrhythmia: Women's bodies, counter rhythms and critique of everyday life. *Gender, Work and Organisation*. 3(5): 1552–1570. https://doi.org/10.1111/gwao.12987

Tillewein, Heather, Namrata Shokeen, Presley Powers, Amaury J. Rijo Sánchez, Sasha Sandles-Palmer and Kristen Desjarlais. 2023. "Silencing the Rainbow: Prevalence of LGBTQ+ Students Who Do Not Report Sexual Violence." *International Journal of Environmental Research and Public Health* 20, no. 3. https://doi.org/10.3390/ijerph20032020

Transport for London. 2016. *Safety and Security Annual Report 2016*. Future Thinking.

Urry, John (2007). Mobilities. Cambridge: Polity Press.

Valan, Michael. L. 2020. "Victimology of Sexual Harassment on Public Transportation: Evidence from India." *Journal of Victimology and Victim Justice* 3, no. 1, 24–37. https://doi.org/10.1177/2516606920927303

Walby, Sylvia. 2001. "Against Epistemological Chasms: The Science Question in Feminism Revisited." *Signs* 26, no. 2, 485–509. https://doi.org/10.1086/495601

Walklate, Sandra. (2001). Gender, Crime and Criminal Justice.London: Willan Publishing.

Welsh, Sandy, Jacquie Carr, Barbara MacQuarrie and Audrey Huntley. 2006. "'I'm Not Thinking of it as Sexual Harassment'. Understanding Harassment Across Race and Citizenship." *Gender and Society* 20, 1, 87–107. https://doi.org/10.1177/0891243205282785

Westmarland, Louise. 2001. "Blowing the Whistle on Police Violence. Gender, Ethnography and Ethics." *The British Journal of Criminology* 41, no. 3, 523–535. https://doi.org/10.1093/bjc/41.3.523

Willott, Sara, Wendy Badger and Vicky Evans. 2020. "People with an Intellectual Disability: Under-Reporting Sexual Violence." *Journal of Adult Protection* 22, no. 2, 75–86. https://doi.org/10.1108/JAP-05-2019-0016

Wood, Dominic, Tom Cockcroft, Stephen Tong and Robin Bryant. 2017. "The Importance of Context and Cognitive Agency in Developing Police Knowledge: Going Beyond the Police Science Discourse." *The Police Journal* 91, no. 2, 173–187. https://doi.org/10.1177/0032258X17696101

Workman-Stark, Angela. 2017. *Inclusive Policing from the Inside Out*. Ottawa: Springer International Publishing.

Zempi, Irene. 2020. "Veiled Muslim Women's Responses to Experiences of Gendered Islamophobia in the UK." *International Review of Victimology* 26, no. 1, 96–111. https://doi.org/10.1177/0269758019872902

5

ON THE CREATION OF NEW ECOLOGICAL WRITING

Alycia Pirmohamed in conversation with Jennifer Cooke

Alycia Pirmohamed and Jennifer Cooke

Cooke: I know you as a poet, but how would you situate your writing and its relation to research? How might we understand what you do as a feminist practice?

Pirmohamed: I think of my work as straddling the creative-critical boundary. My academic research has always greatly informed my creative writing. For example, my doctoral thesis looked at how Muslim second-generation immigrant writers in North America constructed figurative homelands in their poetry. Thematically and formally, this topic was inextricable from my own work as a literary artist. And, in my critical and scholarly work, I have recently become more interested in writing that leans into lyrical modes, that does not shy away from being self-reflective and subjective. This contrasts with when I first pursued academia and research within institutions; back then, I felt like I was in the position where I had to choose between critical or creative writing (and ways of thinking). I believed there was a hierarchy in how these disciplines were perceived, with creative writing on the bottom rung of that ladder. This now, of course, feels like an artificial divide, though I wonder about the quantitative statistics: what type of publications lead to permanent positions at universities; what type of projects receive full-time fellowships and funding?

As someone who has, for the last decade, created poetry within an academic context, I might describe my methodology as a combination of arts-based research and

DOI: 10.4324/9781003399575-6

This chapter has been made available under a CC-BY-NC-ND license.

80 Alycia Pirmohamed and Jennifer Cooke

research-creation practices. I appreciate the broadness of these terms, the way they foster the relationship between critical theory and art while remaining vague enough to suit a variety of artistic practices and methodologies. At their core, they suggest that a creative practice is informed by research and can have a specific line of inquiry and address specific research questions. As a writer and academic, I find footing in the hyphenated creative-critical space they provide.

More recently in my research, I am interested in impact work that moves toward a social-justice practice. This includes workshops and events within my local communities. Some of these projects are outlined below, and I hope they show that I am always approaching my work from an anti-racist and feminist perspective. My work in the environmental humanities is influenced by a postcolonial ecological lens, and consequently, I am constantly considering what it means to author new creative work as a woman of colour within a heteronormative, patriarchal society, where Whiteness holds power.

Cooke: You hesitate to call yourself a nature poet, even though your work is often classed or received as nature writing. Tell me about this hesitation, this discomfort, with the label.

Pirmohamed: I've always felt compelled toward poetry where revelation is symbolised by the natural world. A poetics of the environment. In an essay I wrote, 'Fog Theory: Lost in the White Gaze' (2021a), I began to grapple with the question of why, given this impulse to write and read about the natural world, I hesitated to call myself a nature poet. What was it about Western traditions of nature writing, of landscape poetry, of eco-poetry, that felt out of my reach? As I continued to participate in these traditions and began to publish my poetry, my questions morphed in shape: what literary borders – what kind of gatekeeping – perceived me as outside the boundaries of these traditions? And subsequently, into what narrative frameworks does the Western literary industry more agreeably place my work so as to easily translate or digest my experience? My poetry is, to various degrees, intertwined with all of the aforementioned traditions of ecological writing and modes of ecological thought, even as the persistent Whiteness of British poetry constantly displaces racialised bodies like mine from the centre.

Carving out space in the Western context of nature writing as a person of colour involves work – a continuous learning and unlearning, a continuous resistance against an industry that is steeped in Whiteness, where poetry by racialised writers is misread as a 'direct expression of their racial otherness' (Parmar 2019). Though racialised poets have been more frequently published in mainstream outlets within the last decade, there pervades 'the false binary of the "craft vs. identity politics" debate' (Parmar 2020, 9). This argument suggests our work is published not for its literary or technical excellence, but because of its expression, often through subject and voice, of our identities. Of course, this 'debate' ignores the reality that White poets also write about their identities and 'from their socio-political contexts, elevating their content with their lived experiences'. But 'their constructed familiarity ... disguises such content as universal' (Pirmohamed 2021a), and this imitated universality allows the White literary industry to focus, instead, on the craft and formal technique of these works – aspects which are often neglected in reviews and scholarly work written on poetry by racialised writers.

Ultimately, this framing excludes poets of colour as 'non-literary', which in turn fosters their perceived separation from the influence of British lyric traditions within which they might be working. One such tradition is Romantic poetry, historically a White and male-dominated tradition, and because 'British landscape poetry cannot help but define itself in relation to the Romantic poets' (Tarlo and Tucker 2017, 4), there too exists the perceived separation of poets of colour from British landscape poetry, or, I'd argue, even nature poetry more broadly.

I am constantly interrogating what I have internalised about the way my body, a Brown woman's body, takes up space in the natural world. I feel this as I physically move through green spaces. It makes me wonder what I have previously internalised about ecology, about human presence in the environment, and subsequent conversations about that presence.

Cooke: In 2011, Harriet Tarlo edited an anthology, *The Ground Aslant*, which had the subtitle *Radical Landscape Poetry*. How effective is this term in capturing your own approach and writing?

Pirmohamed: *The Ground Aslant* is where I first came across the genre of radical landscape poetry. In her work on radical landscape poetry, Harriet Tarlo similarly considers the porous boundaries between 'landscape poetry' and other subgenres, writing that 'landscape poetry cannot be subsumed within the categories of pastoral, post-pastoral, or ecopoetry or ecopoetics. Its territory lies somewhere betwixt and between' (Tarlo 2009, 197). In my examination of radical landscape poetry by racialised and gender-marginalised writers, I found that such a space – somewhere betwixt and between – is especially useful for these poets to occupy, as they are often simultaneously mapping or considering multiple spaces (generations, homelands, languages, cultural contexts, and so on).

Many other works have influenced my conceptualisation of nature writing, but my recent research has been specifically interested in Tarlo's inclusion of the word *radical* in her terminology, and the opportunity it presents to poets writing in the twenty-first century. I have already gestured toward a number of terms that are within the realm of nature writing and that, although they may be nuanced by way of style and historical usage, often blur and interconnect with one another. While 'landscape poetry' is less frequently used in lieu of more productive terms within the current geological age, like 'eco-poetry', or even like the compelling broadness of the term 'nature poetry', there is an interesting shift in thinking when contemplating the contours of *radical* landscape poetry. Used often to describe experimental and avant-garde traditions of poetry, or poetries that are otherwise edged out of the mainstream, radical poetry at its core resists systems of power and the status quo.

But Tarlo privileges formal and aesthetic elements in her categorisation of poems as radical landscape poetry, writing that 'above all, it is *in* the form that the radical ideas, philosophical or ideological, exist and are made manifest' (2009, 198) and elsewhere that aesthetics and form are the 'dominant concern' (2009, 198). Given the Whiteness of the industry, and the Whiteness of the gatekeeping of this industry, I find myself uneasy about the implications that come with the separation of form and ideology, particularly when considering whose work automatically slips into conversations about form and craft, and whose work is, like mentioned previously, neglected from such discussions, to instead place emphasis on ideology and subject matter. In fact, these strands are inextricably intertwined.

Within this larger context, and within generative spaces like workshops, I saw that it was increasingly difficult for poets not to write against our current heteropatriarchal and capitalist society, even when – or especially when – engaged with nature or landscape writing; in my work as both a poet and scholar, I argue that this particular strand of nature writing then might also be termed radical landscape poetry. In this framing of 'radical' as 'resistance', I find myself looking towards radical landscape poetry as a term flexible enough to encompass the work I am currently engaged in writing and reading.

Cooke: What do you make of the terms 'eco-poetry' and 'eco-poetics' which have gained recent traction? Are they useful? What might they elide? How do they relate to the term you use in your title, 'new ecological writing'?

Pirmohamed: In an interview about his inter-genre poetry collection *Bright Felon*, Kazim Ali refers to genre as a reading practice: 'In the case of publishers, readers and institutions, genre is just a way of organizing or explaining a piece of writing that at its heart is anarchic' (2024). A term like 'eco-poetry' is useful in that it distinguishes writing as having a strong environmental emphasis, often in combination with some kind of political messaging. It provides readers and writers with a tool of categorisation, meaning that we can not only find it more easily, but we can treat it as a subject area with its own branches of scholarship, research, criticism, and funding. Beyond that, these methods of categorisation also cultivate community, where common interests contribute to collaboration, collectives, and special interest groups around the subject of 'eco-poetry'. My title 'new ecological writing' seeks to find an audience interested in conversations relevant to the creation of new work with strong environmental themes in our current global age – where we are writing against the backdrop of an ecological crisis fed by imperialism, capitalism, and settler-colonialism. The 'new' in my title is important because it emphasises the practice of writing itself and the challenges that come with artmaking as a witness.

But what is categorised as 'eco-poetry' nestles within other labels as well. And any kind of categorisation, determined in part by reading practice, will be limited by what elements are privileged over others. In this vein, my post-doctoral research involved reading poetry by racialised gender-marginalised people of colour through a postcolonial ecological lens, defined as simultaneously considering ecological thought with the history of empire (DeLoughrey and Handley 2011, 20). I found that through this lens, the work by these writers often fell within the scope of nature poetry, whether as landscape poetry or eco-poetry, or between and across these porous boundaries. However, they were rarely read as such by the machinery of the Western literary industry. While my research examines British South Asian writers through this particular theoretical framework, it is also largely informed by the scholarly and creative work of Black poets and academics. In the US, for example, Camille Dungy collected four centuries of African American nature poetry for her anthology *Black Nature* (2009). In an interview with the online publication *The Sun Magazine*, Dungy wrote that 'when [she] reached out to poets [she] wanted to publish in the anthology, they were often pleased that someone was finally seeing their work this way' (2018).

Cooke: In 2020–2021, you undertook a postdoctoral research project at the Institute for Advanced Studies in the Humanities (IASH) at the University of Edinburgh. It was called 'Our Time is a Garden'. Can you describe the project, its methods, and its aims? Why was this a particularly important moment to do this research?

Pirmohamed: There persists the assumption that, unless otherwise marked, the speaker of a poem is what Audre Lorde calls the mythical norm: 'white, thin, male, young, heterosexual, Christian, and financially secure' (1984, 116). It is within the mythical norm that the 'trappings of power reside' (ibid); those who stand outside that power are in some way displaced, and therefore stand outside of the perceived universal experience. In the collaborative pamphlet *Threads*, a dialogue between Nisha Ramayya, Bhanu Kapil, and Sandeep Parmar, Parmar asks, relatedly, how do poets of colour 'differently embody the "I"? Or does it come to embody us?' (2018, 11). This question subverts the idea of a universal lived experience and challenges the coded Whiteness of the lyric subject.

This thinking underpinned 'Our Time is a Garden,' which was a project that examined radical landscape poetry by racialised women and non-binary writers in the UK. It investigated, through an analysis of review culture that was largely informed by the work of the Ledbury Poetry Critics Programme, how poetry by poets of colour is rarely engaged with as nature writing. It is instead exoticised or codified under 'identity poetics' and held at a distance from traditions like nature writing, a category that is prescriptive and reluctant to change. All one must do is look at the history of anthologies, awards, scholarship, audiences, and criticism to see that there is a noticeable gap of poets of colour – particularly women of colour – from the British canon, and this is even more stark in traditions like nature poetry, which have long been defined by Whiteness.

However, despite the tradition and history of this work existing in a Eurocentric, White, and dominantly male context, through different initiatives, there has been better representation of published women nature writers of colour more recently. There has been a call to decolonise nature writing and projects like The Nan Shepherd Prize, a biannual prize for nature writing by underrepresented writers, have been set up as recently as 2019 with an aim to bridge this gap. Even my fellowship with IASH was accepted under their initiative, 'The Institute Project on Decoloniality 2021–2024'. These initiatives to decolonise nature writing both within and outside of academic institutions are important in the UK, where the dominance of White and male perspectives are so pervasive that it is often a barrier for women and non-binary writers of colour to even call ourselves nature writers. And, as the term itself – nature writing – becomes more slippery and even contested as outdated, it remains difficult to position oneself within this category. My work as a researcher and an artist attempts to work alongside these initiatives, pursue these changes in representation, and further interrogate the framework within which these changes are occurring.

Cooke: Tell me about the collaborative side of the project and its interest in nurturing the nature writing of women and non-binary poets. How did you do this and what insights did this work provide?

Pirmohamed: The collaborative side of 'Our Time is a Garden' concentrated on the development of nature writing by women and non-binary writers of colour based in Scotland. This strand moved toward a social-justice practice and involved a course on nature poetry in partnership with the Scottish BPOC Writers Network, an organisation I co-founded with Jay Gao in 2018, and which is now co-directed by Jeda Pearl Lewis and Titilayo Farukuoye. It emphasised knowledge exchange between professional artists, academics, and emerging poets. One of this project's objectives was to bridge the gap between arts practitioners and academics within the environmental humanities, and each of the five sessions began with a talk by an invited speaker, which was followed by group discussion and writing exercises.

These workshops were broad in scope: Anthony Ezekiel (Vahni) Capildeo spoke about colonialism's erasures, thresholds, and their experience with dreams as a diagnostic tool; Samaneh Moafi presented some of her work with Forensic Architecture and the Cloud Studies project; Nina Mingya Powles facilitated a conversation on bodies of water, movement, and migration; Churnjeet Mahn outlined her research on queering postcolonial travel writing; and Amanda Thomson discussed her transdisciplinary artistic process and her project, *A Scots Dictionary of Nature* (2018).

At its core, 'Our Time is a Garden' was a project that came from the desire to nurture and develop new nature writing by women and non-binary poets of colour – at all stages of their writing practices. Earlier, I mentioned my own hesitancy to call myself a nature writer and in facilitating this course, I wanted to create a space where other racialised poets with an interest in nature writing felt invited to explore the genre.

The project ultimately culminated in a published anthology of new nature writing titled *Our Time is a Garden* (Pirmohamed 2022), which is freely available on the IASH website as both a print anthology and an e-book. To ensure the widest possible access to anyone who could not join the course, the guest talks are available as recorded videos on the Scottish BPOC Writers Network's YouTube channel.

Cooke: Collaboration seems an important part of your practice. Can you explain what its benefits are for you as a writer? Is there an example that you could give of a significant collaboration and the process it took?

On the creation of new ecological writing 87

Pirmohamed: In the last five years, I have seen how my most accomplished and exciting work comes from collaboration with other artists. In creating and responding to other artists' works – whether the medium is poetry or sculpture or choreography – I discover and pursue new facets of my voice as a writer. To be more specific, even the way I approach the themes that I have always written about changes, as does the style and structure of my writing itself. One of the first and most influential collaborations I was involved in was with the Indo-Swiss poet Pratyusha. Together, we wrote the lyric essay *Second Memory* (Guillemot and Baseline Press 2021); our writing spans similar themes and, in many ways, our experiences are resonant. We were also inspired by the collaborative text *Threads*, which I mentioned earlier. The collaboration between us felt organic and yet the piece we wrote continuously surprised me. I found myself pulling forward unexpected memories and situations from my past. For me, the quality and context of the work changed when writing to another person, when addressing them explicitly in the text. This introduced a layer of intimacy on the page and forced me to consider the contours of meaning-making with not only the varied interpretations of an anonymous audience, but also an active participant and friend.

In November 2021, I collaborated with Dr Lucy Burnett on one of the poetry and walking routes for her project 'Scree', a new digital guidebook of experimental hiking routes in the Lake District. The project was born from her academic research that sought 'to negotiate a new understanding of our [human] relationship with "nature" that is far more entangled and interdependent than we have previously assumed' (Burnett n.d.). She crafted the route based on my input: my fitness level, my hiking experience, my accessibility needs, what gear I had available, and so on. One of the objectives for 'Scree' was bringing environmental conservation and art together. Thus, for my contribution on the arts side, I came up with the writing and photography prompts that we were to complete on our hike, and which would also be published on the website alongside the route for the public to undertake if they wished.

This was a significant collaboration, one that was embodied and intricately layered, one that challenged my usual methods of writing. As part of it, I scribbled free-writes and poems in a rain-soaked notebook, while out of breath

88 Alycia Pirmohamed and Jennifer Cooke

after a hillside climb, and beside foliage I was just learning to name. While walking on a loop above Grasmere, from Stone Arthur to Nab Scar, my writing and thinking entwined with the landscape as it existed in that moment (foggy, wet, slippery, quiet). I was also influenced by the conversations I had with Dr Burnett while we walked. Through her knowledge of local language and ecological science, she offered a precision to the environment that I wouldn't have had otherwise. And as we embarked on the route, I found myself documenting a host of field notes and reflections on how, as a woman of colour, I could begin to find space in nature writing, challenging the assumptions of Whiteness and wildness that I have grown up with. A few months after the walk, I shaped these field notes into a lyric essay. I also revised the poetry drafts into a lyric poem that I now categorise as new radical landscape poetry.

Since these projects, I have pursued collaborative work more actively. Last November, I worked with the choreographer Gwynne Bilski on an ecopoetic poetry-movement piece. There is much more to say about this, but in my knowing the outcome would be a performance piece that another person would physically move their body to, I found myself experimenting with my diction and syntax. I allowed myself to play with breath, sentence structure and length, and sound – particularly sibilance – in differently purposeful ways.

Cooke: For the 'Scree' project, you worked with writing prompts. Can you explain what these are and why you used the work of feminist Sara Ahmed and poet Bhanu Kapil? Is there a connection that you see between their work, even while it takes very different forms? Were these writers new to Burnett or was she familiar with their writing?

Pirmohamed: Writing prompts are a method of stimulating new work from writers by suggesting a specific topic or idea for them to respond to. They have many purposes, all of which are generative: they encourage writers to think differently about certain subjects, they invite us to explore new forms and structures, and they can also provide writers with focus and a narrowed scope, which can be especially helpful for breaking through writers' blocks. In the case of 'Scree', the writing prompts I suggested were primarily thematic. Dr Burnett invited me to participate in the project under a

On the creation of new ecological writing **89**

specifically decolonial objective, and many of our conversations leading up to the hike in November circled around how the collaboration could explore my thoughts about being a person of colour in nature. My writing prompts were inspired by two South Asian women writers: Bhanu Kapil and Sara Ahmed, and the poetic structure was modelled off literary critic M.H. Abrams's greater romantic lyric.

In *Strange Encounters*, Sara Ahmed writes that 'migration stories are skin memories: memories of different sensations that are felt on the skin'. In her conceptualisation of 'skin memories', Ahmed also writes that 'the physical sense of moving through space is enough to trigger a memory of another place. Memory hence works through the swelling and sweating of the skin' (2000, 92). These ideas resonate deeply with how my writing might hold multiplicity and have presented me with a way to explore my own place in a range of different landscapes. For example, the sensations of walking up the fell, Stone Arthur, surrounded by a thick mist might trigger memories of moving through the thick heat in Dar es Salaam, or walking through the near-zero visibility fog in Vilna, Alberta. These ideas are also explored explicitly in my lyric essay about the 'Scree' project, 'Reflections in Lake District Mist', a shortened version of which is published in the *New Ohio Review* (2021). The longer piece will be part of *A Beautiful and Vital Place*, my forthcoming collection of nature essays with Canongate.

I wanted the writing prompts to foreground memory and movement based on Ahmed's 'skin memories'. More specifically, I wanted the prompts to foreground trans- and intergenerational memories, and to illustrate how different landscapes trigger certain memories, and how memories shape our interpretation of landscape. Ahmed's ideas feel, to me, like they are in conversation with Bhanu Kapil's *The Vertical Interrogation of Strangers*, where Kapil interviews South Asian women writers in India and across the diaspora. One of the questions Kapil asks her interviewees is: 'What do you remember about the earth?' (2001, 9). This question, when asked in the specific environment of the Lake District, had the potential to provoke Dr Burnett and I to think more deeply about memory, movement, and landscape, both in the present environment and in consideration of our personal or intergenerational histories.

The final writing prompt, as outlined on the 'Scree' website, is as follows: 'at intervals while hiking the suggested route, write a poem that answers Bhanu Kapil's question "what do you remember about the earth?" in the style of a greater romantic lyric poem' (Burnett and Pirmohamed, n.d.).

Cooke: Why did you choose M.H. Abrams's conception of lyric as a prompt for thinking about form? He's a scholar with whom an older generation of literary critics will be very familiar, but he is probably far less read now. What was it about his ideas that attracted you to use them for this project in particular?

Pirmohamed: M.H. Abrams coined the term 'greater Romantic lyric' (1965), a form that is characterised by movements between descriptions of landscape and internal reflections. The greater Romantic lyric has a (loose) three-part structure, briefly summarised as 'out–in–out': where a poet looks out at the landscape, then reflects inwardly, and then turns back to the landscape again. In his essay 'Structure and Style in the Greater Romantic Lyric', Abrams analysed the works of Romantic poets like Samuel Taylor Coleridge and William Wordsworth in his identification of this structure (1965, 529–531). Below is my iteration of the greater Romantic lyric structure, which was published on the 'Scree' website. I provided this description as context for those who are unfamiliar with M.H. Abrams's work – perhaps because this is a generational divide, but also because I wanted to make the writing prompt as accessible as possible to emerging writers and people outside of academia not as familiar with this specific niche of poetic terminology. This context is published alongside the writing prompt:

- Out: the speaker describes the landscape. An aspect of the landscape will trigger a memory, meditation, or reflection of some kind.
- In: the poem shifts inward, and the speaker meditates on this memory or experience. They may come to a revelation or epiphany or resolve an emotional problem.
- Out: the poem shifts back to the exterior landscape. The exterior world is implicitly or explicitly altered by the internal reflection.

(Burnett and Pirmohamed, n.d.)

The website reproduces this structure for writing that I followed myself in order for readers to reproduce the experiment. The plan was to provide a way of exploring Sara Ahmed's idea that place triggers memory of other places. The three steps invite others to intertwine thoughts about nature with their own specific memories, experiences, inheritances, and ideas about the migrations that have comprised their own lives. This exercise asks them to reflect on their own cultural and historical contexts by overlaying the notion of skin memory upon this Romantic poem structure while out on a walk.

Cooke: Can you describe the process of the walk and the writing? Did both you and Dr Burnett write, or just you? Did you stop, read a prompt, and write, or was it a less structured experience? What were the challenges in this method?

Pirmohamed: On the day of the hike with Dr Burnett, I came prepared with a few writing prompts that were designed for us to consider our personal histories as well as the present ecological environment we were in. These were in addition to the primary writing prompt described above and Dr Burnett knew what the prompts were in advance. Early in the morning, we parked at the Rydal Water carpark and began our hike from there. The route Dr Burnett prepared for us, based on my interests and my physical ability, climbed up to Alcock Tarn, then descended again to the Greenhead Gill valley before climbing up to Stone Arthur, Heron Pike, and down to Nab Scar.

At intervals throughout the hike, at appropriate spots (for example, flatter areas that were less muddy) and when the weather was moderately clear, Dr Burnett would pause our walk so we could write. Although we stopped in certain places that she must have decided in advance, I suspect the weather and landscape dictated some of this on the day as well. There was also the possibility that one of us might ask to stop when inspiration unexpectedly found us. These stops weren't timed, as such, but because the day was fairly wet and cold, I suspect a few stops were cut short by the need to start moving again and warm up.

At those stopping points, of which there were four or five, I would select one of the prompts I prepared for us and we would generate new writing individually in our own books. We didn't share this nascent work with one another at the time, though we often chatted about the direction our writing took once we continued on our walk. At the time, I did know that a sample of my work would be published online as part of the 'Scree' project's outcomes. It wasn't an expectation that I publish the field notes or early drafts straight from my notebook; there was an opportunity to rework and revise these observations before they were shared with the public. The poem that was eventually published straddled this boundary: it was further shaped and crafted in the few weeks after the walk, but I also attempted to capture the immediacy of the first draft and challenged myself to keep some lines and stanzas unchanged aside from grammatical fixes.

Dr Burnett is also a photographer, so along with written work, she responded to my prompts through visual images. Because of this, alongside our thoughts about memory and history, we also spoke about the technical aspects of photography. For instance, I remember many conversations about the changes in light and how that impacted the quality of the image.

Cooke: Did the fieldnotes go towards other types of writing? If so, how? And could you share some excerpts or examples for us?

Pirmohamed: The field notes – and I'm also including the poetry drafts under this terminology – contributed to two major pieces of work: a lyric essay published in *New Ohio Review*, and a greater Romantic lyric poem. I always knew my participation in 'Scree' would produce a version of the latter piece, the poem, but the lyric essay came forth more unexpectedly. There was quite a bit of time – months – in between the hike itself and the crafting of my prose from the haphazard notes I scrawled on the day of the hike. The first version of the essay was very fragmented and philosophical. Essentially, those early versions attempted to provide a structure to the various field notes, piecing together the most interesting and influential observations in order to accumulate a kind of story, or even argument, about the experience. In later drafts, I attempted to exercise my more narrative writing muscles and tether the fragments to the description and linearity of the walk itself. I wanted to relay important reflections and meditations about nature writing by also inviting readers to take the hike with me: to not only consider what it means to decolonise nature writing theoretically, but to do so while describing more systematically how, for example, the fog cleared and revealed the Cumbrian hillsides and its Herdwick sheep. Despite these choices and revisions, the essay at its core, and in any form, could never have existed without Dr Burnett's invitation, her presence on the hike, our discussion of the writing prompts beforehand, and the very route she chose.

Eventually, the poem too underwent further revisions. The most recent version of it is different from the published version on the 'Scree' website. It drifts further away from the scrawls in my notebook and towards a more polished structure and deliberate rhetoric when it comes to sound.

Extract from the version of the poem published on 'Scree':

A figure leans forward, moss along her spine,
branches stretched into free space like a stray memory.

In a certain kind of light
at a certain point in history
you would have stepped away from your body.

You would have left your body, shed your body
of its autumn leaves.

Now you tell yourself, "Be kinder
to the woman who has just arrived,"

who has not yet fallen in love with these trees.
Be kinder to the body not yet free
of its misunderstandings or its mythologies.
"Let her extend her arm toward you"

(Burnett and Pirmohamed n.d.).

Extract from a newer version of this poem:

The figure with moss along her spine
reaches into the eddying haze.
Her curious gaze disappears into indistinct
layers of white blank skies.
Slick with quietened downpour

you can only see what is in proximity
or growing close to the muddy path –

the snare of bracken, a bronze sheen
so ubiquitous it begins to fade
into the background, nondescript
like your quickened breathing as you ascend
the path up to Alcock Tarn.

In the fog, you note the invisible and visible
traces of your body.
Its soft folds and contours
are another kind of living landscape.

In a certain slightness of light
at a certain point in your young history
you would have liked to disregard
the atlas of your brown self.

In the past, you would have shed
your skin of its autumnal leaves.

Now you tell yourself, "Be kinder
to the woman who has just arrived,"
who has not yet fallen in love
with the figure of mossy trees.
Be kinder to the body not yet free
of its misunderstandings or its mythologies.
"Let her extend her arm toward you."[1]

	Perhaps this later version of the poem is technically better than some of the original iterations (though I'm not actually sure and my opinion on this changes frequently). But when it comes to the question of authenticity and what the poem is for, I think all the different versions find their foothold in different ways.
Cooke:	It is clearly the case that this embodied response to and from within the environment and in the company of other thinkers of gendered and racialised experience has been incredibly generative for you. Do you need to undertake an experiment like this to engage in new ecological writing? Do you continue to use a similar methodology for other writing you do? What do you think are the benefits of writing like

On the creation of new ecological writing **95**

Pirmohamed: this, and are there negatives or problems with it as a way of thinking and writing?

The invitation to work with Dr Burnett on 'Scree' provided a kind of scaffolding for me to pursue new ecological work. The aims were clear – this was a collaboration firmly situated in the arts and environmental humanities – as was the intended output. Although there was some flexibility in when we underwent the hike and, subsequently, when the collaboration was published on the website, the project gifted me a workable timeline where I could conceptualise a clear beginning, middle, and end. And irrespective of the quality of my work, I knew that once I was on the hike, I would be writing and this writing would find an audience, even if that audience was only Dr Burnett herself. In this regard, while you don't need to undertake an experiment as involved as this to create new ecological work, it does offer resources that make innovating one's poetry practice more attainable. It allowed me to envision new possibilities for my work by making my practice that much more sustainable.

While I have undertaken other embodied experiments to produce new work, including practices as simple as going on my own walks around the different spaces I call 'home' and writing about them, I hesitate to say they are necessary. In thinking about the relationship between my body and the natural world, or how my body is perceived in, for example, various landscapes, an embodied practice feels crucial. But I suspect there are limitations and criticisms about privileging the body, particularly the human body, in these discussions. And although these practices and experiments allow me to carve out my own place in such a vast genre of writing, I acknowledge this is an individual inquiry. I appreciate that a bodily emphasis might be less appealing to other women of colour because our race and gender are often centred to the point of eclipsing all the various other experiments we're doing in our work.

Although many of the practices outlined above are elaborate and entangled partnerships with other women artists, where we worked one-on-one on a specific project, I do think of collaboration more broadly than that. I work within these kinds of methodologies in a diversity of ways. While I continue to pursue projects where I work closely with other artists, I also undertake less obvious methods of collaboration. For example, recently I am drawn to writing poems 'after' the poetry and visual artwork of other writers who have influenced my voice. Or I participate in writing workshops, either as an attendee or as a facilitator, that involve generating new work in a room filled with other artists. These – perhaps quieter – methods of collaboration capture what I think is essential for me as a writer: the exchange of ideas and experiences. It's this exchange that allows me to cross a threshold into new ways of thinking and creating that I could never conceptualise on my own.

Note

1 Published here for the first time.

References

Abrams, M.H. 1965. "Structure and Style in the Greater Romantic Lyric." In *From Sensibility to Romanticism: Essays Presented to Frederick A. Pottle*, edited by Frederick W. Hilles and Harold Bloom, 527–560. Oxford: Oxford University Press.

Ahmed, Sara. 2000. *Strange Encounters: Embodied Others in Post-Coloniality.* New York: Routledge.

Burnett, Lucy. n.d. "About Scree." *Scree*. Accessed March 6, 2024. https://www.scree.uk/abouttheproject

Burnett and Pirmohamed. n.d. "Skin Memories: From Stone Arthur to Nab Scar – a Loop Above Grasmere." *Scree*. Accessed March 6, 2024. https://www.scree.uk/routes/skin-memories

DeLoughrey, Elizabeth, and George Hadley, eds. 2011. *Postcolonial Ecologies: Literatures of the Environment.* Oxford: Oxford University Press.

Dungy, Camille. 2009. *Black Nature: Four Centuries of African American Nature Poetry.* Athens: University of Georgia Press.

Fry, John, and Kazim Ali. 2024. "A Conversation with Kazim Ali." In *Bright Felon Reader's Companion*. https://brightfelonreader.site.wesleyan.edu/interviews/

Kapil, Bhanu. 2001. *The Vertical Interrogation of Strangers.* California: Kelsey Street Press.

Lorde, Audre. 1984. *Sister Outsider.* California: Crossing Press.

Parker, Airica, and Camille Dungy. 2018. "Poetic Justice: Camille T. Dungy on Racism, Writing, and Radical Empathy." *The Sun Magazine.* June 2018. https://www.thesunmagazine.org/issues/510/poetic-justice

Parmar, Sandeep. 2020. "Still Not a British Subject: Race and UK Poetry." *Journal of British and Irish Innovative Poetry* 12, no. 1: 2–44. https://doi.org/10.16995/bip.3384

Parmar, Sandeep. 2019. "A Q & A with Sandeep Parmar: Supporting Emerging Critics of Color." Poets.org. January 24, 2019. https://poets.org/text/qa-sandeep-parmar-supporting-emerging-critics-color

Parmar, Sandeep, Bhanu Kapil, and Nisha Ramayya. 2018. *Threads.* London: Clinic Publishing Ltd.

Pirmohamed, Alycia, ed. 2022. *Our Time is a Garden: New Nature Writing by Women and Nonbinary Poets of Colour.* Edinburgh: The Institute for Advanced

Studies in the Humanities, University of Edinburgh. https://www.iash.ed.ac.uk/sites/default/files/OurTimeIsAGarden_OnlineVersion.pdf

Pirmohamed, Alycia. 2021a. "Fog Theory: Lost in the White Gaze." *Wild Court.* June 10, 2021. https://wildcourt.co.uk/fog-theory-lost-in-the-white-gaze/

Pirmohamed, Alycia, 2021b. "Reflections in Lake District Mist." *New Ohio Review,* no. 31: 194–197.

Pirmohamed, Alycia and Pratyusha. 2021. *Second Memory.* Cornwall: Guillemot Press.

Tarlo, Harriet. 2009. "A Preview of The Ground Aslant: Radical Landscape Poetry." *English: Journal of the English Association* 58, no. 222: 192–198. -https://doi.org/10.1093/english/efp020

Tarlo, Harriet, ed. 2011. *The Ground Aslant: An Anthology of Radical Landscape Poetry.* Swindon: Shearsman Books.

Tarlo, Harriet, and Judith Tucker. 2017. "Off Path, Counter Path: Contemporary Walking Collaborations in Landscape, Art and Poetry." *Critical Survey* 29, no. 1: 105–132. http://doi/org/10.3167/cs/2017.290107

Thomson, Amanda. 2018. A Scots Dictionary of Nature. Salford: Saraband Books.

6

MEMORY WORK AS A COLLABORATIVE INTERSECTIONAL FEMINIST RESEARCH METHOD

Line Nyhagen and Jackie Goode

Introduction

While collaborative memory work is an established feminist method, this chapter advocates for memory work as an intersectional feminist method that enables us to examine intersections between different layers of identity and structures of inequality through the analysis of memory or lived experience stories. The chapter also argues that memory work can be used as a potentially empowering tool in multiple settings, including research, teaching, and other academic contexts such as workshops, conferences, and in the community. After outlining the key characteristics and prescribed methodological steps involved in the method, the chapter discusses extant feminist uses and potentials of memory work as a collaborative research method and pedagogical tool for feminist learning and interventions in the classroom and beyond. The discussion showcases a range of feminist uses of memory work and details the authors' own experiences of memory work in empirical research, in the classroom, and at a feminist research conference. We argue that the method has further potential in developing intersectional feminist knowledge by becoming more embedded in the mainstream social scientific research methods repertoire. Finally, the chapter highlights potential pitfalls in using collaborative memory work as an intersectional feminist method.

Origins and developments of memory work as a collaborative feminist research method

Memory work as a feminist research method has its origins from a group of White socialist feminist women in Germany who worked together as

DOI: 10.4324/9781003399575-7

This chapter has been made available under a CC-BY-NC-ND license.

members of the editorial board of the Marxist journal *Das Argument* in the late 1970s and early 1980s (Haug, 1987). Noting that existing research on socialisation either ignored the socialisation of girls and women or failed to acknowledge women's own agency in the socialisation process, Haug and her colleagues set out to write lived experience stories about their own socialisation as women and to produce new theoretical insights. Their method was based on the writing of personal memory stories about specific situations in the past and subsequent collective analyses and theorisations of the stories. The stories were intentionally written in descriptive form, suspending 'present-day-value-judgement' (Haug, 1987, 71).

Memory work was to have a clear liberatory intent, seeking to

> identify [...] the ways in which individuals construct themselves into existing structures, and are thereby themselves formed; the way in which they reconstruct social structures; *the points at which change is possible*, the points where our chains chafe the most, the points where accommodations have been made.
>
> *(Haug, 1987, 41; our emphasis)*

The liberatory or empowering aspects consisted of applying an analytical lens to everyday experience stories which sought to reveal women's subjugation within a system of patriarchal norms and ideologies about femininity and at the same time examine traces of women's agency and resistance within that system. Their findings highlighted how women's experiences of socialisation are ultimately shaped by both structural forces and their own agency, with women participating in their own subordination as well as articulating 'forms of lived resistance' (Haug, 1987, 50). The method was further developed via research that focused more explicitly on women's bodies and female sexualisation, with experience stories about women's hair, legs, knickers, and bras, and the role of power in women's sexual socialisation.

At its heart, memory work as a feminist method is a collaborative effort, as expressed in initial group discussions that decide the specific theme for the writing of individual experience stories and in the group's subsequent collective analysis and theorisation of the anonymised stories written by its members. As such, the method breaks down the binary between the researcher and the researched, as the research is conducted by a collective in which the members themselves are both investigators and study participants. The collaborative and collective aspects of the method set it apart in some respects from more individualistic autobiographic and auto-ethnographic methods.[1] While autobiography as self-narrative takes a longue durée perspective on an individual's life, memory work is based on stories about specific, concrete life events. Auto-ethnography, on the other hand, has more similarities with memory work, as it is also based on an individual's discrete experience stories, deconstructs the binary between the researcher and the research subject (Goode, 2019; see also Newman, this volume), is seen as having transformative potentials, and is frequently undertaken as part of an explicit social justice agenda (Ellis et al., 2011). Moreover, while auto-ethnography is traditionally conducted by individual researchers, it can also be carried out in a collaborative mode (Hernandez et al., 2017).

The work of Haug and her colleagues was first published in German (see Haug, 1987), with the work on women's bodies later translated into English by Erica Carter in the book *Female Sexualization: A Collective Work of Memory*, edited by Haug (Haug, 1987). In turn, their work inspired White Australian feminists and psychologists June Crawford, Susan Kippax, Jenny Onyx, Una Gault, and Pam Benton to develop the method further, culminating in the book *Emotion and Gender: Constructing Meaning from Memory* (Crawford et al., 1992). In their research, Crawford and colleagues wrote and analysed their own lived experience stories related to a range of different emotions, such as happiness, feeling sorry, and feeling fearful or in danger, from across their childhoods and adult lives. Through the analysis of their own stories, they examined how the social construction of emotions is highly gendered. For example, a theme of responsibility for the well-being of others as being placed on the shoulders of women and girls emerged through an analysis of instances where transgressions of such responsibilities had occurred (Crawford et al., 1992, 185). Since its origin in the 1980s and further developments in the 1990s, memory work has become an established feminist method of collecting and analysing data in the social sciences (Onyx and Small, 2001; Kaufman et al., 2008; Johnson, 2018). Before examining further developments, we now turn to a description of how to use the method.

Memory work in practice: a collaborative feminist research method

The memory work method involves a group of people who decide to write down their own personal memories on an agreed topic and then analyse the memories collectively with the aim of producing new forms of knowledge and understanding of the social world, which may in turn have emancipatory effects. Memory work relies in the first instance on individuals invoking, recalling, constructing, and writing memories about their own lived experiences in the near or distant past, which begs a question about the reliability of our memories over time. Haug, however, advises against the notion that memory work seeks to establish 'how it really happened' (Haug, 2008, 538). Instead, she argues that memory work enables us to ask:

how and with what means and constructions of self and others is a certain meaning and sense of the world produced? What contradictions were taken along, what was ignored in silence, and what kind of ability to act was achieved? Which paths were not taken, and which ones would the author try out today? And so on.

(ibid., 540)

Haug also emphasises the shifting and contested nature of memories, arguing that 'memory is constantly written anew and always runs the risk of reflecting dominant perspectives' (ibid., 538). Similarly, Crawford and colleagues emphasise that memory functions as a continual process of construction and reconstruction in light of shifting temporal and spatial contexts: 'We note for example the effect of the women's movement on our changing consciousness of childhood events. We assume that this process of memory reconstruction continues throughout our lifetime' (Crawford et al., 1992, 8). The collective analysis process is thus crucial and involves a radical element: an 'intention of moving [...] out of a position of subalternity' (ibid.). This clearly articulates the emancipatory intent of memory work as a method (see also Onyx and Small, 2001, 774).

Building on Haug (1987), Crawford et al. (1992, 44-52) and Onyx and Small (2001, 775–777) have developed practical guidance on how to use the feminist method of collaborative memory work by describing its different stages and elements within each stage. These authors indicate three main phases of the method, where the first is the writing of individual memories, the second a collective analysis of the memories, and the third a further theorisation of the memory stories (Onyx and Small, 775-777). It is, however, not necessary to follow their 'recipe' to the letter, as the method can be adapted to specific research projects (Onyx and Small, 2001, 778). In our own practice, we have used simplified versions which are based on the following four key stages.

First, the group members (e.g., a group of researchers or students) come together to discuss and agree the theme or topic that will be the focus of the memory work. There is thus a collective element to start with, where the group agrees on a writing instruction (e.g., 'describe an event/situation related to feeling embarrassed or awkward'). The second stage includes the writing of a memory about a specific event in a descriptive, detailed style, without any interpretation or analysis (Crawford et al., 1992, 45). Writing in the third person enables participants to create a personal distance to their own stories, which may also reduce a temptation to interpret or justify one's lived experiences at this stage.

With the third stage, the group members return to a collective mode where they read and discuss the memory stories, examine similarities and differences, identify themes and patterns, observe what seems 'taken for granted' (e.g., social norms; hegemonic ideas), and explore silences or what is hidden and unsaid (Crawford et al., 1992, 49). Memory work can thus teach us about how we construct ourselves and others, and how we construct social meaning. This may include instances where we conform to existing dominant norms and expectations and/or where we deviate from or challenge them. During the fourth and final stage, the memory stories are subjected to further analysis and theorisation, which can be done by an individual and/or a group. This stage involves a 'recursive process' which builds on earlier discussions and theorisations while aiming to develop additional insights (Crawford et al., 1992, 51). 'Hard' outputs from memory work might include academic articles or books that are authored collaboratively by the co-researchers or by one or more memory work group members. 'Soft' outputs include the lived experience stories and the collaborative process itself, which may create new forms of knowledge that are emancipatory for the participants and others.

Feminist uses of memory work as a collaborative research method: towards an intersectional feminist method

Memory work is 'growing in popularity as a research method by those seeking a method that fits with a social constructionist, feminist paradigm' (Onyx and Small, 2001, 777). The method is being used by scholars in various disciplines including sociology, psychology, education, management, and business studies (ibid., 778), and on a range of different topics such as gender and sport (Clift, Francombe-Webb and Merchant, 2023); feminist belonging (Guest, 2016); gender and sexual identities (Easpaig, 2015); the gendering of space (Bryant and Livholts, 2007); women and nature (Kaufman et al., 2006); women's sweating and pain (Gillies et al., 2004); lived experiences of HIV (Stephenson, 2005); menstruation (Koutroulis, 2001); becoming schoolgirls (Davies et al., 2001); father-son relationships (Pease, 2000a); men's heterosexual identities (Pease, 2000b), and women and leadership (Boucher, 1997). Together, these examples illustrate that memory work has mainly been used to analyse how social constructions of gender are constitutive of norms, behaviours, and relationships, often with an explicit focus on women's lived experiences. The predominance of a gendered lens is reflective of the feminist roots of memory work as a research method.

Some scholars have also begun to use collaborative memory work as a method to research and analyse intersections between gender and 'race', thus demonstrating that memory work has the potential to move beyond the lens of gender to grasp intersections between different forms of identities and inequalities. In a pioneering project, White Norwegian sociologist Anne-Jorunn Berg and colleagues used feminist memory work to explore whiteness as a privileged, yet silenced majority position. At that time, memory work had mainly focused on the silencing of women as women. In contrast, Berg and colleagues decided to focus on the silencing of whiteness as a majority category. The instruction they chose for their own writing of lived experience stories was, 'A point when I experienced myself as white' (Berg, 2008, 219). Reflecting on the choice of this instruction, Berg notes that '[t]o begin with, no memories at all were triggered by the assignment "when I experienced myself as white". Whiteness was not only a silent category "out there" but also in our own memories' (ibid., 221). Having overcome initial difficulties, the collective analysis eventually identified 'silent avoidance, passivity and guilt' as strong themes across the memory stories (ibid.). These strategies and emotions were in turn analysed as 'the privilege of the majority or unmarked position' (ibid., 220), where privilege is viewed as contributing to processes of racialisation.

The work of Berg and colleagues inspired our own memory work within a research project on gendered citizenship and the impact of women's movements in Europe (see Nyhagen Predelli and Halsaa, 2012, 124–125). Most of the around 40 researchers involved in the larger project were White, with only a few from racially minoritised backgrounds. The idea was that, as a collective, the White researchers needed to reflect on their whiteness and privileged locations as White middle-class women working in publicly funded universities. The agreed assignment was 'Describe (concretely!) a situation – preferably in the near past – when you felt/experienced/were made aware of being White/ethnic majority' – an assignment that was repeated at three different time points during the project, with the first writing task undertaken at the annual project meeting at Cumberland Lodge, UK, in September 2007. An excerpt from one of the memory stories Nyhagen wrote about interviewing migrant Muslim women and men in Oslo, Norway, reads:

There were differences between the women's rooms in different mosques. In one of the Pakistani mosques, where women were 'known' to be mostly housewives and from rural areas in Pakistan, she remembers sitting down at several prayers and then trying to recruit women for her research. In this mosque there was also some scepticism about her background [asking if she was a journalist], but the major obstacle was language difficulties as she did not speak Urdu and not all the women there spoke Norwegian or English. For some of the women it was all right to be interviewed in the mosque, while most of them invited her to their own homes. She remembers visiting homes with different smells – lots of spices that were unfamiliar to her. The interior decorations were sometimes very different from a 'regular' Norwegian home. There were usually velvety pictures of Mecca on the walls. In one home, the living room had no furniture except cushions [....]. What was really different was to meet some of the men, she found it to be easiest and most comfortable to talk to those who were middle class and had wives who worked outside the home [...]. The men that were most difficult to talk to were some of the imams who had very patriarchal views of women and very negative and stereotypical views of Norwegian society [...] Her lack of knowledge was again revealed when she once stretched her hand out to greet an imam or religious leader with a handshake and it was refused. She remembers feeling ashamed about having actually stretched out her hand, and then also embarrassed about him not having taken it.

The excerpt shows a novice researcher, from a gendered, racialised, and classed position of privilege, taking the role of an explorer who in a detached manner observes what is 'different from' the majority society as 'exotic', 'alien', and even objectionable. The memory story thus contributes to an awareness and knowledge of the researcher's own subjective and normative positioning. Analysed via an intersectional lens, the memory story also demonstrates intersections between gender, 'race', class, and religion in the lived experiences of the researcher and the researched. With the benefit of hindsight, it is also interesting to read and reflect on the memory work instructions for the researchers who occupied minoritised positions in the large European project: 'Describe (concretely!) a situation – preferably in the near past – when you felt/experienced/were made aware of being "non-white/ethnic minority'. The very instructions can be read as an act of minoritisation (Gunaratnam, 2003) and 'Othering' (Hall, 1997) – with a minoritised position referred to as 'non-white', or lacking. As such, it raises a question about the extent to which whiteness and privilege continued to be taken for granted by the majoritised researchers, in a situation that explicitly asked us to critique these positions. Our ability to apply the memory work method as a potential tool to create empowering knowledge was thus limited by existing hierarchies of power and privilege that remained invisible to us because of our whiteness.

Other scholars have also used collaborative memory work to examine intersections between different forms of identities and inequalities. Rikke Andreassen and Lene Myong (2017, 97), for example, used memory stories to analyse their 'racialized and gendered subjectifications as academic researchers' within Danish university contexts. Furthermore, Canada-based researchers Anneliese Sing and Corey Johnson (2018) have combined memory work and participatory action research in a study involving lesbian, gay, bisexual, transgender, queer, and questioning students which resulted in the creation of the social justice organisation 'Georgia Safe Schools Coalition'. Johnson (2018) discusses further studies of lived experiences of (non-)privilege, power relations, and marginalisation involving memory work with teachers, parents, and other groups in the edited volume *Collective Memory*

Work: A Methodology for Learning with and from Lived Experience. For example, Coes, Gulley, and Johnson (2018) studied the motivations of members of Black and LGBTQ communities for engaging in social justice activism and argue that '[c]olletive memory work is a particularly useful methodology when investigating activist communities because of the inherent empowerment of participants to explore their own lived experiences to those with similar experiences' (ibid., 98). The knowledge produced via memory work was found to be useful both to the activist participants themselves and to the broader activist community.

Feminist uses of memory work as an intersectional feminist pedagogy

While memory work is a time-consuming research method, it can easily be adapted to the classroom and become a powerful pedagogical tool in teaching and learning about different forms of identities and inequalities and their intersections. The format Nyhagen has used builds on Norway-based sociologist Karin Widerberg's (1998) pedagogical technique of 'experience writing' and requires two lecture sessions of a minimum of two hours each, preferably held on two different days. The first session introduces memory work as a research method, engages students in choosing a topic and agreeing on a writing instruction, and includes time for the actual writing of individual memory stories using 'I' or the third person. It is emphasised that the method requires active engagement of all members of the group and a ground rule of confidentiality and anonymity is agreed. The lecturer then ensures that all memory stories are typed up using the third person before the class meets again for a second time to read and analyse the anonymised stories, identifying common themes, differences, and silences, and linking the narratives to relevant sociological theories and concepts.[2] As noted by Widerberg, the 'size of the group, how well the participants know each other and the time one has at one's disposal, set the limits for both the themes that can be chosen and the depth of the analyses' (1998, 196–197).

In Nyhagen's own teaching practice, and again inspired by Widerberg (1998), she has experimented with changing the gender of memory work stories by producing different story versions using he/she/them. Such gender transformations are particularly useful in examining social constructions of gender and sex. Undergraduate students in Nyhagen's second-year research methods module have, for example, written about topics such as food, a drunk person, body hair/shaving, an experience of happiness, a birthday, and a situation related to feeling embarrassed or awkward. Stories about such topics are often gendered, as illustrated in Nyhagen's own memory about hair shaving, written for the research methods class in 2010. In this version, the narrator is a 'he' rather than 'they' or the original 'she' narrator, and the friend, who in real life was a 'he' is changed to a 'she':

The last time he shaved was Sunday morning. He was going to wash his hair and body, but then he realised it was a long time (a week or more) since he had shaved last. So, he thought he'd better shave, as sometimes your hairy legs can show if your trouser leg moves up while you sit on a chair. He also thought that maybe he would wear a skirt one day and so if he shaved, he would have the option of being able to choose wearing a skirt [detailed description of how he shaved his legs]. He looks under his armpits. Is the hair long? It is wintertime, so not often that he shows his underarms in public. But just in case he's going to wear a sleeveless top, he'd better shave there too. That way he will be able to choose a sleeveless top if he wants to [detailed description of how he shaved his armpits]. He remembers exactly when he thought he had to start shaving. He was visiting a female friend in another city. He felt cool and on top of the world, dressed in a linen jacket and linen shorts. His friend casually told him 'you should think about shaving'. He'll never forget that.

Gender reversal techniques can reveal in quite powerful ways how gendered practices are socially constructed. Similar reversal techniques can be used to analyse the racial, ethnic, or national identities of the subjects of memory stories, to foreground the social construction of majority and minority categories and processes of majoritisation and minoritisation (Gunaratnam, 2003). In the same way, memory work can also be used to highlight combinations of identity characteristics and structures of inequality, including intersections between gender, 'race', sexuality, age, disability, and class.

Memory work as a collaborative, intersectional feminist method at an international feminist research conference

In 2018, as part of a two-day 'Feminist Methodologies Symposium', Nyhagen tutored a memory work workshop in which Goode was one of a number of female participants from diverse backgrounds and nationalities. The format was that participants would first be introduced to the method, its origins, uses, potentials, and steps followed in practice. The group would then collectively discuss and agree a topic on which to anonymously write brief experience stories. The tutor would type up the stories written by the participants and circulate them later that evening. The second session would then be devoted to selecting one of the stories to discuss and analyse, initially in small groups and then collectively, with the aim of making sociological observations that linked the story to relevant academic scholarship on gender/intersectional inequalities. At the end of the workshop, informed consent forms would be handed out requesting permission to use anonymised quotes from stories in subsequent academic publications. The intended outcomes were outlined as follows:

Memory work as intersectional method **107**

- an understanding of the role of memory work/experience stories in research
- an understanding of the pedagogical role memory work/experience stories can play in student learning about gendered social behaviour
- the skill to embed memory work/experience stories as a method in your own research
- the skill to embed memory work/experience stories as a pedagogical method in your own teaching about gender as well as other social issues

After collecting and discussing a list of topics suggested by workshop members, that of 'rebellion' was chosen by majority vote and participants were then given a set amount of time to: 'Describe an event/situation/action where you rebelled (against gender norms and/or against other norms, structures, actors)'.

On the second day, from the 18 anonymised stories that had been circulated, Goode's story was selected by majority vote (although she hadn't voted for it herself). As part of the anonymisation, personal pronouns were all changed to 'they' but in her story, reproduced below, her preference for 'she/her' has been restored:

She'd had to decide where to take a job after university. It was in the days when one could choose. Her mother had done her best to stop her going to university. It was about time she went out to work and earned her keep. It was just another example of her selfishness. But now, her mother was alone.

She'd taken a job close enough to visit regularly but far enough away to maintain her hard-won independence. She called ahead of time to arrange the visit. She was greeted as usual with sarcasm. How nice that she'd bothered to call! How nice that she was finding time in her busy schedule to visit! No point in reminding her mother that she visited almost every week.

She drove over with a heavy heart. She felt physically sick the closer she got. She felt herself diminish as she climbed the stairs to the first floor flat. By the time she rang the bell she was a child again. 'Drink Me' said the label on the bottle and she swallowed it every time, shrinking ... shrinking ... It didn't take long for the same accusations to be rehearsed yet again. She couldn't have chosen a university further away if she'd tried. 'Yes, but...' she began justifying herself. She'd come back, hadn't she? She visited regularly, didn't she?

Her mother came back at her. It was clear she only visited out of a sense of duty. That was the case, wasn't it? What was that...? 'Yes', she heard herself say, 'yes, that is the case. And you want to know why?

Because I don't really like you very much! Her mother shrank before her eyes.

In the discussion that followed, various elements were identified and some questions were raised (which Goode was of course inhibited from answering due to anonymity), as participants pondered/offered explanations/analysis and made links to relevant scholarship. There was some speculation about the reasons for the mother's resistance to her daughter's going to university which led on to wider discussion of mother-daughter relationships – rich ground for feminist theorising. There was also some discussion of social class (*'about time she went out to work and earned her keep'*); and observations about the 'storying' itself, along the lines of the writer demonstrating an awareness of what constitutes a story (a narrative arc, use of metaphor, etc); and finally, a note of 'melancholy' was commented on.

Across the board, the stories really did reveal the potential of the method both to illuminate 'the ways in which individuals construct themselves into existing structures, and are thereby themselves formed; the way in which they reconstruct social structures; *the points at which change is possible*, the points where our chains chafe the most, the points where accommodations have been made' (Haug, 1987, 41), and to illuminate intersectional vectors of inequality (e.g., gender, class, religion, sexuality), citing as they did 'instances where we conform to existing dominant norms and expectations and/or where we deviate from or challenge them' (Crawford et al., 1992, 185), by storying a range of pertinent issues. These included: disobeying authority (teachers and/or prescribed curriculum or 'regulatory' constraints); rejecting gender-related religious practices (Jewish in one case, Muslim in another); rejecting gender-prescribed practices in relation to bodies/hair/clothes/appearance/sexualities (and asserting one's own agency by adopting/proudly displaying one's own alternatives); claiming (bodily) space in contravention of prescribed restrictions (skinny dipping with LGBT+ women friends; using 'male-designated' toilets); demanding access to 'boys' domains' (asserting one's right to play with 'construction' toys; playing cricket; demanding – and getting – a place on the football team instead of netball at primary school); disobeying parental restrictions on going out at night; *visibly* practising one's principles by taking strike action; standing up to a rude customer in a retail job.

There was an empowering impulse at play in sharing these experiences by virtue of recognising their 'collective'/socially constructed nature (as well as by 'witnessing' others' agency in the face of constraints). In other cases, however, participants in memory work have shared sensitive material despite an expressed desire to 'forget', as happened in Stine Grønbæk Jensen's (2020) work with Danish care leavers. Care leavers are coping with difficult memories in various ways, she comments, observing that some find

Memory work as intersectional method **109**

it helpful to talk about their most painful memories in order to move on while others attempt to forget them. After having said he wanted to forget, one of her participants, apparently 'inspired by the other participants' stories', told about his worst memories. 'Did he actually want to do that?' she wonders (p. 107).

So what of pitfalls? There is always potential risk to the well-being of the 'subject', if what they have written is of a highly sensitive nature and renders them vulnerable. The workshop in which Goode participated was innovative in that there are no references in the literature to using memory work in the context of a conference. While the feedback from participants suggests that Nyhagen was successful in creating a 'safe-space' for all the participants to write and collectively analyse their stories, there are challenges in doing so in such a short space of time and outside of a context of an ongoing (research or pedagogical) relationship with participants.

Grønbæk Jensen (2020) also identifies risks associated with clashes between diverse interpretations. Memories are often dealt with by composing a certain version of the past that we feel safe with, she observes, and when different interpretations of the past among the participants in her project collided, it wasn't just a question of what actually happened in the past (an issue dealt with by Haug and answered by interpretivist researchers in terms of a focus on the *meaning* of the past and the social conditions that shape its construction - see Snelgrove and Havitz, 2010). 'What was at stake was also a contestation between different existential coping strategies', Grønbæk Jensen (2020, 107) recounts. In situations where the participants' perceptions of the past were challenged by others, some tried to negotiate or nuance their own understandings of the past, while some felt forced to reject the views of the others. Consequently, some aspects of the work 'did not necessarily contribute to a sense of belonging or a feeling of finally being understood. On the contrary, the other members could come to represent a threat towards their sense of credibility, towards their memories, and the stories they felt safe with' (ibid., 107).

In Goode's case, here, she was curious about how others might analyse her story, open to reflecting on any interpretations offered and keen to further any links between her own re/membered experiences and feminist and intersectional theorising; she did not feel 'precious' about any of this. Further, she had already written/published on her relationship with her mother (Goode, 2019) and although she had not 'activated' or recorded this particular memory before, any vulnerabilities had long been 'processed'. What had not been anticipated was that, while she felt flattered by positive observations about the 'aesthetics' of the writing, the comment about the note of melancholy touched a nerve and stuck with her, to be pondered for a long time afterwards. This might also be seen as a potential strength of the method, of course – that it provokes ongoing 'analytic' reflection, after

110 Line Nyhagen and Jackie Goode

an initial sense of 'shock' in the face of what might have been unintentionally revealed in a 'subtext'. Certainly, Nyhagen expressed a measure of relief when Goode revealed to her after the workshop that the story discussed had been hers and offered reassurance that no 'harm' had been experienced.

Conclusion

In this chapter, we have demonstrated and argued for the usefulness of memory work as a collaborative intersectional feminist research method and pedagogical tool due to its potential to create liberating forms of knowledge in multiple contexts including research, classrooms, conferences, and communities. Rooted in lived experience, our memory stories are rich resources for the analysis of social constructions of meaning and of how intersections between different forms of identities and inequalities contribute to the production and reproduction of hegemonic discourses, ideologies, and norms. The collaborative dimension of memory work as a method provides the added value of collective insights that strengthen its analytical power and its feminist and liberationist intent:

> Memory workers understand that the way we come to know and what we come to know is shaped by relationship and power. We come to know the world through interactions with others. What we know and how we know it are formed in the space where discourse and the contents of that discourse are shaped by the values of those who hold power in that community and culture. We are rarely aware of this process.
>
> *(Kaufman et al., 2008, 6)*

While memory work as a collaborative intersectional feminist research method has clear strengths, it also has potential weaknesses. The coming together of memory work group members requires relevant skills (e.g., writing and analytical skills) and a strong commitment due to the dependency on a collective and the time-consuming process involved. The collective aspects also risk an overemphasis on commonalities and the obscurance of differences between group members, for example between Black and White women's experiences. Moreover, while memory group work can be therapeutic, there are also emotional dangers and labour involved in researching sensitive topics. Such dangers may emerge in relation to sensitive topics that provoke unresolved grief or trauma and/or lead to emotional exhaustion (see Lapadat, 2017). Memories themselves are, furthermore, often viewed as unreliable, which from a positivist scientific perspective is a major methodological flaw of the method. In contrast, an interpretivist scientific perspective argues that the very social construction of meaning related to events is at the heart of memory work and that the analysis of social meanings enables a deep understanding of patterns of power and hierarchies, and of dominant discourses, ideologies, and norms. A beautiful aspect of memory work as an intersectional feminist method is its flexibility and adaptability to a wide array of contexts and topics. The absence of a dogmatic approach to the method's implementation also makes it flexible by permitting us to 'bend and break the rules of memory work' (Kaufman et al., 2008, 10). Frigga Haug encourages a diversity of memory work methods as 'the very heterogeneity of everyday life demands similarly heterogeneous methods' (as cited in Kaufman et al., 2008, 11).

Notes

1 See, however, Widerberg (2008), who has also used individual memory work to explore sexual harassment, and sexuality and knowledge.
2 Nyhagen has used the same format in introductory workshops for academic staff and doctoral researchers interested in using memory work in their teaching and/or research.

References

Andreassen, Rikke and Myong, Lene. 2017. "Race, Gender, and Resaercher Positionality Analysed through Memory Work." *Nordic Journal of Migration Research* 7, no. 2: 97–104. https://doi.org/10.1515/njmr-2017-0011
Berg, Anne-Jorunn. 2008. "Silence and Articulation – Whiteness, Racialization and Feminist Memory Work." *NORA – Nordic Journal of Feminist and Gender Research* 16, no. 4: 213–227. https://doi.org/10.1080/08038740802446492
Boucher, Carlene. 1997. "How Women Socially Construct Leadership in Organizations: A Study Using Memory Work." *Gender, Work and Organization* 4, no. 3, 149–158. https://doi.org/10.1111/1468-0432.00031
Bryant, Lia and Mona Livholts. 2007. "Exloring the Gendering of Space by Using Memory Work as a Reflective Research Method." *International Journal of Qualitative Methods* 6, no. 3, 29–44. https://doi.org/10.1177/160940690700600304
Clift, Bryan C., Jessica Francombe-Webb and Stephanie Merchant. 2023. "Remembering Learning to Play: Reworking Gendered Memories of Sport, Physical Activity, and Movement." *Qualitative Research in Sport, Exercise and Health* 15, no. 4, 449–466. https://doi.org/10.1080/2159676X.2022.2161609
Coes, Jemelleh, Needham Yancey Gulley and Corey W. Johnson. 2018. "How Do We Sustain Activism? LGBTQ and Black People Share Their Positive and Negative Experiences." In *Collective Memory Work*, edited by Corey W. Johnson, 85–101. New York: Routledge.
Crawford, June, Susan Kippax, Jenny Onyx, Una Gault and Pam Benton. 1992. *Emotion and Gender: Constructing Meaning from Memory.* London: Sage Publication.
Davies, Bronwyn, Suzy Dormer, Sue Gannon, Cath Laws, Sharn Rocco, Hillevi Lenz Taguchi and Helen McCann. 2001. "Becoming Schoolgirls: the Ambivalent Project of Subjectification." *Gender and Education* 13, no. 2, 167–182. https://doi.org/10.1080/09540250124848
Easpaig, Bróna Giolla. 2015. "Capturing Collective Processes of Analysis in Participatory Research: An Example from a Memory Work Investigation into

How Gender and Sexual Identities are Experienced." *International Journal of Social Research Methodology* 20, no. 1, 49–61. https://doi.org/10.1080/13645579.2015.1111585

Ellis, Carolyn, Tony E. Adams and Arthur P. Bochner. 2011. "Autoethnography: An Overview." *Forum Qualitative Sozialforschung* 12, no.1, Art 10. https://www.qualitative-research.net/index.php/fqs/article/view/1589/3095

Gillies, Val, Angela Harden, Katherine Johnson, Paula Reavey, Vicki Strange and Carla Willig. 2004. "Women's Collective Constructions of Embodied Practices through Memory Work: Cartesian Dualism in Memories of Sweating and Pain." *British Journal of Social Psychology* 43, 99–112. https://doi.org/10.1348/014466604322916006

Goode, Jackie. Ed. 2019. *Clever Girls: Autoethnographies of Class, Gender and Ethnicity.* Palgrave Macmillan. https://doi.org/10.13001/jwcs.v6i1.6453

Goode, Jackie. 2019. "Too Clever By Half." In *Clever Girls: Autoethnographies of Class, Gender and Ethnicity,* edited by Jackie Goode, 89–113. Palgrave Macmillan.

Grønbæk Jensen, Stine. 2020. "Doors, Stairways and Pitfalls. Care Leavers' Memory Work at the Danish Welfare Museum." In *Museums and Social Change: Challenging the Unhelpful Museum,* edited by Adele Chynoweth, Bernadette Lynch, Klaus Petersen and Sarah Smed, 96–111. Routledge.

Guest, Carly. 2016. *Becoming Feminist: Narratives and Memories.* London: Palgrave Macmillan.

Gunaratnam, Yasmin. 2003. *Researching 'Race' and Ethnicity – Methods, Knowledge and Power.* London: Sage.

Hall, Stuart. 1997. "The Spectacle of 'The Other'." In *Representation: Cultural Representations and Signifying Practices,* edited by Stuart Hall, 223–279. London: Sage.

Hernandez, Kathy-Ann C., Heewon Chang and Faith Wambura Ngunjiri. 2017. "Collaborative Autoethnography as Multivocal, Relational, and Democratic Research: Opportunities, Challenges, and Aspirations". *a/b: Auto/Biography Studies* 32, no. 2, 251–254. https://doi.org/10.1080/08989575.2017.1288892

Haug, Frigga. Ed. 1987. *Female Sexualization: A Collective Work of Memory.* Translated by Erica Carter. London: Verso.

Haug, Frigga. 2008. "Memory Work." *Australian Feminist Studies* 23, no. 58, 537–541. https://doi.org/10.1080/08164640802433498

Johnson, Corey W. Ed. 2018. *Collective Memory Work: A Methodology for Learning with and from Lived Experience.* New York: Routledge.

Kaufman, Judith S., Margaret S. Ewing, Adrienne E. Hyle, Diane Montgomery and Patricia A. Self. 2006. "Women and Nature: Using Memory-work to Rethink our Relationship to the Natural World." *Environmental Education Research* 12, no. 3–4, 309–326. https://doi.org/10.1080/13504620600942774

Kaufman, Judith S., Margaret S. Ewing, Diane Montgomery and Adrienne E. Hyle. 2008. "Philosophy and Overview of Memory Work." In *Dissecting the Mundane: International Perspectives on Memory Work,* edited by Adrienne E. Hyle, Margaret S. Ewing, Diane Montgomery and Judith S. Kaufman, 3–20. Lanham, Maryland: University Press of America.

Koutroulis, Glenda. 2001. "Soiled Identity: Memory Work Narratives of Menstruation." *Health* 5, no. 2, 187–205. https://doi.org/10.1177/136345930100500203

Lapadat, Judith C. 2017. "Ethics in Autoethnography and Collaborative Autoethnography." *Qualitative Inquiry* 23, no. 8, 589–603. https://doi.org/10.1177/1077800417704462

Nyhagen Predelli, Line and Beatrice Halsaa. 2012. *Majority-Minority Relations in Contemporary Women's Movements: Strategic Sisterhood.* Basingstoke: Palgrave Macillan.

Onyx, Jenny and Jennie Small. 2001. "Memory Work: The Method." *Qualitative Inquiry* 7, no. 6, 773–786. https://doi.org/10.1177/107780040100700608

Pease, Bob. 2000a. "Beyond The Father Wound: Memory-Work and the Deconstruction of the Father-son Relationship." *Australian and New Zealand Journal of Family Therapy* 21, no. 9, 9–15.

Pease, Bob. 2000b. "Reconstructing Heterosexual Subjectivities and Practices with White Middle-Class Men." *Race, Gender & Class* 7, no. 1, 133–145.

Snelgrove, Ryan and Mark E. Havitz. 2010. "Looking Back in Time: The Pitfalls and Potential of Retrospective Methods in Leisure Studies." *Leisure Sciences* 32, no. 4, 337–351. https://doi.org/10.1080/01490400.2010.488199

Sing, Anneliese A. and Corey W. Johnson (2018). "Using Collective Memory Work to Create Safer Schools for Queer and Trans Students: A Story of Love, Liberation, and Transformation." In *Collective Memory Work*, edited by Corey W. Johnson, 102–116. New York: Routledge.

Stephenson, Niamh. 2005. "Living History, Undoing Linearity: Memory-work as a Research Method in the Social Sciences." *International Journal of Social Research Methodology* 8, no. 1, 33–45.

Widerberg, Karin. 1998. "Teaching Gender through Writing 'Experience Stories.'" *Women's Studies International Forum* 21, no. 2, 193–198.

Widerberg, Karin. 2008. "For the Sake of Knowledge: Exploring Memory-work in Research and Teaching." In *Dissecting the Mundane: International Perspectives on Memory Work*, edited by Adrienne E. Hyle, Margaret S. Ewing, Diane Montomery and Judith S. Kaufman, 113–132. Lanham, Maryland: University Press of America.

7

AGEING, CARE, AND WOMEN'S WORK

A world-systems feminist approach to Filipina literature

Jennifer Cooke and Demi Wilton

This chapter showcases the fruitful findings for literary studies that a feminist approach to world-literature can produce, using fiction from the Philippines as our case study. Anglo-American literature in English has long dominated the global publishing landscape, garnering high-profile reviews and international prizes. More is translated from English into other languages than vice versa. If, recently, there have been notable winners from the Global South within the 'Bookerscape' (Masterton 2013, 52), then this has not extended far beyond Commonwealth countries (Booker Prizes 2022). While the 2015 rule changes to the International Booker Prize diversified the winning writers' nationalities, these authors still predominantly hail from developed nations (Booker Prizes, 2023).

The subfield of literary studies that focuses upon 'world-literature' conceives of this canonical hierarchy between the West or Global North and its 'Others' as the product of a singular world-literary system, at once 'one and unequal' (Moretti 2000, 55), in which forms of international literary dependency correlate loosely with the structures of global politico-economic power. Turning to literature produced outside of the dominant Western context, studies of world-literature depend on works in translation, or written in colonially-bequeathed English as the author's second language, to consider the literary from the perspective of its peripheries. Attentive to national and racialised identities, differing geographies, political constellations, and economic conditions, as well as imperial legacies, a world-literature approach already entails significant elements of intersectional thinking, and uses theories from political science to underpin literary critique. Our chapter is thus another example of the productive results when one discipline borrows from another. We further supplement this approach with a feminist

DOI: 10.4324/9781003399575-8

This chapter has been made available under a CC-BY-NC-ND license.

Ageing, care, and women's work **115**

focus on gender, intergenerational care, and ageing, through close readings of two contemporary short stories concerned with unpaid and underpaid women's work: Daryll Delgado's 'Salve' (2018) and Adelaimar Arias Jose's 'Rehearsing Life' (2020). Delgado is an NGO-based researcher in labour rights and an established writer from the Philippines, whose debut collection of short stories, *After the Body Displaces Water* (2012), was awarded the Philippine National Book Award for short fiction in English. Arias Jose is a Filipina lawyer who has published several short stories in English, often with a legal focus. Our chapter's intersectionality manifests as what key UUS intersectional feminist theorists in sociology and legal studies call an 'analytic sensibility' in 'thinking about the problem of sameness and difference and its relation to power' (Cho, Crenshaw, and McCall 2013, 795). The Philippines has over 150 languages, seven thousand islands, a variety of indigenous people, a colonial history of Spanish and American rule and Japanese occupation, significant poverty and wealth inequality, and patterns of huge transnational migration. Taking this together, intersectionality is a strikingly appropriate methodological lens through which to examine its literary production.

The Philippines, the capitalist world-system, and literary production

In 1983, Filipino historian Resil B. Mojares published the first monograph-length study of the Filipino literary tradition, investigating 'the relationship between the system of literature and the culture of which it is a part' (1983, 11). Appearing in the late nineteenth century, the early Filipino novel combined pre-colonial folk narratives and Spanish cultural influence, maintaining a didactic purpose and nationalist idealism until the post-war period, when American rule enforced a second colonial tongue and encouraged further experimentation with form and style, including the short story (Mutia Eusebio 2021, 57). As Filipina creative writer and scholar Jen Mutia Eusebio has noted, Filipino texts generated within the liminal space of colonial upheaval are encoded with the social relationalities that underpin these transitions (2021, 57). In this, both Mojares and Mutia Eusebio offer a pragmatic and thoroughly historicised treatment of the development of fiction in the Philippines through time, noting the parallels between international inequalities and literary development and dissemination.

These pragmatic and materialist approaches to literary investigation are comparable to recent interventions in world-literary studies that attempt to consider the significance of literature from economically peripheral regions of the world, both in terms of literary reception and global social inequalities. Rather than conceiving of world-literature as an expanded canon of masterworks that encompasses literary output from regions beyond Europe and North America, several scholars working in literary studies and the humanities have proposed that world-literature might better be considered a methodological challenge that extends beyond incorporating more literature into curriculums and academic outputs (Graham, Niblett, and Deckard 2012, 466). Speaking to this dilemma, the UK-based Warwick Research Collective (WReC) propose that world-literature should not be perceived as a collection of texts, nor even a mode of reading texts, but instead as a 'system' (WReC 2015, 7). This literary system has the modern capitalist world-system as its horizon, with separate but comparable inequalities existing between literature as between populations (WReC 2015, 11). Under this paradigm, any literature produced within the modern capitalist world-system might be considered an example of world-literature, occupying space within a literary hierarchy characterised by capitalist values. More pragmatically, however, materialist approaches have tended to distinguish works of world-literature as writing in which 'the [capitalist] world-system is not a distant horizon only unconsciously registered in immanent form, but rather consciously or critically mapped' (Graham, Niblett, and Deckard 2012, 468).

These new developments in world-literature follow the lead of north American economic analyst, historian, and sociologist Immanuel Wallerstein, who conceives of modern capitalism as a singular structure characterised by constant accumulation; unequal exchange between cores and peripheries (often through semi-peripheries); and unwaged labour—with racism and patriarchy acting as the underlying power principles allowing for the uneven flow of resources towards metropoles (Wallerstein 2004). Benita Parry, a UK-based postcolonial scholar, explains that 'core' and 'periphery' do not offer relative value judgements but signal 'systemic relation' with 'the periphery existing in an asymmetrical relationship to the older imperialist centres which had pursued capitalism's unilateral intrusion into precapitalist worlds' (2009, 27). It is often difficult to map core and peripheral status neatly onto spaces and regions, given the multiplicity of production and consumption in a globalised world. Rather, core and peripheral zones are best understood through assemblages of dominant logistics, with cores benefiting from the cheaper resources and labour extracted and performed in the latter, ensuring that core needs dictate economic activity conducted in peripheries (Deckard and Shapiro 2019, 9). Where core zones of activity proliferate, they lend imperial strength to nations. Core states have greater sovereignty to impose self-beneficial decisions around international trade, migration, and capital than those characterised primarily by peripheral processes; semi-peripheries tend to combine the two and wield proportional power.

Importantly, for the WReC and its proponents, it is literature produced in the peripheries and semi-peripheries which is most likely to register the 'dynamics and disjunctures of the world-system' – that is, to be world-literature at its most visible (Graham, Niblett, and Deckard 2012, 468). World-literature scholars Sharae Deckard and Stephen Shapiro argue that:

> [...] in the peripheries, the systemic violence and unevenness produced by capitalist development are frequently starker, more brutally manifested [...] Cultural forms mediating these experiences might thus be expected to display a greater apprehension of the inequality and hierarchy that characterises the world-system's divisions.
>
> *(Deckard and Shapiro 2019, 10)*

The Philippines are a traditionally peripheral economy, having pursued an aggressive campaign to increase foreign investment through export-oriented industrialisation since the 1970s (Chin 1998). Exporting labour has been at the forefront of this drive, with over 10% of the country's gross domestic product (GDP) constituted of remittances from overseas workers (Bayangos 2012). As international relations scholar Maria Tanyag notes, labour export is highly gendered, with female workers concentrated in domestic employment, fulfilling global demand for care work as life expectancy increases in developed countries (2017, 46). Recently, there has also been a significant rise in business process outsourcing to the Philippines, as Western companies exploit the comparatively inexpensive labour of Filipino workers to perform the bulk of their administration and customer support services (Lazo 2021); indeed, one of our chosen stories features a call centre worker whose night shifts 'messed with his sense of time' (Arias Jose 2020, 184). This too has been supported by a gendered divide in labour relations in the Philippines; as researcher of Asian-American studies Robyn Magalit Rodriguez observes, more recently women have been encouraged to assume roles in outsourced services industries to allow them to support their dependents without having to divide the family unit by seeking work overseas (2010).

Filipino literature has registered the peripherality of the nation's economic status in a significant body of writing concerned with the experiences of both mobile labourers and workers in outsourced services industries. North American-based cultural studies scholar Alden Sajor Marte-Wood has valuably framed Filipino fiction as world-literature, cognisant of the predatory economic relationship that exists between the Philippines and the capitalist world-system, in work on 'call-centre fiction' and 'Philippine reproductive fiction' (Marte-Wood 2019; Marte-Wood 2022). He argues that Filipino literature attends to the 'crisis of representation in both national identity and literary form' that emerges from the unprecedented scale of the transferal of labour outcomes from the Philippines to Europe and North America (Marte-Wood 2022). Recognising that 'reproductive labourers such as domestic helpers, caregivers and nurses remain the most visible [overseas Filipino workers] within the global imaginary', his criticism has identified the ways in which 'the notion of workplace and home has long been entangled for transnational Filipino workers – their lived experiences give shape to the material feminist insistence that "every sphere of capitalist organization presupposes the home"' (Marte-Wood 2022, 4; Dalla Costa 2019, 32). The stories analysed in this chapter concur insofar as they recognise that the capitalist mobilisation of women's labour extends far beyond the workplace. In this, they offer a distinct but complementary critique of women's care as unwaged work that supports the social reproduction of the Filipino workforce, thereby enabling the continuation of cheap, transnational labour.

In this chapter, we aim to extend recent developments in materialist world-literary studies concerned with social reproduction feminism by exploring the ways in which these arguments and issues have been registered in Filipino fiction. Social reproduction, as defined by north American feminist theorists Barbara Laslett and Johanna Brenner, refers to the 'activities and attitudes, behaviours and emotions, responsibilities and relationships directly involved in the maintenance of life on a daily basis, and intergenerationally' (1989, 382). Care of children, partners, elderly relatives, and other dependents falls within this category as services that maintain existing conditions of production and ensure the creation of a new generation (Laslett and Brenner 1989, 383). Ireland- and UK-based literature scholars Deckard and Kate Houlden have recently placed theories around social reproduction and world-systems analysis into conversation, suggesting that the world-systems model, as conceptualised by Wallerstein, offers a useful framework for thinking through women's work (Deckard and Houlden 2023, 8). While Marx acknowledges the importance of reproductive labour in *Capital, Volume I*, asserting that 'the maintenance and reproduction of the working class remains a necessary condition for the reproduction of capital', he also naturalises this process, assuming that 'the capitalist may safely leave this to the worker's drive for self-preservation and propagation' (Marx 1976, 718-19). Political economist Rebecca Jane Hall historicises the ways that feminists concerned with social reproduction have problematised this assertion in a bid to recast domestic labour as productive labour (Hall 2016, 91-92, see also Endnotes, 2013). According to Deckard and Houldon, world-systems theory differs from Marxist theory:

> in its insistence that nonwaged or poorly waged labour is as essential as fully waged work for the continuation of capitalism: whether the flexible, precarious work of the semi-proletariat, the unpaid work of social reproduction (frequently gendered as 'women's work'), forms of coerced, unfree and unpaid racialised labour in colonies or peripheries or the unvalued work/energy of extra-human nature.
>
> *(2023, 8–9)*

Considering the symbiotic relationship between the world-system and world-literature perspectives outlined earlier, it is not surprising to find that world-literature is particularly sensitive to the unpaid and underpaid forms of labour often assumed by women. As Shapiro writes, world-cultural production can be expected to navigate 'the intersection between the desired social reproduction of class identities and relations' (2008, 36). This might be, as Deckard points out, 'a critically conscious horizon' or, else, encoded at the level of 'the political unconscious' (2023, 12). It is decisively the former in the two short stories analysed here.

A key marker of such intent can be found in the writers' decisions to publish their short fiction in English, rather than Filipino or another of the 183 languages actively spoken in the Philippines. In this, the stories are what scholars of world-literature have termed Global Anglophone writing. North American comparative literary critic Rebecca Walkowitz has claimed that such texts are 'born translated', published with global circulation and commercial success in mind (2015, 16). This is not to say, however, that such texts accede to the logic of the modern capitalist world-system and the comparable hierarchies and inequalities that characterise its world-literary counterpart. Rather, Anglophone world-literature is poised to navigate this landscape while negotiating a new position within it. Responding to Walkowitz, German-based Birgit Neumann and Gabriele Rippl argue that such conditions of production give rise to 'new poetic ontologies' that at once recognise literature's inevitable subsumption to capitalist globalisation and seek to undermine the same power structures that render them marginal (2017, 12). Works of world-literature concerned with 'women's work' in the peripheries of the world-system, written for transmission to a global audience, attest to the imbrication of productive and reproductive labour in under-represented regions of the globe, their words moving in concurrent directions to the flows of global capital they latently register.

The Philippine short story and women writers

An exploration into the publishing landscape in the Philippines reveals the sensitivity of literary production to the nation's peripheral cultural and economic status, as well as its long history of colonisation. Authors from the Philippines are not well-known within Western literary scholarship, even when they choose to publish in English rather than Filipino, both official languages of the Republic. In fact, as Filipina scholar Edna Zapanta Manlapaz states, 'the Philippines has produced a substantial body of literature written in the English language' (2004, 183) and supporting such production are creative writing programmes at the country's leading universities and several national prizes that welcome entries in English and Filipino. Currently gaining in international profile is Filipino American fiction (for example, Castillo 2018; Ramos 2019), which we exclude here since it is produced by Filipinos resident in the United States. Instead, this chapter is interested in the global under-representation of writing in English from the Philippines and how that work registers the related unevenness of material and social conditions within the capitalist world-system. As Filipina author and academic Cristina Pantoja Hidalgo notes, 'all Philippine literature in English is tied up with the experience of colonialism' (Pantoja Hidalgo 2004, 155). While writing in English about lives lived in other Filipino languages puts the author at a remove, Pantoja Hidalgo argues that English is chosen because of educational training and the perceived publishing opportunities, with wider distribution potential offered by producing world-literature (Pantoja Hidalgo 2004, 156). Indeed, according to Zapanta Manlapaz, some authors have viewed their use of English as a form of the 'empire's writing back', and a way to 'raise the consciousness, and perhaps even stir the conscience, of the political elite' (Zapanta Manlapaz 2000, 195) by bringing them representations of everyday Filipino lives. Author Rayji de Guia, in a 2022 artist statement, writes of the English she uses as the 'colonizer's language' (de Guia, 2022). If reading and writing in English in the Philippines is thus inseparable from colonialism, it is similarly intertwined with class and privilege (Shaffer Yamada 2009, 8), and is an expression of cultural and economic capital.

The short story has had a particularly notable place in the development of Philippine literature: '[m]ost literary critics agree' writes Pantoja Hidalgo, 'that it was in the field of the short story that Filipino writers in English quickly began to excel' (2009, 296). When the Carlos Palanca Memorial Literary Award was first launched in 1950, short stories in English and Filipino were the only form solicited and it remains an expansive category within these renowned national prizes, with short story submissions possible in several additional regional languages. One of our writers, Delgado, has won a national award for her writing (Kalatas, 2013). Filipino scholars in the US and the Philippines agree that the country's literary awards perform important political functions. Amanda Solomon Amorao notes that their celebration of English writing is not uncontroversial (2017, 20) or without gendered consequences, and Rosario Torres-Yu has rightly criticised their historical use by those in power to reward representations that steer clear of politics (2009, 326). Nevertheless, the short story continues to be an important literary form in the country compared to its inferior status to the novel that is often assumed in the West. Many major women writers of Filipino literature in English have published influential short fiction collections (e.g., Cristina Pantoja Hidalgo, Kerima Polotan, Rosario Cruz Lucero) and, in the twenty-first century, Filipino short story writers are 'vigorously tackling the many facets of identity formation and ideology by probing such categories as class, gender, ethnicity, and race' (Torres-Yu 2009, 339). The histories of Philippine short story writing in English, Filipino-Tagalog, and other regional languages are different (Torres-Yu 2009; Acuña et al 2021), but authors are increasingly writing in more than one language, and it is widely recognised that the Philippines is a multilingual country and thus a complex context from which to write. If literary journals, such as *Likaan: The Journal of Contemporary Philippine Literature*, from which one of our stories is chosen, publish works written in either English or Filipino, there have also recently been attempts to translate work in regional languages into English to bring them to a greater readership (Acuña et al 2021).

As in many other national literary traditions, even more neglected than their male counterparts are women writers from the Philippines (Zapanta Manlapaz 2004, 183), who we focus upon here. Using English communicates status, which is why Zapanta Manlapaz describes Filipinas writing in English at the turn of the millennium as belonging to the 'middle-class intellectual elite' (Zapanta Manlapaz 2004, 184). She also notes a history of criticism of the subject matter of Filipina writers as too narrowly reflecting 'the middle-class world they know intimately by direct experience' (Zapanta Manlapaz 2004, 186). This critical reception has included the suggestion by one Filipina author that such writing by women is particularly suited to short fiction (Polotan 1998, 236). It is enough, here, to counter-note how ubiquitous marriage and domestic life are as plot drivers of novels penned by men as well as women. Nevertheless, the short story has advantages for our discussion, allowing the inclusion of two different authors, although it is indeed the case that our women writers are not focusing primarily on the lives of poor Filipinos. Yet these short fictions speak to wider issues within Filipino family life, especially its matrifocal organisation (Rodell 2018, 325) and how this ensures that care for the elderly, the ill, and the very young falls largely to women.

It is no surprise that globally women take on more domestic labour in the family home – in aggregate, 60% more unpaid domestic and care work than men (Dowling 2021, 77) – and this has long featured in feminist critiques and campaigning. In the Philippines, historian Paul A. Rodell confirms, 'the traditional "double standard" is still the norm' whereby the domain of women and their daughters is the domestic while men 'spend much of their lives outside the home' (2018, 324). Additionally, since the 1970s the country has worked to brand its considerable overseas workforce, which includes high numbers of Filipinas employed as nannies, cleaners, nurses, and domestic help, as 'compassionate loving super-workers' to cement 'a competitive advantage in the global economy' through 'a racialized and gendered process of commodification' (Romina Guevarra 2014, 131). The substantial remittances these workers pay illuminate not only the reliance the Philippine government has upon them but also the investment political leaders have in painting them as '*bagong bayani*, or national heroes' (Suarez 2017, 7). As north American-based literature specialist Harrod J. Suarez notes, 'sacrifice and love for the nation are expressed as a relation to the maternal' through the idea of service to the mother country (*Inang Bayan*) carried out in employment abroad in domestic and care roles (Suarez 2017,

6). The conception of women as carers, as naturally responsible for family life and the domestic labour required within the home, is thus reiterated and consolidated by the global workforce of Filipinas and their representation both within the Philippines and beyond (Suarez, 2017, 6–7; Romina Guevarra 2014, 30–50). These figurations of Filipina care neatly dovetail with the teachings of the Catholic church, a powerful institution in the Philippines and one that has interfered frequently with reproductive health legislation proposed and supported by women's groups (Mendoza 2018, 423–4). There is, therefore, a formidable array of socio-economic and religious forces exerting pressure upon Filipinas to take up the bulk of responsibility for familial care.

Close readings

What our chosen stories underline is how domestic care continues within kinship networks even after a woman's children have left home. There are elderly mothers, unwell husbands, and young grandchildren who all need care and help, and the stories represent the expectation that female family members in middle-age will facilitate the careers of their adult children by providing free childcare, household help, and financial assistance as well as stepping in to look after ailing relatives. Arias Jose's 'Rehearsing Life' is narrated by Cecelia Cortes as she waits for her asthmatic husband, Chet, to awaken from a coma induced by a recent heart attack. Every day of their marriage Cecelia had prepared Chet's pills, reminded him by text three times a day to take them, and checked he had his inhaler before he left for work, after his doctor warned her about his medication non-compliance. She is wryly resigned to the roles her marriage has entailed: 'So, along with the job of wife, homemaker, housekeeper, mother-in-law-pleaser, and mother, I had also taken on the role of private nurse as well. No, the better word was "babysitter"' (Arias Jose 2020, 187). She keeps her husband in touch with friends and family (Arias Jose 2020, 188–9), and, when their own children are mature, Cecelia helps them with household tasks (Arias Jose 2020, 183–4) and childcare (Arias Jose 2020, 196). Filipino patriarchy and a culture of female domestic familial service, plus a younger generation of women who work outside the home, intersect to keep Cecelia looking after everyone.

We see a similar pattern of grandmotherly help in Delgado's 'Salve'. The eponymous narrator is a professional carer, a nurse employed by a friend to tend to her terminally ill mother, and on her days off supports her daughter, Mela, by looking after her child, Monina. While Monina brings Salve joy, caring for her is tiring, especially after her nursing night shifts. Leaving work, she thinks: 'I wish I could go straight home and collapse on my bed. But I need to get supplies from the bakery: a dozen pan de sal, some sliced bread, coconut jam, and Cheez Whiz for little Monina' (Delgado 2018).

Ageing, care, and women's work **123**

While Salve soothes others, as her name suggests, her own needs take second place. In the story, she has not had time for a foot treatment, resulting in a painful in-growing toenail. In these stories, it is always and only women who are doing the physical and emotional labour of looking after family members.

The men in these families are comatose, absent, or careless. Salve's husband left her for a younger, thinner woman, in spite of the care she took of him and their daughter. Able-bodied Chet wanted a daily dinner 'whipped up from scratch' (Arias Jose 2020, 193), objected to having more than two children because his wife 'only had two hands' (Arias Jose 2020, 188), then was not 'demonstrative' towards them (Arias Jose 2020, 195), and chided Cecelia for helping their daughter with childcare (Arias Jose 2020, 197). Braindead Chet requires continuous administrative care, as health bills must be paid and insurance and other documentation produced and signed. His son, Jumi, does not bother to greet his mother properly when he arrives late to the hospital. Instead, he takes the plate of food from Cecelia's lap and finishes it himself (Arias Jose 2020, 192) as though it is his entitlement, even though he is no longer a child. Familial care is not rewarded in these stories with support, companionship, or reciprocal care. Instead, it is exhausting, time-consuming, and thankless. When a tricycle driver who had lost his father to an unorthodox police killing casually enjoins Salve to 'take care' (*ingat*), it causes her to meditate upon the phrase, linking it to different forms of loss within her crime-ridden Metro Manila neighbourhood:

> Take care. How does one do that these days? How does he do it, still driving around Talipapa, still living in the house where his father was killed? I'm pretty sure the lola [grandmother] taking her apo [grandchild] to school two days ago was taking care. I'm sure she wasn't expecting to get shot in the face that day. I know I was taking care of my family, my husband. He left anyway. Mela, as soon as she could, also went away.
>
> *(Delgado, 2018)*

The pain in this short passage is acute; its versions of care are telling. There is care as a form of living on in the face of loss and injustice and within the orbit of continued threat. Then there is intergenerational care, which in the shooting incident was also a form of quotidian pedestrian vigilance familiar to all adults who have shepherded children through busy streets. Finally, there is the care of reproducing familial life, the household labour and love that goes into maintaining a marriage and raising a child without any assurance that they will not one day reject you. Salve's reflections and Cecelia's predicament demonstrate the factors that intersect to keep middle-aged women tied to the family: obligation, love, gendered roles, financial inequalities between married couples, and a younger generation who need to work but cannot afford the childcare they require and prefer a family member to a stranger. Care in these stories is largely unidirectional, even while it relies on middle-aged women to anchor and deliver it.

Both stories recognise the economic value of the underpaid and unpaid forms of care carried out by women in the Philippines, contributing to the world-literary landscape through their incisive depiction of Filipina women's part in both the national and global economy (Graham, Niblett, and Deckard 2012, 468). 'Rehearsing Life' explores this most overtly, mapping the flow of capital from a metropolitan tax firm in Makati to the personal bank accounts of Chet, the company's 'chief financial officer' (Arias Jose 2020, 187), to Cecelia's purse in the form of a tightly monitored marital 'allowance' (Arias Jose 2020, 196). These financial processes are revealed incrementally: Cecilia recurrently worries over the family's suddenly precarious finances as vast sums of debt are accumulated in the de-facto private healthcare system of the Philippines (Sakamoto 2023, 4). Business process outsourcing has created high numbers of service sector jobs akin to Chet's in the Philippines since the early 2000s; north American and European accounting firms have utilised the comparatively inexpensive services of accountants from the Philippines, given the nation's low wages and significant number of educated workers (Rodolfo 2005). North American imports in accounting and financial services grew at a staggering rate of 21% in the first decade of the twenty-first century, as companies flocked to exploit global discrepancies in wages (The United Nations 2004, 151). The gendered divide of labour in the Cortes household is made explicit by its patriarch: while Cecilia's hands were for holding each child, Chet said his were for 'fishing out his wallet ... to pay bills' (Arias Jose 2020, 188). It is clear, however, that while the wages trickle from the large corporation employing Chet to the family's cupboards, the labour performed for these wages begins with Cecilia. The overwhelmed protagonist silently reflects upon the injustice that while Chet 'paid his secretary at work to send correspondences ... he had expected me to manage his social media for free' (Arias Jose 2020, 189). In this, the story positions the unpaid labour performed by women through acts of marital care as economically equivalent to the value-producing labour performed by those employed in the Philippines service sector.

The protagonist of Delgado's 'Salve' echoes Cecelia's sentiment, declaring from the outset of the story that she 'takes on too much for too little' from her employer (Delgado 2018). As Cecelia worries about family finances in the face of Chet's impending death, the narrator of 'Salve' is notably conscious of her income and outgoings after her separation from her husband, quantifying in the story's second sentence her taxi ride cost – 'fifty pesos' – and, shortly afterwards, the monthly price of her apartment building's security – 'three hundred pesos per household' (Delgado 2018). These inclusions highlight the difficult financial position created by her husband's abandonment.

Ageing, care, and women's work **125**

They also underline the sacrifices made by this working grandmother to raise her daughter, Mela, and later, Monina. Salve recalls her training as a nurse, listing her academic successes: 'I did well in our community working course [...] I got an A in my research paper [...] could have travelled [abroad for work], but then Mela came along' (Delgado 2018). The financial consequence of motherhood for Filipina healthcare professionals is made explicit: the dream is 'not to earn the same kind of money that the daughters of our neighbour earned, but as much as nurses in Saudi, the U.K. or the U.S.' (Delgado 2018). Delgado positions both the underpaid nursing role and unpaid (grand)parental role assumed by Salve within the Philippines' wider political and economic international relations. When Salve loses her job as a nurse, she is forced to turn to caring for an elderly family friend to make ends meet, the result of the ideological vision of national independence set forth by 'the new president' (Delgado 2018). Here, Delgado nods to the controversial policy choice of newly elected Philippine President Rodrigo Duterte in 2017 to refuse foreign intervention, which has had direct negative effects on social security in the nation across several sectors (Reuters 2017). As in 'Rehearsing Life', issues of unpaid care, and of women's disproportionate assumption of the familial burden, intersect with global assemblages of power and finance. The stark inequalities between wages and welfare in the Philippines and the West force the protagonist of 'Salve' to choose between family connections and career success.

Conclusion

Reading Delgado's 'Salve' and Arias Jose's 'Rehearsing Life' as works of world-literature, attentive to the peripheral politico-economic status of the Philippines in the modern world-system, has important implications for understanding the texts' treatment of both women and their work in the nation state. Each narrative explicitly registers the economic contributions of their protagonists through underappreciated and unpaid labour to not only the Philippines' national economy but the global market too, in literary acknowledgements of the unpaid social reproductive work that subsidises the worst effects of low income. In this, Delgado and Arias Jose recognise the exceptional peripherality of unwaged or underpaid women in the Philippines, who are not only subject to marginalisation due to their national identity, with its complex colonial past, but also due to their age, gender, and employment (or, else, a lack thereof). In this, the stories extend and develop the kinds of simultaneous oppression that Denmark-based scholar Kirsten Holst Peterson and Australian-born post-colonialist Anna Rutherford have labelled 'double colonisation' (1986), offering a materialist reframing of international and gendered power structures. The authors' indictments of the suffering and stress assumed by capable, hard-working, and intelligent women for the benefit of their partners and dependents highlight the sacrifices made in the name of social reproduction and economic mitigation. It is not possible to claim, from a reading of just two short stories, that the voices of our chosen authors are representative of all Filipina women concerned with unreciprocated and underpaid care. Our case study shows, however, the importance of attending to literary texts as creative knowledge products entangled within webs of political, economic, colonial, and gendered processes.

References

Acuña, Tilde, John Bengnon, Daryll Delgado, Amado Anthony G. Mendoza III, and Kristine Ong Muslim. 2021. "Introduction." In *Ulirát: Best Contemporary Stories in Translation from the Philippines*, edited by Tilde Acuña, John Bengnon, Daryll Delgado, Amado Anthony G. Mendoza III, and Kristine Ong Muslim, xvii–xlv. New York: Singapore Unbound.

Arias Jose, Adelaimar. 2020. "Rehearsing Life." *Likhaan: The Journal of Contemporary Philippine Literature* 14, no. 1: 183–197.

Bayangos, Veronica B. 2012. *Going with Remittances: The Case of the Philippines.* Manila: BSP Working Paper Series.

Booker Prizes. 2023. "Full List of International Booker Prize Winners, Shortlisted Authors, Translators, and Their Books." Thebookerprizes.com. (January 89, 2023). https://thebookerprizes.com/the-booker-library/features/full-list-of-international-booker-prize-winners-shortlisted-authors-and-their-books

Booker Prizes. 2022. "Full List of Booker Prize Winners, Shortlisted and Longlisted Authors and Their Books." Thebookerprizes.com. (September 16, 2022). https://thebookerprizes.com/the-booker-library/features/full-list-of-booker-prize-winners-shortlisted-and-longlisted-authors

Castillo, Elaine. 2018. *America is Not the Heart.* London: Atlantic Books.

Cho, Sumi, Kimberlé Williams Crenshaw and Leslie McCall. 2013. "Towards a Field of Intersectionality Studies: Theory, Application, and Praxis." *Signs: Journal of Women in Culture and Society* 28 (4): 785–810. https://doi.org/10.1086/669608

Dalla Costa, Mariarosa. 2019. "Women and the Subversion of the Community." In *Women and the Subversion of the Community: A Mariarosa Dalla Costa Reader*, edited by Camille Barbagallo, 17–50. Oakland, CA: PM Press.

Deckard, Sharae. 2023. "Social Reproduction, Struggle and the Ecology of 'Women's Work' in World-literature." *Feminist Theory* (online first). https://doi.org/10.1177/14647001231209901.

Deckard, Sharae, and Kate Houlden. 2023. "Social Reproduction Feminism and World-Culture: Introduction." *Feminist Theory* (online first). https://doi.org/10.1177/14647001231209864

Deckard, Sharae and Stephen Shapiro. 2019. "World-Culture and the Neoliberal World-System: An Introduction." In *World Literature, Neoliberalism, and the Culture of Discontent*, edited by Sharae Deckard and Stephen Shapiro, 1–48. Cham: Palgrave Macmillan.

De Guia, Rayji. 2022. "Artist Statement." Rayjideguia.com. October 16, 2022. https://www.rayjideguia.com/blog/articles/artist-statement/

Delgado, Daryll. July 2018. "Salve." *Cha: An Asian Literary Journal* 40. https://www.asiancha.com/content/view/3214/673/

Dowling, Emma. 2021. *The Care Crisis: What Caused It and How Can We End It?* London: Verso.

Endnotes. 2013. "The Logic of Gender: On the Separation of Spheres and the Process of Abjection." *Endnotes* 3 (September 2013). https://endnotes.org.uk/translations/endnotes-the-logic-of-gender

Graham, James, Michael Niblett, and Sharae Deckard. 2012. "Postcolonial Studies and World Literature." *Journal of Postcolonial Writing* 48 (5): 465–471. http://dx.doi.org/10.1080/17449855.2012.720803

Hall, Rebecca Jane. 2016. "Reproduction and Resistance: An Anti-colonial Contribution to Social-Reproduction Feminism." *Historical Materialism* 24 (2): 87–110. https://doi.org/10.1163/1569206X-12341473

Kalatas. 2013. "Winners of the 32nd National Book Awards." *Kalatas: Philippine Literature, Culture, Ideas.* October 24, 2013. https://kalatasliteraryezine.wordpress.com/2013/10/24/winners-of-the-32nd-national-book-awards/

Laslett, Barbara, and Johanna Brenner. 1989. "Gender and Social Reproduction: Historical Perspectives." *Annual Review of Sociology* 15: 381–404.

Lazo, Kristyn Nika M. 2017. "BPO Revenues to Outpace OFW Remittances by 2018—ING Bank." *Manila Times.* (January 27, 2017). manilatimes.net/2017/01/27/business/bpo-revenues-outpace-ofw-remittances-2018-ing-bank/309043. Accessed 12 March 2024.

Magalit Rodriguez, Robyn. 2010. *Migrants for Export: How the Philippine State Brokers Labor to the World.* Manila: University of Philippines Press.

Marte-Wood, Alden Sajor. 2022. "Domestic Shifts: Reproducing Peripheral Realism in Philippine Call-Center Fiction." *Ariel: A Review of International English Literature* 53 (4): 1–39. https://doi.org/10.1353/ari.2022.0031

Marte-Wood, Alden Sajor. 2019. "Philippine Reproductive Fiction and Crises of Social Reproduction." *Post45* 1. https://post45.org/2019/01/philippine-reproductive-fiction-and-crises-of-social-reproduction/

Marx, Karl. 1976, *Capital: A Critique of Political Economy. Volume One,* translated by Ben Fowkes. Harmondsworth: Penguin.

Masterton, John. 2013. "Aravid Adiga: The White Elephant? Postliberalization, The Politics of Reception and the Globalization of Literary Prizes." In *Postliberalization Indian Novels in English: Politics of Global Reception and Awards,* edited by Aysha Iqbal Viswamohan, 51–66. London: Anthem Press.

Mendoza, Diana J. 2018. "The Women's Movement: Policy Issues, Influence and Constraints." In *Routledge Handbook of the Contemporary Philippines,* edited by Mark R. Thompson and Eric Vincent C. Batalla, 418–426. Oxford: Routledge.

Mojares, Resil B. 1983. *Origins and Rise of the Filipino Novel: A Generic Study of the Novel Until 1940.* Quezon City: University of the Philippines Press.

Moretti, Franco. 2000. "Conjectures on World Literature." *New Left Review* 1: 54-68.

Mutia Eusebio, Jen. 2021. "Literary Contact Zones and Transnational Poetic Space in the Philippine Commonwealth Era: The Poetry of Rafael Zulueta da Costa and José Garcia Villa." *Humanities Diliman* 18 (1): 33–59.

Neumann, Birgit, and Gabriele Rippl. 2017. "Anglophone World Literatures: Introduction." *Anglia* 135 (1): 1–20. https://doi.org/10.1515/anglia-2017-0001

Palanca Awards, 2024. "Winning Works". Palancaawards.com. http://www.palancaawards.com.ph/index.php/palanca-awardee/winning-works Accessed March 21, 2024.

Pantoja Hidalgo, Cristina. 2004. "The Philippine Short Story in English: An Overview." *World Englishes* 23 (1): 155–168. https://doi.org/10.1111/j.1467-971X.2004.00341.x

Pantoja Hidalgo, Cristina. 2009. "The Story of the Philippine Short Story in English." In *Modern Short Fiction of Southeast Asia: A Literary History,* edited by Teri Shaffer Yamada, 293-320. Ann Arbor, MA: Association for Asian Studies, Inc.

128 Jennifer Cooke and Demi Wilton

Parry, Benita. 2009. "Aspects of Peripheral Realism." *Ariel* 40 (1): 37–55.
Peterson, Kirsten Holst, and Anna Rutherford. 1986. *A Double Colonization: Colonial and Post-colonial Women's Writing.* Mundelstrup: Dangeroo Press.
Polotan, Kerima. 1998. *Author's Choice: The Selected Writings of Kerima Polotan.* Quezon: University of Philippines Press.
Ramos, Joanne. 2019. *The Farm.* London: Bloomsbury.
Reuters. 2017. "Philippines Declines Aid from Europe to Assert Independence – Official." *Reuters.com.* (May 18, 2017). https://www.reuters.com/article/idUSKCN18E0CA/
Rodell, Paul A. 2018. "A Syncretic Culture." In *The Routledge Handbook of the Contemporary Philippines,* edited by Mark R. Thompson and Eric Vincent C. Batalla. Oxford: Routledge. 321–329.
Rodolfo, Caferino S. 2005. *Sustaining Philippine Advantage in Business Process Outsourcing.* Quezon City: Philippines Institute for Development Studies.
Romina Guevarra, Anna. 2014. "Supermaids: The Racial Branding of Global Filipino Care Labour." In *Migration and Care Labour: Theory, Policy and Politics,* edited by Bridget Anderson and Isabel Shute, 130–150. Basingstoke: Palgrave Macmillan.
Sakamoto, Haruka. 2023. *The Role of the Private Sector in Asia: Challenges and Opportunities for Achieving Universal Health Coverage.* New Delhi: World Health Organization.
Shaffer Yamada, Teri, ed. 2009. *Modern Short Fiction of Southeast Asia: A Literary History.* Ann Arbor, MA: Association for Asian Studies, Inc.
Shapiro, Stephen. 2008. *The Culture and Commerce of the Early American Novel: Reading the Atlantic World-System.* University Park, PA: Pennsylvania State University Press.
Solomon Amorao, Amanda. 2017. "Writing Against Patriarchal Philippine Nationalism: Angela Manalang Gloria's 'Revolt from Hymen'." In *The Southeast Asian Woman Writes Back: Gender, Identity and Nation in the Literatures of Brunei Darussalam, Malaysia, Singapore, Indonesia and the Philippines,* edited by Grace V. S. Chin and Kathrina Mohd Daud, 19–40. Singapore: Springer.
Suarez, Harrod J. 2017. *The Work of Mothering: Globalization and the Filipino Diaspora.* Urbana: University of Illinois Press.
Tanyag, Maria. 2018. "Depleting Fragile Bodies: The Political Economy of Sexual and Reproductive Health in Crisis Situations." *Review of International Studies* 44 (4): 654–71. https://doi.org/10.1017/S0260210518000128
The United Nations. 2004. *World Investment Report: The Shift Towards Services.* New York: The United Nations Conference on Trade and Development. https://investmentpolicy.unctad.org/publications/43/world-investment-report-2004---the-shift-towards-services
Torres-Yu, Rosario. 2009. "The Contemporary Short Story in Filipino." In *Modern Short Fiction of Southeast Asia: A Literary History,* edited by Teri Shaffer Yamada, 321–349. Ann Arbor, Mass.: Association for Asian Studies, Inc.
Walkowitz, Rebecca L. 2015. *Born Translated: The Contemporary Novel in an Age of World Literature.* New York: Columbia University Press.
Wallerstein, Immanuel. 2004. *World-Systems Analysis: An Introduction.* Durham, NC: Duke University Press.
Warwick Research Collective. 2015. *Combined and Uneven Development: Towards a New Theory of World-Literature.* Liverpool: Liverpool University Press.
Zapanta Manlapaz, Edna. 2004. "Filipino Women Writers in English." *World Englishes* 23 (1): 183–190. https://doi.org/10.1111/j.1467-971X.2004.00343.x
Zapanta Manlapaz, Edna. 2000. "Literature in English by Filipino Women." *Feminist Studies* 26 (1): 187–200. https://doi.org/10.2307/3178598

8

BECOMING A STRONGWOMAN

An auto/ethnographic study of the pursuit of strength, power, and gender aesthetics

Hannah J.H. Newman

Ethnography is a research method that aims to understand the culture of a particular pre-existing group from the perspective of the group members, with the group culture therefore lending insight into the behaviours, values, emotions, and mental states of those within it (Krane & Baird 2005). Ethnographic research explores a culture or social group for an extended period of time, including commitment to the first-hand experience and exploration of the particular group or culture (Sparkes & Smith 2013) via a process of knowing and becoming through immersed observation (Atkinson 2012). Autoethnography is a method which draws on the researcher's own personal lived experience, specifically in relation to the culture and subcultures of which they are a member (Allen-Collinson 2012). It is an approach that seeks to describe and systematically analyse the personal experiences of the researcher to understand cultural experience (Ellis 2004).

In this chapter, I utilise a case study of a methodological approach incorporating and combining elements of both ethnography and autoethnography which was used to explore and investigate the subculture of the sport of strongwoman in the UK (Newman 2020). I focus on how this methodological approach engages with feminist research that values making oneself vulnerable and embracing emotion in the research experience, as well as how it enables the exploration of intersectional identities and experiences, and thus its potential for enabling a feminist intersectional lens.

Case study – becoming a strongwoman

Strongwoman is a strength and power-based sport and the female counterpart of strongman; collectively, but less commonly, they are referred to

DOI: 10.4324/9781003399575-9

This chapter has been made available under a CC-BY-NC-ND license.

as strength athletics. The sport tests competitors' physical capacity, combining static tests of strength with dynamic tests that require power, speed, and endurance. The rising profile and success of strongman has in part encouraged the more recent development of strongwoman, with a distinctive growth in opportunities to train and compete at all levels. Participation rates vary hugely, but the women's competition is most popular in Sweden, Norway, Britain, and the United States (Shilling & Bunsell 2014).

Strongwoman, like other strength sports for women, has seen a steady increase in interest and participation. Strength and muscle have long been perceived as the antithesis of femininity (muscle = masculinity) (Shilling & Bunsell 2014). However, in recent years this trend has begun to change and there has been increasing media interest in strength sports and strength-based fitness activities for women. Despite an increase in women's participation in such activities, gendered expectations and implications are still influencing how these strength- and muscle-based activities are negotiated, experienced, and sometimes recuperated into heteronormative gender roles, an illustration of the complex layers of power that exist at the intersection of gender and sexuality. Strongwoman has no aesthetic focus and is judged entirely on physical capacity. However, in both research and societal contexts it is often conflated with aesthetically judged, muscularity-based sports such as bodybuilding.

While bodybuilding research (discussed further below) has enabled exploration and understanding of gender via an extreme example of visible transgression of what is widely considered 'the norm' of gender aesthetics, the study of other strength- and muscularity-based sports has the potential to expand and deepen our understanding of gender, particularly when a hyper-muscular appearance, and/or appearance more broadly, is not the primary focus of the activity. British sociologists Chris Shilling and Tanya Bunsell (2014) called for further research into this unexplored area. Their study documented one female bodybuilder's transition from female bodybuilding to strongwoman and suggested that its focus on practical achievement as opposed to aesthetics helped to provide an escape from the dominance of gendered aesthetics within bodybuilding. Hence, they posited that strongwoman may have the potential to be more empowering or liberating than bodybuilding.

My subsequent strongwoman research aimed to explore participants' motivations for and experiences of training and competing in strongwoman, including their negotiation of gender and gender aesthetics. This formed an integral part of a wider exploration of the subculture of this small, niche sport. The study of the dynamic between sport and gender has been gaining momentum, for example through the work of British sociologists Victoria Robinson (2008) (rock climbing and masculinity) and Maddie Breeze (2015) (roller derby). This research on strongwoman was, on the one hand, a detailed exploration of a sport and its specific subculture. On the other, it was about sport and how it helps us to understand gender better, exploring stories about gender and embodiment, and examining how cultural ideals create expectations for and influence the form of our bodies. Gender was thus the privileged lens for the research, but throughout this chapter I also reflect on the intersections between gender and sexuality, race, ethnicity, and class.

The auto/ethnographic approach

The combined ethnographic and autoethnographic approach to this research was taken due to my own pre-existing status within the strongwoman culture. Prior to the research, I was already an established member of the strongwoman community, having trained and competed for three years prior to the beginning of the formal fieldwork period. This meant I had a pre-existing relationship with the culture, community, and those within it that differs from many examples of traditional ethnographic research, where the researcher enters a community or culture that they are not familiar with or a part of, stays immersed within it for a set period of time, and then leaves once the 'data collection' or fieldwork is complete (O'Reilly 2012).

Therefore, it seemed logical and useful to embrace and use my own personal experiences in the sport and as part of that community to contribute to and help to further understanding of the culture. However, it remained important to capture and utilise not just my relation to this culture, but also to explore the stories and experiences of others. While I recognised that there was value to be added through the contribution of my own personal experiences, with insight deeper than that I could get from talking to other competitors, I also felt that my story alone could never fully explore all the nuances of the strongwoman culture or give justice to the diversity of experience that I had witnessed. This was particularly so as a White, gender diverse, queer person amongst the array of different women involved, which although predominantly White and heterosexual, included a range of intersecting identities and experiences in relation to class, race, ethnicity, and sexuality, with different reasons and journeys that led them to find their place in this community.

Intersectionality was defined by US Black feminist legal scholar Kimberlé Crenshaw as 'a metaphor for understanding the ways that multiple forms of inequality or disadvantage sometimes compound themselves and create obstacles that often are not understood among conventional ways of thinking' (Crenshaw 1989, 139). I used the autoethnographic approach described in combination with key aspects and features of a traditional ethnographic approach, partly in acknowledgement that my story alone could not seek to address or understand the impact of intersectional identities such as race, class, and sexuality on lived experience within the sport. Ethnography employs the use of multiple methods, with participant observation providing the basis, but supplemented by other methods such as qualitative interviews, and the collection and analysis of textual, photographic, or online data (LeCompte & Schensul 1999). In this research, I adopted some of these methods, including participant observation, interviews with 23 strongwoman competitors, and the use of online data. Hence, I called my approach to this research undertaking 'auto/ethnographic', with the slash deliberately used to signify the combination of these methods. This research therefore comprised of the co-construction of knowledge from both my own personal experiences and the experiences of others, allowing for interactive exchanges and joint reflection. This was a two-way dyadic process – some topics or points of interest were driven by my own personal experience and reflection (e.g., the potential conflict between aesthetic- and strength-based goals), while other topics arose from my observations or interviews with others (e.g., performance-enhancing drugs), in turn leading me to reflect on my own experience of those topics.

It has been argued by some that autoethnography does not need to be seen as a distinct methodology from ethnography, based on the principle that if ethnography is done well, the full immersion of an ethnographer within the culture being studied would produce personal experiences and levels of personal reflection comparable to those detailed in what others term autoethnography (e.g., Moors 2017). My view, and hence my approach to this research, is that the experiences and position of a researcher who has a pre-existing relationship with the topic of study or who is a pre-existing member of the culture being studied will have differences to those of a researcher who has entered the culture purely to conduct that research. To exemplify this, if I had never competed in strongwoman before, but did so for the purpose of this research, I may be able to reflect on my experiences, such as changes to my body, but the meaning I attached may be different considering I would not be driven in the same way by any previous motivation for and experiences of involvement in the sport that were not for the purpose of research. In summary, the experiences of those who embark on the research from a pre-existing position of being a cultural member (insider) will hold differences to the experiences of those who, without the motive of research, would be a cultural stranger (outsider) (Maso 2001). This is not to discount the experiences of the latter, but to recognise the distinction between the two. Considering these differences in motivations and experiences, the combined auto/ethnographic approach lends itself well to the application of an intersectional lens in analyses of the construction of athletes' identities and experiences.

Embracing emotion

My approach to this auto/ethnographic research was underpinned by an interpretivist epistemological perspective, which accepts that the researcher is inseparably a part of what is studied (Smith 1989). British methodologists Andrew Sparkes and Brett Smith (2017) describe this as an interdependency between the knower and the known, which are 'fused together in such a way that the "findings" are the creation of a process of interaction between the two' (13). This basic belief influenced my decision to combine both autoethnographic and ethnographic methods, enabling the co-construction of data, drawing on interactively produced, collaborative, and shared knowledge.

The typical positivist paradigm to research on humans requires a separation between the researcher(s) and the participant(s) based on the idea that any kind of personal involvement would bias the research, disturb the natural setting, and/or contaminate the results. However, UK-based scholars Helen Owton and Jacquelyn Allen-Collinson (2014), along with many others taking an interpretivist position, argue that emotional involvement and emotional reflexivity can provide a rich resource in ethnographic research and do not necessarily constitute a 'problem' that needs to be avoided. Furthermore, US-based scholars Sherryl Kleinman and Martha Copp (2003) argue there are significant costs associated with ignoring feelings in this context and therefore encourage their exploration. US critical media scholar Lisa Tillmann-Healy (2003) proposed the concept of friendship as method, described as being built upon the principles of interpretivism, taking reality to be both pluralistic and constructed in language and interaction. Friendship as method is described not as a strategy aimed at gaining further access but as 'a level of investment in participants' lives that puts fieldwork relationships on par with the project' (735).

I did not plan to adopt the concept of friendship as method prior to the beginning of my study; however, during and after the official fieldwork period it became clear that there was an overlap between my position as researcher and as a friend in the case of many of those strongwomen who contributed. Like other researchers, such as Owton and Allen-Collinson (2014), I recognised that the friendship dimension I had with many of those contributing both enhanced my research relationships but also generated challenges. Hence friendship as method became a relevant approach to my research and the decisions I made regarding ethical considerations such as maintaining anonymity, what stories and experiences I could or should use, and the level to which those relationships continued or didn't continue after the end of the formal fieldwork period.

The ways that different forms and types of autoethnography are categorised has been a point of debate amongst ethnographic and autoethnographic researchers. These debates have centred largely upon the distinction between 'evocative' and 'analytical' autoethnographies. Evocative autoethnography can be described as a *'show* stories' rather than a *'tell* stories' approach to autoethnography (Smith 2017). In this approach, theory is shown through emotionally-driven stories with the goal of creating an emotional resonance with the reader, letting the story do the theoretical work on its own. Analytic ethnography (Anderson 2006), on the other hand, tells the reader what the story aims to theoretically do. There is a theoretical dissection of the story that does not occur in evocative autoethnographies (Smith 2017). Regarding this debate, I would agree with US communication scholars Carolyn Ellis and Arthur Bochner's (2006) statement that evocation should be a quality of all autoethnography, as opposed to a type, and thus in this research evocation was a central aim of the use of autoethnographic vignettes.

This debate also relates to how autoethnography is evaluated or assessed. Criticisms of autoethnography have described it as unscientific, entirely personal, and full of bias (Denzin 2000). Autoethnographers have in turn sought to 'rethink' the ways in which we determine the validity of research. This argument for different ways of knowing has been strongly made by US Black feminist sociologist Patricia Hill Collins (2000), who suggests that knowledge is built upon lived experience and thus all knowledge is based upon beliefs. Some have also expressed concerns of methodological policing around placing too much emphasis on criteria (e.g., Bochner 2000). In their book on autoethnographic methodology, Tony Adams, Stacy Holman Jones, and Carolyn Ellis (2015) suggested four goals for evaluating and assessing autoethnographic work, asking does it: make a contribution to knowledge; value the personal and experiential; demonstrate the power, craft, and responsibilities of stories and storytelling; and take a relationally responsible approach to research practice and representation. Using these four goals, the approach to this research can be judged as valid because it made a conscious effort to use personal narratives and autoethnographic reflections as a tool to extend existing knowledge, as well as to give a deeper level of insight into the experience of being a strongwoman. These goals also link to US communication scholar Amber Johnson's (2021) criteria for intersectional praxis in autoethnography, which include the connection of the personal to the political, in which the body is positioned by examination of the social categories tied to it and the systems of power that are complicit in how bodies move through the world (see also Mirza with Nyhagen, this volume). The personal stories featured in this research were used to help explore the subculture of strongwoman through its reflexive, two-way dyadic approach. Great care was taken to be relationally responsible, for example through using ideal types (Runciman 1978), a conceptual tool used to understand the social reality of the lived experiences of participants involving the amalgamation of stories to create characters or narratives that reflect such experience. Ideal types were used here to combat the risk of the narratives of individual participants being recognisable to others in a relatively small, close-knit community (see Newman 2020 for further discussion).

Embodiment

The body of the female athlete is an integral part of their identity and plays a crucial role in the formations of other people's perceptions of them . The symbolic meanings that bodies convey are important; the physical body is a message in social communication (Brace-Govan 2002). Much feminist reflection on female embodiment has been built upon the sociohistorical fact that the differences in women's bodies to men's have served as excuses for structural inequalities (Young 2005, 4), as has the assumption that differences between women and men are biological as opposed to cultural. American Philosopher Iris Marion Young's (1990) paper 'Throwing Like a Girl' explores the societal restriction of women's movement and motility that exemplifies this difference between bodily experiences. Young describes 'that feminine existence experiences the body as a mere thing – a fragile thing … a thing that exists as *looked at* and *acted upon*' (39).

This notion of a woman's body as something to be 'looked at' is linked to British film theorist Laura Mulvey's (1975) concept of the 'male gaze', which refers to the depiction of the world from a masculine perspective, presenting women and their bodies as objects of male pleasure. Women's sport has at times been suggested as an attraction due to its opportunity to 'expose bare flesh' (Boddy 2014, 254) as opposed to its demonstration of skill and/or power. Women with large muscles evoke strong reactions from both men and women, including disgust, discomfort, anger, and threat, and are perceived as unattractive to heterosexual men (Bunsell 2013), an example of the inextricable connection between intersecting identities and experiences of gender and sexuality. Also, some female athletes have considered their muscular bodies as the primary hindrance to being perceived as heterosexually feminine (Krane et al. 2004). Thus, the bodies of women who are involved in muscularity and strength-based sports do not 'fit' with the masculine perspective of the 'male gaze'. Inevitably, then, participants are subject to negative perceptions and reactions, as well as societal expectations to conform to hegemonic standards of beauty and contain their strength and muscularity by avoiding or holding back on strength training. This is in line with the notion of a 'glass ceiling' of women's strength, where US sociologist Shari L. Dworkin (2001) suggested that women may find their bodily agency limited by ideologies of emphasised femininity. Women's bodies are not only gendered but racialised, with some feminist sport theorists historically calling for greater interrogation of sport as both a racialised and engendered arena in which Black women are marginalised (Scraton, 2001).

Some philosophers have suggested that humans can only understand themselves 'by comparing themselves with others or seeing themselves through the eyes of others' (e.g., Merleau-Ponty 1962). An extension of this concept postulates that external eyes are not only important in the understanding of ourselves but also for our lives to have meaning and purpose, as positive approval is needed for this to occur (Mead 1962). The concept of the 'looking glass self' (Cooley 1922) has been used to illustrate how identities of individuals are formed via the 'gaze of the other', and British sociologist Nick Crossley (2006) suggested the significant influence of the perception of this gaze, stating that 'it is difficult to find yourself beautiful if others do not' (97). Furthermore, Canadian-American sociologist Erving Goffman (1979, 1987) proposed that the first impression is crucial in the preservation of both social and personal identities. Social expectations, norms, values, and roles are constantly being maintained, with the strongest evidence of this being in the case of culturally acceptable notions of gender. Individuals are thought to make an automatic 'gender attribution' every time they see a human being, consigning that person to the sex of male or female based upon Western assumptions of masculine and feminine (Kessler & McKenna 1978). Hence it is reasonable to suggest that female athletes, particularly those in muscularity and strength-based sports, may place high value on the opinions and perceptions of others and experience self-consciousness in relation to their bodily presentation.

The bodies of female athletes then, especially if they are perceived as 'masculine', play an integral role in their marginalisation and stigmatisation, including heterosexism and homophobia, highlighting the inseparability and interdependence of intersecting identities and experiences. Successful athletes need to be powerful and strong, yet outside of the sporting community obvious signs of this power are construed negatively, and previous studies have described an arbitrary line that separated too much muscle from attractive muscle in women (Krane et al. 2004). In a culture where the 'appearance and (re)presentations of women's bodies are key determinants of feminine identity and cultural acceptability' (Brace-Govan 2002, 404), female athletes are therefore condemned because of their deviant aesthetic and are forced to negotiate their desire to be strong for sporting success while attempting to maintain a body that is socially accepted (Wright & Clarke 1999).

The strongwoman identity

Strongwomen in this research suggested that being a strongwoman was an identity that seeped into many different aspects of their lives. This became visibly evident in both social and work situations in which disclosure of their strongwoman activity became a novel point of discussion and in some cases, a commonly used form of identifier. At the point at which an individual decided to take part in their first novice strongwoman competition, there seemed for many to be a significant shift towards embracing their identity as 'a strongwoman', as opposed to strongwoman being something they do ('being' a strongwoman, rather than 'doing' strongwoman). In many ways, this apparent pride in the strongwoman identity conflicted with fears of stigma and negativity towards muscularity, and negotiations of gendered appearance. However, this could also be linked to the notion that it was not the 'doing' of the sport (i.e., the act of lifting weights) that was deemed a transgression of gender norms, but instead the changes to appearance that can accompany it.

Intersectionality and autoethnography together affect what stories we choose to tell, our understanding of ours and others' bodies in stories, and how those bodies and stories are connected to larger political structures and systems of power (Johnson & Lemaster 2020). Given the earlier high-lighted complexity of the intersecting identities of gender and sexuality, I had thought that sexuality, or perceptions of sexuality, might have been more salient in the research. Previous research has suggested that there is an association often made between female athleticism and lesbianism such that 'Female athlete = masculine = lesbian' (Lenskyj 1995). Given that strength has been so strongly associated with masculinity, I had expected more discussion around sexuality. Instead, any explicit discussion of sexuality in this research was very rare, it was simply not made salient. Johnson (2021) posited that autoethnographers can establish a rigorous intersectional praxis by addressing four criteria: narrative fidelity, narrative cohesion, self-reflexivity, and connection of the personal to the political. The combined auto/ethnographic approach taken in this strongwoman research facilitated narrative fidelity, enabling me to locate my truth as one possible truth within a complex system of power and perceptions, rather than positioning it as a universal truth applicable to all taking part in strongwoman. Self-reflexivity in this context refers to an intentional and rhetorical process of analysing our own research processes, biases and story, word, and analytic choices, also described as a constant process of perception checking (Johnson & LeMaster 2020). The auto/ethnographic approach taken, through its bringing together of stories, co-construction of knowledge, and space for interactive exchanges and joint reflection, created a research process that was conducive to self-reflexivity and perception checking regarding intersecting identities and experiences. The connection of the personal to the political also provides a theoretical framework for understanding the complexity and overlap of a single body's social identity categories and their political ramifications, acknowledging not just explicit discussion, but also the implicit or unspoken stories or experiences in relation to intersecting identities, such as that of sexuality and race (Johnson & LeMaster 2020).

This intersectional lens also highlighted how issues of social class intersected with gender, which was more explicitly and openly discussed than the intersections of sexuality and race. This intersection between social class and gender has been demonstrated in other exercise spaces such as pole fitness (Fennell 2018). For strongwomen, access to appropriate gym facilities, equipment, and kit costs money that not all could equally afford. For those already in the sport, the point at which cost became a significant barrier to participation was when qualifying or being invited to one of the more prestigious international competitions. Often held in the United States or outside of Europe, these competitions required a large level of self-funding and financial commitment for travel and accommodation in order to participate, as well as potentially unpaid time off work. This was not achievable for all.

The empowerment debate

The perceived 'masculine' nature of strength sports, and the discernment that women's participation in these sports can be considered a transgression of gender norms, has provoked debate over their empowering nature. As recognised by Bunsell (2013) in her ethnography of female bodybuilding in the south of England, empowerment is a difficult concept to operationalise, and explicit definitions are rare. She posited that Sarah Mosedale's (2005) definition of women's empowerment was useful in this context: 'the process by which women redefine and extend what is possible for them to be and do in situations where they have been restricted, compared to men, from being and doing' (252). Bunsell (2013) also drew on sport feminist definitions of bodily empowerment, specifically the following interpretation:

> Bodily empowerment lies in women's abilities to forge an identity that is not bound by traditional definitions of what it 'means to be female', and to work for a new femininity that is not defined by normative beauty of body ideals, but rather by the qualities attained through athleticism (such as skill, strength, power, self-expression).
>
> *(Hesse-Biber 1996, 127)*

Bunsell's approach to empowerment, which I build upon, is underpinned by the notion that it is a complex, multi-dimensional concept, and a process rather than an event. The debate as to whether bodybuilding is an empowering endeavour for women is complex, as posited by Bunsell (2013) in her ethnography of female bodybuilding, which implied that female bodybuilders are not simply either empowered or oppressed, but that for most, elements of both would be present.

As within the female bodybuilding literature, the debate as to whether any muscularity- or strength-based sports are liberating and empowering or restrictive and oppressive for women is ongoing. There appears to be a constant conflict between the empowerment associated with building a body for themselves, or one which is capable of huge feats of physical sporting success, and the restriction and oppression imposed by societal expectations of how a woman's body 'should' and 'ought' to look, placing a cap, or a 'glass ceiling' (Dworkin 2001), on potential liberation and empowerment. In addition to the previously described empowering benefits, such as the opportunity to create a body for their own pleasure (Frueh 2001) and to experience achievement previously unavailable to them, muscularity- and strength-based sports can also be viewed as symbolically and physically empowering for some women due to their potential to reduce the physical power imbalances on which patriarchy and the oppression of women have been founded (Custelnuovo & Guthrie 1998).

However, evaluations of empowerment must consider potential differences and limitations due to intersecting identities such as race, given the historical dehumanisation and defeminisation of Black female athletes, and navigation of multiple conflicting body ideals within sports culture, Black culture, and the dominant culture (Landgrebe 2022). Additionally, considering intersecting identities of gender and sexuality, others have cited concern that strength- and muscularity-focused activities can become recuperated into heterosexual normative gender roles. For example, the femininity rules instigated by bodybuilding federations, which state that competitors should look 'feminine' and not 'too big', encourage the absorption of subversive femininity back into the mainstream (e.g., muscular women as subjects of the male gaze) (Brace-Govan 2004). Heterosexual desirability was also identified as a strategy for recuperation in women's bodybuilding (Schulze 1990). This was implemented by allaying fears of 'excessive muscles' using assertions of biological impossibility and linking the activity to self-improvement, self-confidence, and self-control (Brace-Govan 2004). Furthermore, although the recent increase in media attention can be seen as a positive step for strength-based sports, much of this appears to use sexualisation and a focus on aesthetic attractiveness as tools to promote the benefits of participation. Examples include references to 'beauty' in newspaper headlines (Oliver 2015) and social media campaigns featuring phrases such as 'strong is the new sexy'. Some journalists have even suggested that 'strong' may be a rebrand of 'skinny', representing a shift in the type of body women are expected to conform to but ultimately still creating a new desired aesthetic and pressure to conform (Kessel 2016).

Throughout my research, insights into the processes of strongwoman showed them to be transgressive in relation to social norms of femininity. There were many points where strongwomen appeared to be negotiating these transgressions in relation to their gendered appearance. While the sport itself does not focus on aesthetics, increased muscularity is an unavoidable side effect of 'becoming strong' or 'being strong'. It is this aesthetic impact of strongwoman participation that appears to be more noticeably transgressive, and which requires the most negotiation rather than the act of 'becoming strong' or 'being strong'. My understanding is that, generally, most of the strongwomen involved in this study did not feel much negativity towards their strength as long as their gendered aesthetic remained aligned with societal expectations of femininity. This fear of gaining excessive musculature has been seen in other sporting contexts, for example the female wrestlers in Norwegian scholars Mari Sisjord and Elsa Kristiansen's (2009) study. Again, their study aligns with Dworkin's (2001) concept of the 'glass ceiling' for musculature for women, whereby women can gain strength and muscle, but then struggle to reconcile seemingly incompatible expectations about musculature and femininity. If sexuality, ethnicity, and class are taken into account, it appeared that White, middle-class women who identified as heterosexual were privileged in the strongwoman context, with these intersecting identities and experiences being powerful and important in perceptions of transgressions of femininity and social norms.

Despite strength often becoming a key tenet of identity, it was evident that those in this research still felt the need to negotiate aspects of being a strongwoman in relation to their gendered aesthetic. For example, negotiations of eating enough for good performance versus not wanting to eat too much (because of the perception that 'big is bad' for women), practices of dieting down post-competition, self-consciousness about bodily changes, particularly visible musculature (even if they liked it themselves), and negotiations around performance-enhancing drug (PED) use and the risks to gendered appearance that these pose. Therefore, despite an increasing openness and acceptance of women's strength, power, and muscularity, in this strongwoman context there still appeared to be a 'glass ceiling' (Dworkin, 2001) to what is deemed acceptable regarding these physical characteristics. The negotiations made, and the perceived need that the strongwomen felt in making these, suggest that 'being strong' and/or muscular as a woman is still viewed as a transgression because importance is still placed on traditional norms of femininity. Although we appear to be at a point when attitudes are shifting, there are still constraints to this and hence there is some tension preventing many strongwomen from being completely content with the identity they have constructed in current society, and hence the potential for social empowerment is reduced.

Concluding comments

The case study presented in this chapter explored a combined auto/ethnographic methodology, focusing on how it engages with feminist research approaches that value making oneself vulnerable and embracing emotion, as well as how it can enable a feminist intersectional lens on identities and experiences, taking into account intersecting identities such as gender, sexuality, class, and ethnicity. The combination of autoethnographic and ethnographic elements gave space for narrative fidelity, self-reflexivity, and connection of the personal to the political, all deemed key components in the development of an intersectional praxis. The methodology adopted allowed space for the co-construction of knowledge with others, and acknowledgement and analysis of differing experiences and truths beyond my own, positioning this combined approach as one that could be valuable in the development of an intersectional lens across a range of research topics. This intersectional lens is, in turn, useful in auto/ethnographic research as it provides a framework for exploring and understanding the intricacies and multifaceted nature of lived experiences.

References

Adams, Tony E., Stacey Holman Jones, and Carolyn Ellis. 2015. *Autoethnography: Understanding Qualitative Research*. New York: Oxford University Press.

Allen-Collinson, Jacquelyn. 2012. "Autoethnography: Situating Personal Sporting Narratives in Socio-cultural Contexts." In *Qualitative Research on Sport and Physical Culture (Research in the Sociology of Sport, Vol. 6)*, edited by Kevin Young and Michael Atkinson, 191–212. Bingley, UK: Emerald Group Publishing Limited.

Anderson, Leon. 2006. "Analytic Autoethnography." *Journal of Contemporary Autoethnography*, 35 (4): 375–395. https://doi.org/10.1177/0891241605280449

Atkinson, Michael. 2012. "The Empirical Strikes Back: Doing Realist Ethnography." In *Qualitative Research on Sport and Physical Culture*, edited by Kevin Young and Michael Atkinson, 23–50. Bingley, UK: Emerald Group Publishing Ltd.

Bochner, Arthur P. 2000. "Criteria Against Ourselves." *Qualitative Inquiry*, 6: 266–272. https://doi.org/10.1177/107780040000600209

Boddy, Kasia. 2014. "Watching Women Box." In *The Routledge Handbook of Sport, Gender, and Sexuality*, edited by Jennifer Hargreaves and Eric Anderson, 254–262. London: Routledge.

Brace-Govan, Jan. 2002. "Looking at Bodywork: Women and Three Physical Activities." *Journal of Sport and Social Issues*, 24 (40): 404–421. https://doi.org/10.1177/0193732502238256

Brace-Govan, Jan. 2004. "Weighty Matters: Control of Women's Access to Physical Strength." *The Sociological Review*, 52: 503–551. https://doi.org/10.1111/j.1467-954X.2004.00493.x

Breeze, Maddie. 2015. *Seriousness and Women's Roller Derby: Gender, Organization, and Ambivalence*. New York: Springer.

Bunsell, Tanya. 2013. *Strong and Hard Women: An Ethnography of Female Bodybuilding*. London: Routledge.

Collins, Patricia Hill. 2000. *Black Feminist Thought: Knowledge, Consciousness, and the Politics of Empowerment* (2nd ed.). New York: Routledge.

Cooley, Charles H. 1922 [1902]. *Human Nature and Social Order*. New Brunswick: Transaction Publishers.

Crenshaw, Kimberlé. 1989. "Demarginalising the Intersection of Race and Sex: A Black Feminist Critique of Antidiscrimination Doctrine." *University of Chicago Legal Forum*, 139–168. https://doi.org/10.4324/9780429500480-5

Crossley, Nick. 2006. "In the Gym: Motives, Meanings and Moral Careers." *Body & Society*, 12 (3): 23–50. https://doi.org/10.1177/1357034X06067154

Custelnuovo, Shirley, and Sharon R. Guthrie. 1998. *Feminism and the Female Body: Liberating the Amazon Within*. London: Lynne Rienner.

Denzin, Norman K. 2000. "Aesthetics and the Practices of Qualitative Inquiry." *Qualitative Inquiry*, 6 (2): 256–265. https://doi.org/10.1177/107780040000600208

Dworkin, Shari L. 2001. "'Holding Back': Negotiating a Glass Ceiling on Women's Muscular Strength." *Sociological Perspectives*, 44: 333–350. https://doi.org/10.1525/sop.2001.44.3.333

Ellis, Carolyn. 2004. *The Ethnographic I: A Methodological Novel About Autoethnography*. Walnut Creek, CA: AltaMira Press.

Ellis, Carolyn, and Arthur P. Bochner. 2006. "Analyzing Analytic Autoethnography: An Autopsy." *Journal of Contemporary Ethnography*, 35 (4): 423–449. https://doi.org/10.1177/0891241606286979

Fennell, Dana. 2018. "Pole Studios as Spaces Between the Adult Entertainment, Art, Fitness and Sporting Fields." *Sport in Society*, 21 (12): 1957–1973. https://doi.org/10.1080/17430437.2018.1445995

Frueh, Joanna. 2001. *Monster/Beauty Building a Body of Love*. London: University of California Press.

Goffman, Erving. 1979. *Gender Advertisements*. London: Macmillan.

Goffman, Erving. 1987. "The Arrangement Between Sexes." In *Interaction*, edited by Mary Jo Deegan and Michael R. Hill, 51–78. Winchester, MA: Allen and Unwin.

Hesse-Biber, Sharlene. 1996. *Am I Thin Enough Yet? The Cult of Thinness and the Commercialization of Identity*. New York, NY: Oxford University Press.

Johnson, Amber. 2021. "How Intersectional Autoethnography Saved My Life: A Plea for Intersectional Inquiry." In *Handbook of Autoethnography*, edited by Tony E Adams, Stacy Holman Jones, and Carolyn Ellis. New York: Routledge.

Johnson, Amber L, and Benny LeMaster. 2020. *Gender Futurity, Intersectional Autoethnography: Embodied Theorizing from the Margins*. New York: Routledge.

Kessel, Anna. 2016. "Why Has Women's Fitness Become a Beauty Contest?" *The Guardian*, August 22, 2017. https://www.theguardian.com/commentisfree/2016/aug/22/sport-is-supposed-to-be-about-fun-not-body-image

Kessler, Suzanne J, and Wendy McKenna. 1978. *Gender: An Ethnomethodological Approach*. Chicago: University of Chicago Press.

Kleinman, Sherryl, and Martha A Copp. 1993. *Emotions and Fieldwork*. London: Sage Publications.

Krane, Vikki, and Shannon M. Baird. 2005. "Using Ethnography in Applied Sport Psychology." *Journal of Applied Sport Psychology*, 17 (2): 87–107. https://doi.org/10.1080/10413200590932371

Krane, Vikki, Precilla Y. Choi, Shannon M. Baird, Christine M. Aimar, and Kerrie J. Kauer. 2004. "Living the Paradox: Female Athletes Negotiate Femininity and Muscularity." *Sex Roles*, 50 (5/6): 315–329.

LeCompte, Margaret D., and Jean J. Schensul. 1999. *Designing and Conducting Ethnographic Research*. New York: AltMira Press.

Lenskyj, Helen. 1995. "Sport and the Threat to Gender Boundaries." *Sporting Traditions*, 12 (1): 48–60.

Maso, Ilja. 2001. "Phenomenology and Ethnography." In *Handbook of Ethnography* edited by Paul Atkinson, Amanda Coffey, Sara Delamont, John Lofland and Lyn Lofland, 136–144. Thousand Oaks, CA: Sage.

Mead, George. 1962 [1934]. *Mind, Self and Society*. Chicago, IL: Chicago University Press.

Merleau-Ponty, Maurice. 1962. *Phenomenology of Perception*. London: Routledge.

Moors, Annelies. 2017. "On Autoethnography." *Ethnography*, 18 (3): 387–389. https://doi.org/10.1177/1466138117723354

Mosedale, Sarah. 2005. "Assessing Women's Empowerment: Towards a Conceptual Framework." *Journal of International Development*, 17: 243–257. https://doi.org/10.1002/jid.1212

Mulvey, Laura. 1975. "Visual Pleasure and the Narrative Cinema." *Screen*, 16 (3): 6–18.

Landgrebe, Lindsey. 2022. *"Exploring Body Image at the Intersection of Racial, Gender and Sport Identities: Giving Voice to Black Female Athletes' Experiences."* PhD diss., University of Missouri.

Newman, Hannah J. H. 2020. *"Becoming a Strongwoman: An Auto/ethnographic Study of the Pursuit of Strength and Power, and the Negotiation of Gender Aesthetics in the UK Strongwoman Community."* PhD diss., Loughborough University.

O'Reilly, Karen. 2012. *Ethnographic Methods*. London: Routledge.

Oliver, Brian. 2015. "'Strong is Beautiful': The Unstoppable Rise of Crossfit." *The Guardian*, December 6, 2015. https://www.theguardian.com/lifeandstyle/2015/dec/06/crossfit-weightlifting-strong-is-beautiful

Owton, Helen, and Jacquelyn Allen-Collinson. 2014. "Close But Not Too Close: Friendship as Method(ology) in Ethnographic Research." *Journal of Contemporary Ethnography*, 43 (3): 283–305. https://doi.org/10.1177/0891241613495410

Robinson, Victoria. 2008. *Everyday Masculinities and Extreme Sport: Male Identity and Rock Climbing*. New York: Berg.

Runciman, Walter G. 1978. *Max Weber: Selections in Translation*. Cambridge University Press.

Schulze, Laurie. 1990. "On the Muscle." In *Building Bodies*, edited by Pamela Moore, 9–30. New Brunswick, NJ: Rutgers University Press.

Scraton, Sheila. 2001. "Reconceptualising Race, Gender and Sport." In *'Race', Sport and British Society*, edited by Ben Carrington and Ian McDonald, 170–187. London: Routledge.

Shilling, Chris, and Tanya Bunsell. 2014. "From Iron Maiden to Superwoman: The Stochastic Art of Self-transformation and the Deviant Female Sporting Body." *Qualitative Research in Sport, Exercise, and Health*, 6 (4): 478–498. https://doi.org/10.1080/2159676X.2014.928897

Sisjord, Mari K., and Elsa Kristiansen. 2009. "Elite Women Wrestler's Muscles: Physical Strength and a Social Burden." *International Review for the Sociology of Sport*, 44 (2/3): 231–246. https://doi.org/10.1177/1012690209335278

Smith, Brett. 2017. "Narrative Inquiry and Autoethnography." In *The Routledge Handbook of Physical Cultural Studies*, edited by Michael Silk, David Andrews and Holly Thorpe, 205–215. New York, NY: Routledge.

Smith, John K. 1989. *The Nature of Social and Educational Inquiry: Empiricism Versus Interpretation*. Norwood, NJ: Ablex.

Sparkes, Andrew C, and Brett Smith. 2013. *Qualitative Research Methods in Sport, Exercise and Health: From process to product*. London: Routledge.

Tilmann-Healy, Lisa M. 2003. "Friendship as Method." *Qualitative Inquiry*, 9: 729–749. https://doi.org/10.1177/1077800403254894

Wright, Jan, and Gill Clarke. 1999. "Sport, the Media and the Construction of Compulsory Heterosexuality." *International Review for the Sociology of Sport,* 34: 227–243. https://doi.org/10.1177/101269099034003001

Young, Iris M. 2005. *On Female Body Experience: Throwing Like a Girl and Other Essays.* Oxford: Oxford University Press.

Young, Iris M. 1997. *Intersecting Voices: Dilemmas of Gender, Political Philosophy, and Policy.* Princeton, NJ: Princeton University Press.

9

THE ARCHIVAL IS PERSONAL IS POLITICAL

Historiography, the archive, and feminist research methods

Charlotte Riley

This chapter makes a case for intersectional feminism as a methodology for 'doing history', drawing on the author's experience of working in a British university on contemporary British history. Women's history has been a part of the historical canon in British academia since the 1970s, when women involved with the British women's liberation movement (WLM) and labour movements started to recover stories of women in the archive. Today, most history departments in the UK offer some form of gender history, and most general histories include gender – and women – within their analysis. It can be striking how often these stories end up bolted on to the main event, how often male histories are understood as the default, how often female historians still find themselves forgotten when it comes to roundtables, colloquia, and special issues. But the idea that women's stories are part of history, and that gender history is a valid framework, has been widely accepted (even if some historians think that this work can be left to other people). However, 'sex' or 'gender' is often identified as part of the list of identities that might diversify a history curriculum (alongside 'race', class, and sometimes topics such as age or disability) without a sustained effort to explore how these identities might intersect or how these intersections might inform academic research. Within the field of feminist historiography, however, an intersectional approach must be recognised as the most effective, most valuable way to explore the complexities of (gender) history.

This chapter argues that as well as women's and gender history, we need to support and reinvigorate *feminist* history in the profession: history that takes feminism as its organising theoretical and methodological principle. An intersectional approach has been and should be a critical driver of work in this field, by helping to avoid a homogeneous approach to women's

DOI: 10.4324/9781003399575-10

This chapter has been made available under a CC-BY-NC-ND license.

stories, instead acting as a lens that reveals the differences among women, and foregrounds how their identities and experiences are linked to different biographical and social histories in specific contexts.

What does it mean to be an intersectional feminist historian, to research, write, and teach feminist history? Intersectional feminism has shaped my research in three ways: firstly, in the topics I am drawn to and the stories I want to tell; secondly, in my relationship to these topics and figures, particularly drawing on a concept of archival empathy as espoused in the work of Michelle Caswell and Marika Cifor (2016); thirdly, in my work with collaborators and the idea of the feminist collective. Feminist history, like the Marxist history that was one of its forebears – encapsulated in the *History Workshop Journal*'s shifting self-identification from 'a journal of socialist historians' to 'a journal of socialist and feminist historians' in 1982 – is simultaneously a methodology, an interpretative framework, and a lived and theorised political position. The relationship between the feminist historian and feminist history is not straightforward.

This chapter begins with a short history of the historical method, before examining how feminist thought and methodology has been adopted by historians. I then present the ways my work has been shaped by an intersectional feminist approach. The chapter concludes by exploring how historians' affective relationship with the archive might be understood through this lens, and the wider context of intersectional feminist identity and practice within the academy, drawing on the experiences of British and American historians, departments, and organisations. The chapter ends with some thoughts about the potential for intersectional feminism in the future of historical scholarship.

The history of historical methodology

Historians' discussion of methodology was once framed through an identification with the skills and experience of archival documentary research, assumed to be common to all professional historians. Knowledge of the past, for these 'historicists', was both the means and the end of historical research; 'historicism' as a form of knowledge and writing about the past was rooted fundamentally in a 'command of the sources' (Tosh 2009, 3). The development of post-structuralist and postmodern theories, with their focus on the discursive and the subjective, led to both the linguistic and cultural turns in historical research, as well as, in hindsight, somewhat alarmist panics that these approaches meant the imminent death of the discipline.

Despite these fears, historians still, mostly, follow a process of research echoing that set out in the nineteenth century: we 'read' sources, and write about them. But the instruction, passed down by the nineteenth-century historian Leopold von Ranke, to write the past *wie es eigentlich gewesen* [how things really were] has been rejected not only as impossible, but also undesirable. Academic history has long accepted the idea that historians are subjective in their relationship to the past and that their interpretation is shaped by their ideological position – the 'bee' in the historian's 'bonnet' set out by E.H. Carr, the British historian and influential historiographer (1987, 23).

And yet, as the 'Theory Revolt' collective (Kleinburg et al. 2018) make explicit, some historians remain extremely conservative in their methodology, and in gatekeeping acceptable ways of approaching the past. For Ethan Kleinberg, Gary Wilder, and Joan Wallach Scott (all historians working in the United States), academic history is limited by its attachment to a 'realist epistemology and empiricist methodology'. The subject and its practitioners are trapped in a narrow methodology, guilty of 'archival fetishism', an 'insistence on the primacy of chronological narrative', and a 'maintenance of reified boundaries between present and past' (Kleinburg et al. 2022, 91). It certainly is true that historians have often instinctively recoiled from the idea of 'theory' in their work. In an early review of the writing of Joan Wallach Scott alongside that of British philosopher Denise Riley, the British feminist historian Catherine Hall argued 'it is hard work for historians, even feminist historians, to do theoretical work since ... our training is so embedded in empiricism': importantly, she followed this up with the caveat that empiricism itself is 'a theory that is rarely recognised as such' (Hall 1991, 207).

In fact, the 'historical method' of archival research is a methodology, an ideology, and a theory: an approach to the sources, a way of justifying the work that historians do, and a framework that sets out the difference between The Past and History. Suggesting new methodologies in this context can be especially fraught; it is always difficult to engage with an ideology masquerading as common sense. Furthermore, although there is surface acceptance that a historian is subjective in their relationship to the past and that their interpretation is shaped by their ideological/historiographical position, there is less interrogation of how this position is shaped by the historian's conditions of labour, or identity. This can leave feminist historical methodology, which builds a theoretical approach to the past on a contemporary political position, in a difficult and defensive position. Whilst many historians consider themselves feminists, fewer (especially outside the fields of women's or gender history) explicitly identify their work as 'feminist history', or as explicitly 'intersectional'. And yet – as this chapter argues – feminist approaches to the study of the past, and an engagement with intersectional analysis as part of this, has had and must continue to have a critical influence on the wider field.

Feminism as historiography and methodology

The north American feminist historian Susan Pedersen, addressing the American Historical Association in 2000, characterised the challenges and opportunities facing feminist historiography in that moment. She argued that feminist historiography was characterised by 'that cast of mind that insists that the differences and inequalities between the sexes are the result of historical processes and are not blindly "natural"'. As such, she argued, feminist history is animated by a 'dual mission':

> on the one hand to recover the lives, experiences, and mentalities of women from the condescension and obscurity in which they have been so unnaturally placed, and on the other to re-examine and rewrite the entire historical narrative to reveal the construction and workings of gender.
>
> *(Pedersen 2000)*

From this mission comes a methodology. Initially, this was a focus on sources that relate specifically to women's lives and experience, often using different archives than those that relate to normative (male) histories. Connectedly, there was an attempt to read both with and 'against the grain' of archival materials to re-insert women into these stories; an approach to historical narratives prioritising previously ignored spaces such as the home, the marriage, and the nursery. Of course, this work largely accepts the existence of a gender binary – and it also had the potential, although this was not always the case, to flatten and homogenise 'women's histories' into a single experience, ignoring the intersections of other identities such as class, race, or sexuality.

Feminist methodology as an explicit, declared approach to historical research and writing has its origins in the women's liberation movement (WLM) of the late 1960s onwards, particularly in Britain. As Natalie Thomlinson and Jeska Rees have made clear, in their histories of the moment, the WLM was itself struggling to reflect properly the intersectional identities of its participants and their motivations and experiences (Thomlinson 2012; Rees 2010). But the WLM was galvanising for feminist historians, many of whom were associated with the British socialist and labour movements. As they engaged with the literature and communities of feminist liberation in Britain, they questioned how and why women had been omitted from the historical canon. In a path-breaking piece on the topic, the British feminist socialist historian Anna Davin declared that history had been shaped by class and patriarchy to the exclusion of many of its historical subjects: 'In a class society, history has meant the history of the rulers, and in a male dominated society the history of men' (Davin 1972, 216).

Feminist historians were initially motivated by the promise of recovering women's lost stories, which had not been captured in the archive and had therefore not been included in the books written by men who did not care very much about what was happening to female historical subjects. (This was often a lonely, undervalued pursuit by isolated early-career female

The archival is personal is political **149**

historians: Ann McGrath, in an article reflecting on Australian research cultures, writes that 'Once upon a time, in history departments it had always been like this: one nervously heard the echo of one's voice, the lone feminist historian in the room, and often the only woman' (McGrath 2014, 205)). The activities of women had not been 'legitimated' by historical writing (Hall 1992, 6); to be captured in the work of historians is to be witnessed, and women had been ignored and therefore invisible to much of the historical profession. To respond to the scale of this absence, early feminist history writing was often 'a broad historical sweep' (Hall 1992, 7): British historian Sheila Rowbotham's *Hidden From History* (1973), for example, sought to write women back into 300 years of British history. But this was soon replaced by more considered, specific, primary-source focused histories, which looked to replicate the methods of 'traditional' historical writing but to apply it to female subjects.

As well as this shift to more specific, limited stories, there was a movement to broaden or shift the focus of feminist history from 'women' to the broader category of 'gender'. This encompassed both an attempt to think about the experience of men *as men* rather than as the default historical actor, such as in the work of John Tosh on men and masculinity in nineteenth-century Britain (Tosh and Roper 1991; Tosh 1999), but also a focus on the relationships between men and women and the ways that gender might be understood to exist as a social construction and a political pressure in the world. A key text here is the pioneering *Family Fortunes* by Catherine Hall and Leonore Davidoff, with its subtitle *Men and Women of the English Middle Class* (1987); by situating women within the family and the family within British society, work by Hall and others in the field opened the door for more feminist historical engagement with themes of class and race – particularly, in the case of British history, through the lens of empire.

The shift from 'women' to 'gender' was not, however, without its controversies. When Penny Corfield wrote a piece in which she referred to women's history as 'mutating into gender history' (Corfield 1997, 241) – presenting this as a widening of scope, and thus as a *positive* development – she was met with criticism from those who argued that 'gender history is yet another variation of men's history, peppered with frequent references to "gender" but with little reference to women's lives' (Purvis and Weatherill 1997, 334). 'Gender history' has become the dominant term, not least perhaps because students of history are now used to thinking about the ways that identities such as gender, race, and class shaped historical experience; 'women's history' still exists as a field, though, not least in publications such as the *Journal of Women's History* and *Women's History Review*.

As gender history developed in the UK, feminist historians in Britain also began to engage with developments primarily in the United States which sought to apply post-structuralist scholarship to historical enquiry. In women's history, this was predominately received through the work of pioneering scholars such as Joan W. Scott and Denise Riley. Perhaps their most enduring contribution was the insistence that 'woman' was not a fixed category of identity – Riley memorably reframing the Black American abolitionist and women's rights activist Sojourner Truth's demand 'Ain't I a woman?' as 'Ain't I a fluctuating identity?' (1988, 1) – and that the categories of gender, but also sex and race, had been socially constructed.

Scott, in particular, also pushed back against the increasing focus on 'experience' in women's history, arguing that although this approach had enabled the addition of different stories to the canonical historical narrative, it had also rendered various categories of experience (race, gender) curiously ahistorical, and had 'reproduc[ed] rather than contest[ed] given ideological systems' (Scott 1991, 778). Not all feminist historians embraced the values and approaches of post-structuralism. Some pointed out that post-structuralism was dominated by theorists who were no friends to feminists or women (Jackson 1992, 25) whilst others expressed concern that de-stabilising the category of 'woman' would undo the political and academic work that had been done to recover women's stories and take women's experience seriously both as historic subjects and as historians (Laura Lee Downs pointedly titling her piece on the topic 'If "Woman" Is Just an Empty Category, Then Why Am I Afraid to Walk Alone at Night?' (1993)). But feminist historians have, increasingly, taken on board the idea that to write histories of women there must be an interrogation of the category of 'woman' at any given historical time.

This has necessarily created an impetus towards intersectional approaches to feminist history writing, in which 'woman' and 'man' are not taken for granted as stable historical categories, and in which a wider range of identities and experiences can be reflected and interrogated. These histories reject narratives which take White, straight, middle-class lives as the default and which challenge this default only through inserting a female subject. Instead, feminist histories now intersect with queer histories and the histories of people of colour, to think about how different marginalised identities interacted to shape lives and experiences (see, for example, Vicinus (2004) and Jennings (2007) for pioneering research on lesbianism, the path-breaking scholarship by historians such as Dadzie, Bryan, and Scafe (1985) and Thomlinson (2016) on Black British women's history, and agenda-setting work on masculinity (Sinha 1995) and feminism and colonialism (Burton 1994)). This shift has also helped historians to explore how women might find power within patriarchal, capitalist, heteronormative, and racist societies and how some were able to leverage aspects of their identity to do so; Hannah Young's work on White female slave owners, for example (Young 2020), problematises the idea of the historical female subject only as oppressed rather than oppressor.

The archival is personal is political **151**

In my own work, then, I engage with this intersectional feminist methodology in history research and writing. Firstly, and perhaps foundationally, feminist methodology requires that historians focus on the uncovering of women's stories, and 'writing women in' to narratives that have previously omitted their contributions. Sometimes these omissions reflect women's absence from moments in history where their presence was unusual or unrequired; sometimes these absences have clearly been imposed by historians who have failed to notice or to consider the very visible role that women played in the past. For example, in British Labour Party history there is a well-known text, Must Labour Lose? (1960), produced in response to the party's poor showing in the 1959 general election. This text is often referred to by political scientists and historians as having been written by the researchers Mark Abrams and Richard Rose; it is attributed to Abrams and Rose in many library catalogues and contemporary reviews. And yet the book actually had three authors: Abrams, Rose, and Rita Hinden, who wrote in its entirety the final section and conclusion to the text; Hinden's contribution is rarely acknowledged by political scientists. In an article re-evaluating the book in light of Brexit, I explored Hinden's central role in its formation, notably, her writing of the conclusion, the section of the book that suggested what the party should do to improve their chances in future elections (2021a).

Hinden is a central figure in my research, a woman with a critical role in socialist politics but also in contributing to anti-imperial activism in Britain in the mid-twentieth century. A recent project by Patricia Owens et al., 'Women and the History of International Thought', sought to re-evaluate the male-dominated field of international relations (IR) 'to write women back in' to the subject and its history. The project took women's contributions to political thought seriously, thinking critically about the definition of 'political thought' and how a canon has been historically constructed that excludes women's work. By opening up this definition, the project moved beyond simply adding elite White women to the canon, engaging instead with women doubly excluded because of their race, class, or non-professional status. It resulted in an anthology of writing (Owens, Rietzler, Hutchings, and Dunstan 2022), an edited collection on key female thinkers (Owens and Rietzler 2021), and a special issue of a journal. My contribution to the latter was again focused on Rita Hinden and argued that imperial history can be productively written into IR, not least because it was a space in which female theorists, as well as actors from the Global South, were active and engaged (2021b). I built here on the work of Cynthia Enloe, and her demand that we use 'feminist curiosity' to ask questions about how power works in the world (Enloe 2004).

My work as a modern and contemporary historian adds another layer to my feminist engagement with these histories of Britain and empire. For most of the period under my study, women were agitating for equality; as Dale Spender's book would have it, *There's Always Been A Women's Movement This Century* (Spender 1983). My article tracing the ways that the British feminist magazine *Spare Rib* engaged with the UN International Women's conferences involved reading material that was produced in the context of, and explicitly engaging with, the tenets of the women's liberation movement that would also shape women's history and feminist historiography (2022). Working with *Spare Rib* and taking it seriously as a political text is an act of feminist methodology that seeks to redress material produced by political historians and IR scholars based on sources that did not centre female actors. *Spare Rib* provides a rich and valuable account of the International Women's conferences, which were covered only cursorily in mainstream British media. This work also upends the frequent assumption in British political histories that the British women's movement was parochial and inward-looking. This analysis is necessarily intersectional; the conferences brought together women from across the world and forced debates around topics that highlighted the ways that, for example, racial identity or global economic inequality shaped women's lives but also divided the global category of 'women' into smaller groups (women of the Global South and women of the Global North, for example), which could be deeply oppositional or stand in solidarity with one another. And *Spare Rib* as a magazine consistently reflected intersecting identities in women's lives, for example, in its work to highlight the challenges posed for women in Northern Ireland by sectarian violence, or its engagement with the global campaign against the contraceptive injection Depo Provera.

Recovering sources can itself be a feminist scholarly act. When feminist histories were framed around writing women into histories that had ignored them, the traditional archives were abandoned in favour of different sources: oral histories, material culture, life-writing. The archive itself was recognised as a patriarchal space, a site 'of power and privilege' that had 'long been implicated in acts of violence and erasure' (Dever 2017, 1); this was amplified in the case of women who were excluded from this narrative still further because of their class, their race, or sexuality. And yet, as Maryanne Dever makes clear, for feminist historians the archive is also still a site 'of promise and desire', a space that feels rich with possibility (2017, 1). The feminist historian enters these spaces motivated by the desire 'to unlock stored meanings, allowing the voices of the past to speak, especially the voices of those conventionally silenced in official discourses, the fabled voices of the "Other"', even as they simultaneously recognise 'the impossibility of recovering the lost voices of the past in their original meaning' (Bradley 1999, 114 and 117).

Seeing and feeling the archive through an intersectional lens

The way in which we engage with the archive as feminist historians should be understood through an intersectional lens that accounts for the multiple different identities a historian is bringing to their work. Emily Robinson has written about the affective relationship between historians and their sources, the way that the archival experience is shaped as much by a desire to physically experience the documents as by the need to read their contents (Robinson 2010).

For me, this emphasis on the affective nature of the historian's relationship with the archive owes something important to feminist methodology: not only because the act of taking emotions seriously as historical subjects is clearly rooted in feminist theory – although it has not always been acknowledged as such during the 'affective turn' (Åhäll 2018) – but because Robinson's focus on the historian as an emotional actor challenges the assumption of the neutral researcher. If we accept that a historian's relationship with the archive, and thus the past, is affective, we can explore this emotional messiness more deeply as part of our research practice. My emotional relationship with the archive is shaped by my feminism, not least by a type of empathy with women who sit in different historic contexts but whose experiences echo mine. Reading the personal papers of the British Labour politician Judith Hart and coming across her to-do lists – including 'cleaning lady', 'fix hairdo', and 'make mince', alongside 'aid brief for Scotland' and 'ring ACAS' (Judith Hart Papers, PHM) – led me to reflect on the fact that she was the first mother to serve in the British cabinet, and to consider the challenges that we might share as working mothers; exploring the archives of her Labour colleague Barbara Castle and reading the hate mail sent to her at multiple times during her career (Castle Papers, Bodleian Library) evoked my own experiences receiving hate mail after writing newspaper articles related to my research. These reflections have shaped the direction of my research: for example, participation in a collaborative workshop funded by the Royal Historical Society in 2023 exploring the Labour Party's relationship to mothers and the maternal (RHS 2023).

An awareness of the ways that our interaction with sources is shaped by our own experiences and emotions – an assertion which owes much to the feminist insistence on the blurring of lines between the personal and the wider world, as well as an intersectional analysis of the different identities that we bring to our work and lives – forces us to confront the fact that the histories that we write are subjective, acts of interpretation. Knowing my relationship to the sources is based on my feelings is an important reminder that my engagement with the past is personal and partial. Making this personal dimension explicit is an acknowledgement that other historians may well see these histories differently.

154 Charlotte Riley

There is also a wider context to feminist methodology in history that goes beyond the written and the published. The north American theorist bell hooks in 1986 set out the necessity of feminist solidarity which would involve women learning to 'actively struggle in a truly supportive way' to understand differences and to build a community of interest (1986, 138). For hooks, feminist solidarity was a long-term project that would not diminish the different experiences and challenges that women faced because of their intersecting identities of race, class, disability, or sexuality, but would instead build a 'sustained, ongoing commitment' between different groups: a true 'sisterhood' (1986, 138). I see this as applicable to academia in two ways. Firstly, resisting institutional pressures on researchers to engage in competition in pursuit of individual 'excellence', in favour of collaborative working with other scholars. This does not just mean setting up research networks or bidding for funding to host PhD or postdoctoral researchers (although this can be an important part of this process) but also quieter, more subtly generative work to build connections with and support other scholars, especially those in precarious positions. Catherine Hall has written about how the 'model of the lone researcher' was 'alienating and disappointing' to her when she first embarked on doctoral studies; women's history was so engaging for her partly because its topics and focus were 'collectively' developed (1992, 4, 8). Working with other scholars such as Emily Baughan (University of Sheffield), Emma Lundin (University of Malmo), Anna Bocking-Welch (University of Liverpool), Tehila Sasson (Emory University), and Eve Colpus (University of Southampton) has been central to my development as a feminist historian.

Using a feminist methodology also requires that we call out behaviour and institutions that do not support the goals of feminist solidarity. Using our voices to demand and effect change is part of the responsibility of doing feminist work in the academy. In my work on sexual abuse and harassment in academia (2020a) and the aid industry (2020b) and on patriarchal cultures in the historical profession (2024), I have tried to hold that imperative in my mind.

In her analysis of the development of feminist historical methodology up until the early 1990s, Hall noted 'the gradual move away from thinking primarily about feminist history as part of a political movement towards thinking of it as an academic subject' (1992, 7). In many ways this shift was part of a legitimation of feminist history as an approach that belonged in the academy alongside other modes of historical enquiry. It also perhaps marked one of the distinctions between feminist history and women's history: a shift towards a history that focused on women's stories and wrote women into previously male-dominated narratives, but that was not necessarily marked explicitly by a feminist (political) approach. Given the focus, especially at graduate level, of finding the 'holes' in historical writing, with new work being legitimated by its role in identifying and filling in a gap that previously existed in the accounts of a particular period or event, 'recovering women's stories' could be understood as a pragmatic rather than political act. But perhaps we lost something when we stopped explicitly identifying feminist history with a progressive, even revolutionary, political movement.

We might agree with Afsaneh Najmabadi when she argued provocatively that, 'in making certain methodological and epistemological choices and refusing others in our grand endeavour to rethink radically the enterprise of writing history, we have entrapped ourselves into a mode of critique' that has prevented us from becoming 'radical re-doers' of the field, and has instead placed feminist historians in a passive, perhaps even 'parasitic', relationship to history more broadly (2004, 33). When Pendersen (2000) addressed the American Historical Association at the turn of the century, she argued that feminists had become part of the establishment that they used to critique: 'it is no good, anymore, pretending that we are brave outsiders valiantly challenging patriarchal institutions: that is, the institutions may still be patriarchal, but we are right in the middle of them'. Instead, feminist historians must see, name, and declare their own power within the academy, and use it to work in service of more marginalised groups, rather than pretending to still hold the powerlessness but also the kudos of an edgy outsider status.

However, as Najmabadi points out, the impact of feminist history on the field has been uneven. Feminist histories have been concentrated in specific areas, such as cultural history, and particular periods and regions, namely 'modern Euro-America'; we have thus produced 'our own appendices and afterthoughts, our own margins and absences' (Najmabadi 2004, 30–1). This remains true, although some progress has been made by feminist historians in, for example, the fields of political and diplomatic history, which at the time Najmabadi was writing still seemed profoundly untouched by this approach. As for the importance of acknowledging the power commanded by feminist historians in academic institutions: since 2000, Pedersen's generation of feminist historians has only become more entrenched in academic power structures. But what of those who have come after them, in a job market that is increasingly precarious, in an academy that has been under attack by right-wing political forces, both in the US, where Pedersen is based, and in the UK? In a world in which 'critical theory' and 'identity politics' can be thrown around as insults on the right, and in the context of a sustained right-wing attack on feminists, trans people, and anybody who challenges conservative hetero-norms of gender identity, is feminist historiography really safe? Are feminists really assured of their position within the historical profession?

The recent Royal Historical Society report on gender in the historical profession in Britain (RHS 2018) would seem to caution against triumphalism. The report found 'gender based discrimination and abusive behaviour

156 Charlotte Riley

was widely reported' in the discipline, and 'gender inequality' could be seen in 'all the main fora of intellectual exchange' including journal editorships, seminar programmes, and teaching practices; it also acknowledged that 'race and gender ... intersect to exacerbate particular challenges faced by BME female historians'. Over 18 per cent of female historians responded to the RHS survey to say that they had been sexually harassed in the previous five years in the discipline (RHS 2018). In light of these figures, it is difficult to argue that feminist historians have captured the academy.

We do not live in a post-feminist age: it is still true, 50 years later, that 'men and women *do* inhabit different worlds' (Alexander and Davin 1976, 5). But although this means that feminist history is still necessary, it is also harder to understand *why* this might be the case. Why, if we have been doing this feminist work for so long, are both the discipline in which we are working and the society in which we are living still so resistant to the lessons that we uncover? But the continued conservatism of gender relations in the discipline and our wider society is not a surprise to feminist historians. We understand better than most that institutions and cultures can be stultifyingly slow to change.

A better question might be how we should continue to motivate ourselves, if the revolution is still so far away. Ultimately, we need to understand the potential of feminist history not only in terms of the topics that it uncovers, but also the methodologies it opens up to us. The work that feminist historians do is important not only because of its outcomes, but because of the process itself: a methodology that recovers and writes the stories of the marginalised, and the fluid and interrelated politics of different identities, whilst also drawing attention to the historian's subjectivities, and the conditions of historical production. Catherine Hall declared in 1992 that by the mid-1970s, 'the utopian moment was over' in feminism, replaced by the 'long haul' of the fight for gender equality (1992, p. 11). Thirty years later, feminist historians are still in it for the long haul; only through a conscious, continual effort to sustain this fight will it ever be won.

References

Åhäll, Linda. 2018. "Affect as Methodology: Feminism and the Politics of Emotion." *International Political Sociology* 12 (1) (March): 36–52. https://doi.org/10.1093/ips/olx024

Alexander, Sally and Anna Davin. 1976. "Feminist History." *History Workshop Journal* 1 (1) (Spring): 4–6. https://doi.org/10.1093/hwj/1.1.4

Bradley, Harriet. 1999. "The Seductions of the Archive: Voices Lost and Found." *History of the Human Sciences* 12 (2): 107–122. https://doi.org/10.1177/09526959922120270

Burton, Antoinette. 1994. *Burdens of History: British Feminists, Indian Women, and Imperial Culture, 1865–1915*. Chapel Hill: The University of North Carolina Press.

Carr, E. H. 1987. *What Is History?* London: Penguin.

Caswell, Michelle and Marika Cifor. 2016. "From Human Rights to Feminist Ethics: Radical Empathy in the Archives." *Archivaria* 81 (May): 23–43.

Corfield, Penelope J. 1997. "History and the Challenge of Gender History." *Rethinking History* 1 (3): 241–258. https://doi.org/10.1080/13642529708596318

Dadzie, Stella, Beverly Bryan, and Suzanne Scafe. 1985. *The Heart of the Race: Black Women's Lives in Britain.* London: Virago.

Davin, Anna. 1972. "Women and History." In *The Body Politic: Writings from the Women's Liberation Movement in Britain 1969–72*, edited by Michelene Wandor, 215–224. London: Stage 1.

Dever, Maryanne. 2017. "Archives and New Modes of Feminist Research." *Australian Feminist Studies* 32 (91–92): 1–4. https://doi.org/10.1080/08164649 .2017.1357017

Downs, Laura Lee. 1993. "If 'Woman' Is Just an Empty Category, Then Why Am I Afraid to Walk Alone at Night? Identity Politics Meets the Postmodern Subject." *Comparative Studies in Society and History* 35 (2): 414–437.

Enloe, Cynthia. 2004. *The Curious Feminist: Searching for Women in a New Age of Empire.* Oakland: University of California Press.

Hall, Catherine. 1991. "Politics, Post-structuralism and Feminist History." *Gender & History* 3: 204–210. https://doi.org/10.1111/j.1468-0424.1991.tb00125.x

Hall, Catherine. 1992. *White Male and Middle Class: Explorations in Feminism and History* London: Polity.

Hall, Catherine, and Leonore Davidoff. 1987. *Family Fortunes: Men and Women of the English Middle Class.* Abingdon, Oxford: Routledge.

hooks, bell. 1986. "Sisterhood: Political Solidarity between Women." *Feminist Review* 23: 125–138. https://doi.org/10.2307/1394725

Jackson, Stevi. 1992. "The Amazing Deconstructing Woman: The Perils of Postmodern Feminism." *Trouble and Strife* 25: 25–31.

Jennings, Rebecca. 2007. *A Lesbian History of Britain: Love and Sex Between Women Since 1500.* Westport: Greenwood World Publishing.

Kleinberg, Ethan, Joan W. Scott, and Gary Wilder. 2018. "Theses on Theory and History." Accessed February 27, 2024. https://historyandtheory.org/theoryrevolt

Kleinberg, Ethan, Joan W. Scott, and Gary Wilder. 2022. "Theses on Theory and History." In *Historical Understanding: Past, Present, and Future*, edited by Lars Deile, Zoltán Boldizsár Simon, 91–101. London: Bloomsbury Academic.

Lester, Alan. 2021. "The Common Sense Group's Culture War, the 'Woke' and British History." Snapshots of Empire. Accessed February 27, 2024. https://blogs .sussex.ac.uk/snapshotsofempire/2021/05/28/the-common-sense-groups-culture -war-the-woke-and-british-history/

Matthews, Jill. 1986. "Feminist History." *Labour History* 50 (May): 147–153. https://doi.org/10.2307/27508788

McGrath, Ann. 2014. "The Loneliness of the Feminist Historian." *Australian Feminist Studies* 29 (80): 204–214. https://doi.org/10.1080/08164649.2014 .928400

Najmabadi, Afsaneh. 2004. "From Supplementarity to Parasitism?" *Journal of Women's History* 16 (2) (Summer): 30–35.

Owens, Patricia, and Katharina Rietzler. 2021. *Women's International Thought: A New History.* Cambridge: Cambridge University Press.

Owens, Patricia, Katharina Rietzler, Kimberley Hutchings, Sarah C. Dunstan, eds. 2022. *Women's International Thought: Towards a New Canon.* Cambridge: Cambridge University Press.

Pedersen, Susan. 2000. "Perspectives on Feminist History." *Perspectives on History* 38 (7). Accessed Febraury 27, 2024. https://www.historians.org/

158 Charlotte Riley

research-and-publications/perspectives-on-history/october-2000/the-future-of
-feminist-history

Purvis, June, and Amanda Weatherill. 1999. "Playing the Gender History Game: A Reply to Penelope J. Corfield." *Rethinking History* 3 (3): 333–338. https://doi.org/10.1080/13642529908596357

Rees, Jeska. 2010. "A Look Back At Anger: The Women's Liberation Movement in 1978." *Women's History Review* 19 (3): 337–356. https://doi.org/10.1080/09612025.2010.489343

Royal Historical Society. 2018. *Promoting Gender Equality in UK History: A Second Report and Recommendations for Good Practice.* London: RHS.

Royal Historical Society. 2023. "'Labour Pains: Mothers and Motherhood on the Left in the Twentieth Century' – Workshop." Accessed Febraury 27, 2024. https://royalhistsoc.org/calendar/workshop-labour-pains-mothers-and-motherhood-on-the-left-in-the-twentieth-century/

Riley, Charlotte Lydia. 2020a. "Men Behaving Badly." *Tortoise.* Accessed February 27, 2024. https://www.tortoisemedia.com/2020/02/19/campus-justice-riley-day-two/

Riley, Charlotte Lydia. 2020b. "Powerful Men, Failing Upwards: The Aid Industry and the MeToo Movement." *Journal of Humanitarian Affairs* 2 (3) (September): 49–55. https://doi.org/10.7227/JHA.052

Riley, Charlotte Lydia. 2021a. "Must Labour Lose? The 1959 Election and the Politics of the People." *Historical Reflections/Reflexions Historiques* 47 (2): 65–77. https://doi.org/10.3167/hrrh.2021.470206)

Riley, Charlotte Lydia. 2021b. "Writing like a Woman: Rita Hinden and Recovering the Imperial in International Thought." *International Politics Reviews* 9 (2): 64–271. https://doi.org/10.1057/s41312-021-00127-9

Riley, Charlotte Lydia. 2022. "Spiritualists, Ideologues, Pragmatists, Feminists and Women of All Descriptions: The British Women's Liberation Movement, the UN Decade For Women and Feminist Transnationalism in *Spare Rib.*" In *Resist, Organize, Build: Feminist and Queer Activism in Britain and the United States in the Long 1980s,* edited by Sarah Crook and Charlie Jeffries, 117–143. New York: SUNY.

Riley, Charlotte Lydia. 2024. "Male Historians Explain Things To Me." In *Men and Masculinities in Modern Britain,* edited by Matt Houlbrook, Katie Jones, and Ben Mechen, 111–118. Manchester: Manchester University Press.

Riley, Denise. 1988. '*Am I That Name?*': *Feminism and the Category of 'Women' in History.* Houndmills, Basingstoke: Palgrave Macmillan.

Robinson, Emily. 2010. "Touching the Void: Affective History and the Impossible." *Rethinking History* 14 (4): 503–520. https://doi.org/10.1080/13642529.2010.515806

Roper, Michael and John Tosh, eds. 1991. *Manful Assertions: Masculinities in Britain Since 1800.* Abingdon: Routledge.

Scott, Joan W. 1991. "The Evidence of Experience." *Critical Inquiry* 17 (4): 773–797.

Sinha, Mrinalini. 1995. *Colonial Masculinity: The "Manly Englishman" and the "Effeminate" Bengali in the Late Nineteenth Century.* Manchester: Manchester University Press.

Spender, Dale. 1983. *There's Always Been A Women's Movement This Century.* Sydney: Harper Collins.

Thomlinson, Natalie. 2012. "The Colour of Feminism: White Feminists and Race in the Women's Liberation Movement." *History* 97: 453–475.

Thomlinson, Natalie. 2016. *Race, Ethnicity and the Women's Movement in England, 1968–1993.* London: Palgrave Macmillan.

Tosh, John. 1999. *A Man's Place: Masculinity and the Middle-class Home in Victorian England*. New Haven: Yale University Press.

Tosh, John, ed. 2009. *Historians on History*. London: Pearson.

Vicinus, Martha. 2004. *Intimate Friends: Women Who Loved Women, 1778–1928*. Chicago: University of Chicago Press.

Young, Hannah. 2020. "Negotiating Female Properly and Slave Ownership in the Aristocratic World." *The Historical Journal* 63 (3): 581–602. https://doi.org/10.1017/S0018246X19000402

10

CONDUCTING SURVEY RESEARCH WHILE A FEMINIST

Taking intersectional and decolonial approaches

Shan-Jan Sarah Liu

Introduction: political science as a gendered discipline and knowledge

Women have historically been under-represented in the field of political science. Few women were political scientists and few political science studies focused on women. For example, in the first few decades since the American Political Science Association (APSA) was founded in 1903, on average only 9% of the PhD recipients were women (Tolleson-Rinehart and Carroll 2006). Even in recent decades when gender progress has been made in the discipline, men still out-publish women significantly (Mathews and Andersen 2002; Breuning and Sanders 2007). Women authors are also cited less than men (Atchison 2017; Maliniak et al. 2013; Teele and Thelen 2017). The type of scholarship political scientists generate and publish is also gendered (Sawer 2004; Tolleson-Rinehart and Carroll 2006). For example, few doctoral programmes allow students to focus solely or mainly on feminist approaches to studying political science (Hawkesworth 2005). As women political scientists attain PhD degrees, they are also confronted with gendered labour in their institutions and are oftentimes forced to leave academia (Kantola 2008). Political science scholarship is also gendered. Traditionally, the public opinion and political behaviour of men have been the default focus in the study of politics. When research on mass attitudes and behaviour is produced, the assumption has been that the findings would apply to all individuals when in reality, they apply only (or mostly) to men.

Progress has been made in the discipline, starting with the vibrant women's movements in the United States and elsewhere in the 1960s and 1970s. Political scientists started realising that biased conclusions would be drawn if half of the population were ignored. Feminist political scientists petitioned

DOI: 10.4324/9781003399575-11

This chapter has been made available under a CC-BY-NC-ND license.

the APSA to study the status of women in the discipline (Mitchell 1990) and studies based on survey research[1] began incorporating women's political opinions and behaviour. Findings from research on gender show that gender differences indeed exist (Whitaker 2008). Political scientists also began investigating *why* women and men might think and behave differently in politics. For example, U.S.-based scholar Susan Welch's (1977) study showed that women participate less than men in politics because unemployed women being homemakers prevents them from establishing and accessing networks that could motivate them to engage in politics. While Welch's study was pioneering in that it explained why gender gaps in political participation were prevalent between American women and men, any attention to how race and ethnicity might also play a role in shaping the differences was lacking. In particular, while the theoretical argument focused on barriers to employment for women in the 1970s, the reality that many women of colour were employed was neglected in research (Brown 2014). Thus, had race and ethnicity been considered, the findings on the impact of employment on gender gaps in political participation might have been different.

Since women's movements raised demands both within and beyond academia, political science has undergone decades of positive, incremental changes, illustrated by the inclusion of women as a category in survey research. Recently, political science has made more significant progress as current works incorporate intersectionality as an approach or even as a paradigm.[2] For example, US-based scholar Kimberlé Crenshaw (2017), urges researchers to apply an intersectional frame of analysis to a wide range of research. Intersectionality allows us to understand the ways that multiple forms of inequality, disadvantage, and oppression compound themselves based on one's various identities, which often intersect with one another. Crenshaw and colleagues want researchers to think about how questions and debates about intersectionality have been developed, adopted, and changed in different disciplines, specifically how the subject is 'statistically situated in terms of identity, geography, or temporality, or is dynamically constituted within institutions and structures' (Cho et al. 2013, p.786). Also, US-based scholar Patricia Hill Collins (2019) provides a set of analytical tools for those wishing to develop intersectionality. Specifically, she argues that the critical analysis using this tool does not only criticise but also reaches for ideas and practices that are crucial for changes to happen. Thus, intersectionality is no longer a concept but a tool that can be utilised to challenge the status quo and transform it towards a more equal structure.

Similarly, building on Crenshaw's and Hill Collins's concepts of intersectionality, US-based scholar Ange-Marie Hancock (2007a and 2007b), argues that intersectionality as an approach helps answer 'questions left unanswered by the unitary and multiple approaches' (2007b, p.71). Hancock lays the foundation for a coherent set of standards based on which political scientists could use intersectionality as a research approach, particularly for policy purposes, as intersectionality avoids the overemphasis on generalisability and instead examines the relationships between actors and institutions. Specifically, while scholars recognise the limitations of research that previously only focused on gender differences and ignored other variations of identities and structures of inequality, there are few studies which examine how survey research on public opinion and political behaviour could and should incorporate intersectionality as a paradigm.

This chapter, thus, explores the following: (1) what challenges exist in conducting intersectional feminist survey research; (2) how incorporating feminist epistemologies in survey research can address gender and intersecting social structures and identities; (3) how feminist epistemologies can contribute to social critiques that address contemporary forms of inequality and social injustice. The chapter argues that, albeit challenges exist, feminist survey research is possible if using feminist epistemologies to guide us. Rethinking and redesigning the questions we ask allows us to achieve insights that might otherwise not have come to light within the androcentric, heteronormative paradigm which has historically predominated in political science. The current paradigm produces knowledge about cis white men and ignores knowledge about the marginalised. Therefore, taking an intersectional approach allows us to shift the existing paradigm and broaden the way we design our surveys so they can be more inclusive of the experiences and opinions of minoritised[3] participants. Being inclusive means rethinking how we conceptualise gender, race, ethnicity, country of origin, citizen status, disability, sexuality, and so on, as it enables us to gain a more comprehensive picture of different groups of people's political attitudes and behaviour. Lastly, to ensure that our feminist survey research contributes to social critiques that address contemporary forms of inequality and social injustice, particularly in a time when white supremacy has been heightened across the globe (Wright and Hubbard 2022), we need to focus on the impact of whiteness, rather than white people. Doing so allows us to decolonise survey research, which is crucial if our goal as feminist political scientists is to dismantle the existing power structures through which hegemonic masculinity sustains itself and benefits.

Drawing from a brief review and reflection on feminist epistemologies that anchor my scholarship, this chapter begins by exploring the challenges that quantitative scholars, and particularly survey researchers, face in taking on feminist approaches. It then discusses what conducting feminist research means for political scientists and presents an argument for why political scientists should take an intersectional approach. It then concludes with some possible future directions of feminist survey research, particularly with an emphasis on mechanisms to decolonise survey research.

The limitations and possibilities of feminist survey research

Political science research has increasingly focused on gender by paying attention to women's representation and participation in political processes and institutions; nevertheless, not all of this strand of literature can be considered feminist. According to Brooke Ackerly and Jacqui True (2019), based in the United States and Australia, respectively, feminist research is guided by critical feminist perspectives using 'critical inquiry and reflection on social injustice by way of gender analysis to transform, and not simply explain, the social order' (p.1). Feminist research is also guided by a feminist research ethic, which is:

> a methodological commitment to any set of research practices that reflect on the power of epistemology, boundaries, relationships, and the multiple dimensions of the researcher's location throughout the entire research process and to a normative commitment to transforming the social order in order to promote gender justice.
>
> *(Ackerly and True 2019, p.2).*

Although gender and politics research may pay attention to gender, not all are committed to critiquing and dismantling patriarchy. Particularly in quantitative research where attention is paid to gender differences, gender is often treated merely as a category of analysis. Most of this research takes a unitary approach (Hancock 2007a), where one single category of identity is seen as the only (or the most) relevant. In this instance, researchers ignore the multiple identities shaping one's political experiences and attitudes; instead, they focus either on gender or race. Such scholarship also assumes that everyone who shares one common identity has the same political experiences. Although this type of research is aware that gender is a social construct and affects the way women and men behave, the attention to gender does not necessarily make this research feminist. Furthermore, while some scholars understand that multiple axes of identities can co-exist at any one time, they tend to treat them, e.g., gender, race, and class, as having the same weighting, assuming that they have an equivalent impact on one's political attitudes and behaviour.

Conversely, intersectionality transcends the unitary and multiple approach by treating the relationship among various axes of identities as interactive and mutually constitutive. That is, intersectionality investigates beyond categories of difference and instead examines the relationship among the categories. Intersectionality also conceptualises categories of differences as dynamic productions of both individual and institutional factors (Hancock 2007b). Thus, intersectionality as a concept and practice broadens our knowledge, including in quantitative methods, which are historically contentious in feminist research. Traditionally, quantitative scholars take a positivist approach, centring on their belief that the nature of political behaviour is objective and can be scientifically measured. Consequently, quantitative methods strive for objective measures through numbers, allowing individuals to understand how a phenomenon might operate or work 'on average'. Conversely, feminist research builds on the interpretive approach, emphasising human agency and the subjectivity of research participants (Gorelick 1991). Feminist research also emphasises reducing hierarchies between researchers and the people they study, which is almost inevitable in large-scale quantitative studies. Therefore, these two approaches often seem incompatible, thus forcing scholars to choose to be either feminist researchers or quantitative researchers.

Although balancing being positivist and feminist can be challenging, several scholars have also examined the myriad of quantitative methods and approaches that are and can be used by feminist scholars. For instance, US-based scholars Stauffer and O'Brien (2018; 2019) have written extensively on how gender and politics scholars and quantitative methodologists could collaborate to achieve innovations in scholarship in both gender and politics research and methodologies. While some studies may offer nuanced insights into how feminist epistemologies can be adopted to make feminist political science more comprehensive, very few studies calling for feminist approaches focus on survey research. Also lacking is a profound examination of why attention to intersectionality is needed in current research and how taking an intersectional approach can enable scholars to ask feminist questions and obtain answers helpful to feminist aims, leading to impacts on the academic discipline, as well as on policymaking regarding gender equality.

Why should we take an intersectional approach?

Taking an intersectional approach when conducting survey research is important for several reasons. First, minoritised individuals, including women, are often ignored in political science research. As discussed earlier, if we do not consider people's experiences with multiple and intersectional forms of oppression in survey research, we only understand a small segment of how people think and behave politically. As US-based scholar Jordan-Zachery (2007) writes, one cannot separate people's different identities into neat and unitary categories. People's identities (e.g., gender, ethnicity, sexuality) interlock and thus shape the way they view and experience the world. These experiences range from exposure to politics to interactions with faculty and students in academia (Liu 2019). As intersectionality is an approach used to evaluate the differences among group members, taking an intersectional approach in survey research allows us to understand how different groups of women, for example, white women vs. Black women, experience the world differently. Such an understanding allows us to minimise the way we essentialise women as a whole or as a group. It also helps ensure the representation of the minoritised in both politics and academic research. More importantly, an intersectional approach offers insights and policy suggestions, informing the creation of policies that are more inclusive of the vulnerable.

Feminist epistemologies in survey research

Survey research uses questionnaires that consist of a list of questions regarding participants' political attitudes and can be carried out on paper, online, and by interview. Survey researchers conduct statistical analyses of collected data and draw meaningful conclusions; this process is largely gendered (Ackerly and True 2019). The gendering ranges from how survey questionnaires are designed to how surveys are carried out. Moreover, survey research often does not take an intersectional approach as some challenges might exist in examining the opinion and behaviour of individuals and groups of multiple marginalised identities. Below, I discuss in greater detail some of the shortcomings in existing research and challenges for feminist survey researchers, with a particular focus on the consideration and incorporation of intersectionality.

Intersectionality has been increasingly incorporated in recent survey research. Gender and politics scholars do so by examining how different axes of identities beside gender also play a role in people's attitudes and behaviour. Scholars like US-based Leslie McCall and Ange-Marie Hancock have called for the adoption of intersectionality as a research paradigm. Specifically, McCall (2005) suggests three approaches to understanding the complexity of intersectionality in real life: anticategorical complexity (based on a methodology that deconstructs analytical categories); intracategorical complexity (focusing on particular social groups at neglected points of intersection); and intercategorical complexity (requiring that scholars provisionally adopt existing analytical categories to document relationships of inequality among social groups and changing configurations of inequality along multiple and conflicting dimensions). McCall (2005) argues that the categorical approach, which emphasises comparisons for different groups along various types of identity-markers, is essential to comprehending the fullest range of complexities of inequality.

In response, critics label McCall's approach as seemingly good but inherently detrimental, arguing that it has harmed Black women scholars by decentring their experiences (Alexander-Floyd 2012). In particular, McCall advocates for revisiting the contributions of women scholars of colour; however, such a call puts individuals in different categories and compares them in the emerging developments of inequality. That is, Black women's suffering is compared to that of white women's. McCall situates the works of women of colour on intersectionality as subjugated knowledge without recognising the insights they offer (Alexander-Floyd 2012). Furthermore, a large part of McCall's research takes an additive rather than intersectional approach. For example, scholars may examine women's voting preferences and Black people's voting preferences, but rarely Black women's voting preferences. Moreover, race is not the only axis of identity that gender intersects with to have an impact or mediating effect on how one views or experiences politics. An intersectional approach, where gender and other multiple axes of identity are treated as interlocking (Hill Collins 2019), is still lacking. This means that marginalised groups continue to be essentialised. An additive approach prevents us from understanding the unique experiences and views of certain groups.

Thus, my own research (e.g., Abdellatif et al. 2021; Liu 2021; Blell et al. 2022; Blell et al. 2023; Liu 2019; Fang and Liu 2021) is guided by Hancock's (2007a and 2007b) study on intersectionality as a research approach where she observes that additions of identities do not work in understanding the complex experiences of the marginalised in political science research. Specifically, as she suggests, more than one category of difference shapes the current political and social problems experienced by different individuals. Nonetheless, scholars should not assume that all identities are completely equal in affecting individuals. That is, the impacts of gender and race, for example, can be fluid, individual, and context-specific. My research follows Hancock's principles by recognising cross-group differences as well as within-group differences and, most importantly, by understanding that these differences are the by-products of structural and institutional inequalities.

While I have tried my best to account for intersectionality without using an additive approach, it does not mean that challenges no longer exist for quantitative scholars, including survey researchers conducting feminist research. Notably, it is difficult to reconcile the different methodological proclivities of feminist and positivist research and even more challenging to navigate in practice. Below, I reflect on my own experiences of using existing surveys, as well as conducting my own surveys. I discuss the challenges that I have faced and offer some possible solutions for survey researchers to be more mindful and proactive about being inclusive.

First, it is difficult to consider multiple axes of identities and take an intersectional approach when conducting surveys unless the sample size is statistically sufficient to test the differences across groups with multiple identities. For example, examining the differences on average between disabled women and able-bodied men requires an interaction in the statistical analysis. If we were to add another dimension – such as age – the tests for differences among older disabled women and younger able-bodied men become more difficult. As including gender, disability, and age requires a

Conducting survey research while a feminist **167**

three-way interaction, the statistical model gets complicated even if the sample size is big enough. While this challenge exists, it does not mean that scholars should not account for multiple axes of identities. However, how might scholars determine which identities to include when studying identity politics? I recommend that identities that have strong theoretical underpinnings need to be examined. For example, in the recent political climate where reproductive rights, trans inclusion, and racial justice are salient issues, particularly in conservative states in the United States, it is important to understand how voter identities might matter for their support for state governor candidacy. Voter identities and backgrounds that could shape their support include race, gender, and trans identity or contact with trans people. In this instance, researchers need to take these multiple identities into consideration instead of focusing overly on one group of people, such as women. While focusing on women allows for understanding women's support for political candidates who are e.g., anti-abortion or anti-trans-inclusion, it does not enable a more nuanced understanding of, for example, how cis white women might differ politically from non-binary Black men.

Second, existing surveys are heteronormative as most questions are designed for cis heterosexual people. I contend that surveys need to be designed to be inclusive by considering gender alongside other axes of identities, as the current androcentric, heteronormative approaches to questions hinder attainment of comprehensive responses. These limited approaches could also cause biases in research findings. For example, traditionally, research has shown that women are less knowledgeable about politics than men. This kind of understanding has been used to explain women's alleged lack of political interests, leading to the assumption that women are unsuited to participate in politics. It has also been used to argue that women are not as capable political leaders as men are. However, as US-based scholar Kathleen Dolan (2011) demonstrates, the previous survey questionnaires that asked women and men about their political knowledge were biased as they tested default knowledge, which was male-centred. Moreover, when questions were changed to ask more about the gender dimensions of politics, such as the percentage of women holding legislative seats in the United States, then women were found to be more knowledgeable than men (Dolan 2011). Other researchers (Ferrin et al. 2022) have also shown that women tend to answer 'I don't know' if they are hesitant about their knowledge, whereas men tend to take a guess. Thus, removing the 'I don't know' option also removes the gender differences in political knowledge gaps. Dolan's (2011) findings showcase the importance of creating balanced and comprehensive survey questions, although her study focuses only on gender. Depending on the purpose of the surveys, studies should also tailor towards the target audience. For example, if the goal is to test the differences among racial and ethnic groups, then the researchers need to ensure that comprehensive questions are asked.

Third, in addition to paying attention to how questions are designed and asked to different groups of people, it is also crucial to think about how we conceptualise certain issues. For example, I work largely with the World Values Surveys, which have a wide range of questions on protest propensity for participants across the globe.[4] However, questions in these existing large-scale, cross-sectional surveys are often androcentric. Specifically, many of the measures that test public engagement are often visible, recognised, and require collective action. Peaceful demonstration, for instance, is one form of public engagement that is studied by many scholars (e.g., Liu 2022; Liu and Banaszak 2017; Desposato and Norrander 2009; Dim 2023; Coffee and Bolzendahl 2011; Liu 2018; Valenzuela et al. 2016). Yet, the participation in peaceful demonstration can be gender-exclusive as the cost is high – women with caring responsibilities are less available for this form of political engagement. On the contrary, other types of political engagement are often ignored in existing survey research, such as activism that takes place in the private sphere, e.g., online. A few exceptions exist, including media and communication scholars Saifuddin Ahmed and Dani Madrid-Morales's study on gender inequality in online political engagement in Kenya, Nigeria, and South Africa (Ahmed and Madrid-Morales 2020). Using the 2016 Pew Global Attitudes Spring Survey, their study shows that the gender divide in online political engagement is the most significant among the higher educated groups of participants. Virtual peaceful assembly might attract more women participants as the costs and risks are lower; yet the exclusion of questions on virtual peaceful assembly in existing surveys also means that women's political engagement is not documented. Such an exclusion suggests that our current understanding of women's involvement in public affairs is biased. Therefore, questions that ask women and other minority groups about their participation in conventional ways leave out significant groups of people who may engage in politics in other, less conventional ways. This is particularly excluding when it comes to disabled and other minoritised women.

Furthermore, survey questions on political engagement can also be Western-centric, neglecting how individuals in countries in the Global South might engage in politics differently. For example, World Values Surveys include a question on how often participants contact their government officials or legislators regarding their political concerns. While this type of political action is a norm in the Global North, it might not be in other parts of the world. Therefore, when scholars examine cross-sectional differences, a conclusion might be drawn that people outside the Global North are less familiar with the democratic process or less inclined to utilise their power to influence their representatives. Such a conclusion might be biased as individuals outside the West might have other ways to pressure their representatives. Thus, including questions that take contexts into account also matters for scholars' ability to draw comprehensive conclusions.

Fourth, surveys are also often exclusive of certain marginalised groups, perhaps because the population sizes are not huge. Currently, because there is a lack of data on minoritised groups (e.g., minoritised ethnic and LGBT+ groups), the conclusions we can draw from survey research about how people (assuming everyone in the society) behave are very limited. Thus, to truly depart from heteronormative and androcentric approaches, surveys need to be inclusive of minoritised groups, including trans people and racial and ethnic minorities. For example, in most surveys, gender questions only ask if participants are male or female, neglecting non-binary and trans individuals. Given the current anti-trans climate across the Global North, we need to be trans-inclusive in our surveys to broaden our understanding of the situation transgender people face. Questions on gender need to be included, allowing us to mainstream trans inclusion, recognising the existence of the trans community and normalising accounting for them in survey research. The inclusion of minoritised individuals should also extend to other groups, such as immigrants. Very few national or cross-national surveys ask about participants' immigrant status. Questions about immigrants do not only allow us to understand their political opinion and behaviour; they also reveal how researchers view citizenship, for example, whether citizenship is strictly about having the legal status to stay and naturalise in a country or more about being members of and feeling a sense of belonging to a society. This is important, as it has implications for how immigrants view politics. One way to mainstream the inclusion of minoritised individuals is to include them, in as specific detail as possible, in existing surveys. For example, a challenge in studying the indigenous community in Canada has been that the Indian Register only records enfranchised 'Indians'. Such a narrow definition of the indigenous community does not capture a comprehensive understanding of the First Nations and Inuit populations (Hayward et al. 2021). Therefore, to be inclusive in greater detail also addresses the lack of data issue, allowing us to draw a more comprehensive picture of how different members of society view and experience politics.

Future directions: decolonizing survey research

Feminist epistemologies have social equalities and justice as goals. Above, I have discussed several ways in which to address the shortcomings in extant survey research. In addition, I want to argue that the way forward is to decolonise survey research as a feminist act. Decolonisation allows scholars to challenge the hegemonic ways knowledge is produced and reproduced, which primarily comes from Eurocentric perspectives (Bhambra et al. 2018; Liu and Estampador-Hughson 2023; Hill Collins 2019). While feminist scholarship and political science have benefitted and enriched each other (Weldon 2019), I further contend that to continue such an enrichment of the field, we must decolonise the discipline. Here I offer some suggestions to decolonise survey research while being feminist scholars.

First, I contend that researchers must keep these questions in mind: Who benefits from this research? That is, before fielding surveys, researchers must be aware of the power dynamics between them as researchers and the participants as subjects. How surveys are conducted, particularly if in-person or face-to-face, matters for the results that are obtained. Researchers' gender and race, for example, play a role in how participants respond to survey questionnaires. More importantly, most of the time, researchers go into the field with the hope of gathering data that they can analyse to advance their academic careers. How their studies can potentially translate into policies or provide important implications for the improvement of the status quo often remains a secondary concern. Therefore, I argue that the voices of the marginalised must be at the centre of the research process. Researchers can achieve this by maximising the agency of survey participants. This could mean that pilot studies are conducted before survey questionnaires are designed. It could also mean providing space for participants to offer (qualitative) feedback on the surveys.

Second, scholars often believe that they can be 'neutral', as survey researchers are largely trained to utilise a positivist research paradigm. However, it is crucial to recognise that complete neutrality or objectivity does not exist in the research process. The researcher's own identity, positionality, and experiences play a major role in how survey questions are asked and how survey responses are analysed. Thus, the challenge is not necessarily for the researchers to remain neutral. Rather, it is for them to recognise that they may also be biased. Such recognition is a first step to address the issues that imbalanced power dynamics might bring, which allows researchers to understand the salient issues that participants might face, both during the research process and in their everyday political lives. Such recognition also ensures that researchers are held accountable for the effects their research might have on participants.

Third, as discussed above, the conventional approach to survey research is to take white, male bodies as the default, resulting in the generalisation of how different groups of people function collectively as societal members. That is, prior to the 1970s, when people's political opinion and behaviour were studied via surveys, they primarily focused only on white men without highlighting the white identity of survey participants. While it is important

Conducting survey research while a feminist **171**

to examine the experiences of minoritised individuals as I have argued in this chapter, racial minorities in the Global North are often othered in survey research, while white remains the default. Nevertheless, I argue that rendering whiteness invisible is inherently colonial and functions to centre and hegemonise whiteness. Thus, in addition to ensuring that non-white people are represented in survey research, it is also crucial to examine how white people operate politically, but without treating white people as the default. Paying attention to whiteness differs from treating everyone as white, male, and able-bodied. Instead, focusing on white people also allows us to examine the impact of their whiteness on politics. Shifting the existing research patterns allows us to decolonise a long-standing research agenda that treats whiteness as the default and consequently allows us to move towards equality and justice. Such a shift to paying attention to whiteness is vital given the recent rise of right-wing populism and white supremacy as they shape many of the political decisions in much of Europe (Byman 2022).

Fourth, while whiteness is the default in most Global North contexts, it may not be so in other contexts. For example, in many countries in the Global South, where racial and ethnic compositions do not include white people as the majority, it is important to also pay attention to how those who hold hegemonic power have also been treated as the default. Removing them as the default enables the centring of ethnic minorities in specific contexts.

Overall, as decolonisation creates a space to challenge acts of oppression, appropriate collaborations can be built between white and non-white scholars and scholars in the Global North and South (Datta 2018). Specifically, decolonising critically challenges the status quo that informs survey research, suggesting that feminist and decolonial approaches are not and cannot be mutually exclusive. To decolonise is also to critically challenge the idea that research stemming from the Global North is the only objective and scientific way of understanding the political world. Holding such beliefs prevents scholars from knowing the voices and values of minoritised individuals and groups, and subsequently creates barriers to achieving social justice and equality. Without decolonisation, perhaps only justice and equality for certain groups of minorities can be achieved in the Global North, which would contradict the goals of feminist epistemologies. More importantly, linking back to Ackerly and Brooke's (2019) principles of feminist epistemologies, which suggests that the purpose of feminist research is to transform the existing social order, decolonisation allows for such a dismantling of the existing power structure.

Notes

1 Survey research is a method used to collect information from individuals, which in turn can be categorised into different groups (e.g., based on identity, income, geography, and so on.).

2 Paradigms represent a set of basic beliefs that precede any questions of empirical investigation (Guba and Lincoln 1994).
3 Minoritized are those who are made subordinate in status to a more dominant group or its members who are thus vulnerable due to their lack of access to privileges and resources. The term "minoritized" indicates the active process of categorisation based on the power differentials that are socially constructed (Gunaratnam 2008).
4 The World Values Survey can be accessed via https://www.worldvaluessurvey.org/wvs.jsp

References

Abdellatif, Amal, Maryam Aldossari, Ilaria Boncori, Jamie Callahan, Uracha Chatrakul Na Ayudhya, Sara Chaudhry, Nina Kivinen et al. 2021. "Breaking the Mold: Working through our Differences to Vocalize the Sound of Change." *Gender, Work & Organization* 28, no. 5, 1956–1979. https://doi.org/10.1111/gwao.12722

Ackerly, Brooke A. and Jacqui True. 2019. *Doing Feminist Research in Political and Social Science*. Bloomsbury Publishing.

Ahmed, Saifuddin and Dani Madrid-Morales. 2020. "Is it Still a Man's World? Social Media News Use and Gender Inequality in Online Political Engagement." *Information, Communication & Society* 24, no. 3, 381–399. https://orcid.org/0000-0002-1522-5857

Alexander-Floyd, Nikol G. 2012. "Disappearing Acts: Reclaiming Intersectionality in the Social Sciences in a Post—Black feminist era." *Feminist Formations* 24, no. 1, 1–25.

Atchison, Amy L. 2017. "Negating the Gender Citation Advantage in Political Science." *PS: Political Science & Politics* 50, no. 2, 448–455. https://doi.org/10.1017/S1049096651/000014

Bhambra, Gurminder K., Dalia Gebrial and Kerem Nişancıoğlu. 2018. *Decolonising the University*. Pluto Press.

Blell, Mwenza, Shan-Jan Sarah Liu and Audrey Verma. 2022. "'A One-Sided View of the World': Women of Colour at the Intersections of Academic Freedom." *The International Journal of Human* Rights 26, no. 10, 1822–1841. https://doi.org/10.1080/13642987.2022.2041601

Blell, Mwenza, Shan-Jan Sarah Liu and Audrey Verma. 2023. "Working in Unprecedented Times: Intersectionality and Women of Color in UK Higher Education in and Beyond the Pandemic." *Gender, Work & Organization* 30, no. 2, 353–372. https://doi.org/10.1111/gwao.12907

Breuning, Marijke and Kathryn Sanders. 2007. "Gender and Journal Authorship in Eight Prestigious Political Science Journals." *PS: Political Science & Politics* 40, no. 2, 347–351. https://doi.org/10.1017/S1049096507070564

Brown, Nadia E. 2014. "Political Participation of Women of Color: An intersectional Analysis." *Journal of Women, Politics & Policy* 35, no. 4, 315–348. https://doi.org/10.1080/1554477X.2014.955406

Byman, Daniel. 2022. *Spreading Hate: The Global Rise of White Supremacist Terrorism*. Oxford University Press.

Cho, Sumi, Kimberlé Williams Crenshaw and Leslie McCall. 2013. "Toward a Field of Intersectionality Studies: Theory, Applications, and Praxis." *Signs: Journal of Women in Culture and Society* 38, no. 4, 785–810. https://doi.org/10.1086/669608

Coffe, Hilde and Catherine Bolzendahl. "Gender Gaps in Political Participation Across Sub-Saharan African Nations." *Social Indicators Research* 102 (2011): 245–264. https://doi.org/10.1007/s11205-010-9676-6

Crenshaw, Kimberlé W. 2017. *On Intersectionality: Essential Writings*. The New Press.

Datta, Ranjan. 2018. "Decolonizing Both Researcher and Research and its Effectiveness in Indigenous Research." *Research Ethics* 14, no. 2, 1–24. https://doi.org/10.1177/1747016117733296

Desposato, Scott and Barbara Norrander. 2009. "The Gender Gap in Latin America: Contextual and Individual Influences on Gender and Political Participation." *British Journal of Political Science* 39, no. 1, 141–162. https://doi:10.1017/S0007123408000458

Dim, Eugene Emeka. 2023. "Openness of Political Structures and Gender Gaps in Protest Behaviour in Africa." *Cogent Social Sciences* 9, no. 1. https://doi.10.1080/23311886.2023.2194731

Dolan, Kathleen. 2011. "Do Women and Men Know Different Things? Measuring Gender Differences in Political Knowledge." *The Journal of Politics* 73, no. 1, 97–107. https://doi.org/10.1017/S0022381610000897

Ferrín, Mónica, Gema García-Albacete and Irene Sánchez-Vítores. 2022. "How Long Does it Take to Admit that You Do Not Know? Gender Differences in Response Time to Political Knowledge Questions." *Research & Politics* 9, no. 3. https://doi.org/10.1177/20531680221117454

Fang, Nini and Shan-Jan Sarah Liu. 2021. "Critical Conversations: Being Yellow Women in the Time of COVID-19." *International Feminist Journal of Politics* 23, no. 2, 333–340. https://doi.org/10.1080/14616742.2021.1894969

Gorelick, Sherry. 1991. "Contradictions of Feminist Methodology." *Gender & Society* 5, no. 4, 459–477.

Guba, Egon and Yvonne Lincoln. 1994. Grounded Theory. In *Handbook of Qualitative Research*, ed. Yvonne Lincoln and Norman Denzin. Thousand Oaks, CA: Sage Publications.

Gunaratnam, Yasmin. 2008. "From Competence to Vulnerability: Care, Ethics, and Elders from Racialized Minorities." *Mortality* 13, no. 1, 24–41. https://doi.org/10.1080/13576270701782969

Hancock, Ange-Marie. 2007a. "Intersectionality as a Normative and Empirical Paradigm." *Politics & Gender* 3, no. 2, 248–254. https://doi.org/10.1017/S1743923X07000062

Hancock, Ange-Marie. 2007b. "When Multiplication Doesn't Equal Quick Addition: Examining Intersectionality as a Research Paradigm." *Perspectives on Politics* 5, no. 1, 63–79. https://doi.org/10.1017/S1537592707070065

Hawkesworth, Mary. 2005. "Engendering Political Science: An Immodest Proposal." *Politics & Gender* 1, no. 1, 141–156. https://doi.org/10.1017/S1743923X0523101X

Hayward, Ashley, Larissa Wodtke, Aimée Craft, Tabitha Robin, Janet Smylie, Stephanie McConkey, Alexandra Nychuk, Chyloe Healy, Leona Star and Jaime Cidro. 2021. "Addressing the Need for Indigenous and Decolonized Quantitative Research Methods in Canada." *SSM-Population Health* 2021 Aug 18, 15: 100899.https://doi.org/10.1016/j.ssmph.2021.100899

Hill Collins, Patricia. 2019. *Intersectionality as Critical Social Theory*. Duke University Press.

Jordan-Zachery, Julia S. 2007. "Am I a Black Woman or a Woman Who is Black? A Few Thoughts on the Meaning of Intersectionality." *Politics & Gender* 3, no. 2, 254–263. https://doi.org/10.1017/S1743923X07000074

Kantola, Johanna. 2008. "'Why Do All the Women Disappear?' Gendering Processes in a Political Science Department." *Gender, Work & Organization* 15, no. 2, 202–225. https://doi.org/10.1111/j.1468-0432.2007.00376.x

Liu, Shan-Jan Sarah. 2019. "Chinese Migrant Wives in Taiwan: Claiming Entitlements, Resisting Inequality, and Rejecting Citizenship." *International*

Feminist Journal of Politics 21, no. 4, 617–638. https://doi.org/10.1080/14616742.2018.1522964

Liu, Shan-Jan Sarah and Lee Ann Banaszak. 2017. "Do Government Positions Held by Women Matter? A Cross-National Examination of Female Ministers' Impacts on Women's Political Participation." *Politics & Gender* 13, no. 1, 132–162. https://doi.org/10.1017/S1743923X16000490

Liu, Shan-Jan Sarah. 2021. "Framing Immigration: A Content Analysis of Newspapers in Hong Kong, Taiwan, the United Kingdom, and the United States." *Politics, Groups, and Identities* 9, no. 4, 759–783. https://doi.org/10.1080/21565503.2019.1674162

Liu, Shan-Jan Sarah. 2022. "Gender Gaps in Political Participation in Asia." *International Political Science Review* 43, no. 2, 209–225. https://doi.org/10.1177/0192512120935517

Liu, Shan-Jan Sarah. 2018. "Are Female Political Leaders Role Models? Lessons from Asia." *Political Research Quarterly* 71, no. 2, 255–269.

Liu, Shan-Jan Sarah and Sharleen Estampador-Hughson. 2023. "Why Does Political Representation of the Marginalised Matter? Teaching Classic Literature Using Intersectional and Decolonial Approaches." *European Political Science* 22, 496–510. https://doi.org/10.1057/s41304-023-00433-w

Maliniak, Daniel, Ryan Powers and Barbara F. Walter. 2013. "The Gender Citation Gap in International Relations." *International Organization* 67, no. 4, 889–922. https://doi.org/10.1017/S0020818313000209

Mathews, A. Lanethea and Kristi Andersen. 2002. "A Gender Gap in Publishing? Women's Representation in Edited Political Science Books." *PS: Political Science & Politics* 34, no. 1, 143–147. https://doi.org/10.1017/S1049096501000221

McCall, Leslie. 2005. "The Complexity of Intersectionality." *Signs: Journal of Women in Culture and Society* 30, no. 3, 1771–1800. https://doi.org/10.1086/426800

Mitchell, Joyce M. 1990. "The Women's Caucus for Political Science: A View of the 'Founding'." *PS: Political Science & Politics* 23, no. 2, 204–209.

Sawer, Marian. 2004. "The Impact of Feminist Scholarship on Australian Political Science." *Australian Journal of Political Science* 39, no. 3, 553–566. https://doi.org/10.1080/103614042000295147

Stauffer, Katelyn E. and Diana Z. O'Brien. 2019. "Fast Friends or Strange Bedfellows? Quantitative Methods and Gender and Politics Research." *European Journal of Politics and Gender* 2, no. 2, 151–171. https://doi.org/10.1332/251510819X15538595080522

Stauffer, Katelyn E. and Diana Z. O'Brien. 2018. "Quantitative Methods and Feminist Political Science." In *Oxford Research Encyclopedia of Politics*. https://doi.org/10.1093/acrefore/9780190228637.013.210

Teele, Dawn Langan and Kathleen Thelen. 2017. "Gender in the Journals: Publication Patterns in Political Science." *PS: Political Science & Politics* 50, no. 2, 433–447. https://doi.org/10.1017/S1049096516002985

Tolleson-Rinehart, Sue and Susan J. Carroll. 2006. "'Far From Ideal': The Gender Politics of Political Science." *American Political Science Review* 100, no. 4, 507–513.

Valenzuela, Sebastián, Nicolás M. Somma, Andrés Scherman and Arturo Arriagada. 2016. "Social Media in Latin America: Deepening or Bridging Gaps in Protest Participation?" *Online Information Review* 40, no. 5, 695–711. https://doi.org/10.1108/OIR-11-2015-0347

Welch, Susan. 1977. "Women as Political Animals? A Test of Some Explanations for Male-Female Political Participation Differences." *American Journal of Political Science* 21, no. 4, 711–730. https://doi.org/10.2307/2110733

Weldon, S. Laurel. 2019. "Power, Exclusion and Empowerment: Feminist Innovation in Political Science." In *Women's Studies International Forum* 72, 127–136. https://doi.org/10.1016/j.wsif.2018.05.014

Whitaker, Lois Duke, ed. 2008. *Voting the Gender Gap.* University of Illinois Press.

Wright, Gwendolyn L., Lucas Hubbard and William A. Darity, eds. 2022. *The Pandemic Divide: How COVID Increased Inequality in America.* Duke University Press.

11

CLOSE READING

Critical feminist method and pedagogical process

Sophia Kier-Byfield

Close reading, which is the in-depth interrogation of the details and qualities in passages of written text, is a fundamental method of analysis in literary studies. Despite fading in and out of fashion and having had different relationships to literature's production and reception contexts over time, it remains an essential tool for scholars to make sense of the meanings, politics, and effects of fiction (Herrnstein Smith 2016). Although it has primacy in literary studies, scholars have argued that close reading is also a way of interrogating non-fiction texts, content, and cultural objects in other disciplines (Gallop 2007; Stang 2022). Its role as a method also continues to be debated and defended in feminist knowledge production more specifically (Lukić Espinosa and Andelina Sánchez 2011). Recent scholarship by US Black feminist theorist Jennifer Nash, for example, has observed how close reading is used to uphold and defend the reputation of intersectionality in defensive debates about how intersectionality should or should not be done (Nash 2019). For intersectionality's defenders, the close reading of particular origin texts – namely US legal scholar Kimberlé Crenshaw's key articles from the 1980s – is a means of locating the original articulation of 'true' intersectionality. Nash expresses frustration with this trend: she argues that the insistence that intersectionality be protected through close reading of and reference to origin texts hinders its expansive potential as a concept and keeps it locked into a quest for singular meaning.

Nash's claims about the ways in which close reading is utilised in feminist debates situates the method at the heart of a struggle over issues of truth, authenticity, and correctness in feminist reading and theorising, in this case centred upon the concept of intersectionality. This positioning raises questions about what purposes close reading serves, how it relates to other

DOI: 10.4324/9781003399575-12

This chapter has been made available under a CC-BY-NC-ND license.

Close reading **177**

methods, and what its role in intersectional feminist learning and scholarship might be moving forward. However, the epistemological struggles about reading and interpretation that Nash's observations point to are not new: close reading's history is troubled by similar issues, as early proponents argued for and against certain ways of reading English literature well. It is possible to identify deeper apprehensions in close reading's intellectual history about the implications of scholarly reading and methods as they relate to the role of the self and desire in research. This chapter considers in greater detail some of the methodological tensions surrounding subjectivity, positionality, and interpretation in close reading and how these are subtly present in current feminist debates. It goes on to argue that when embraced as an unpredictable method of enquiry that acknowledges subjectivity, its attachments to knowledge, and the multiplicity of meaning, close reading can be deployed to analyse the textual and interpersonal manifestations of feminism in unexpected yet accountable and reflexive ways. Ultimately, the chapter argues for close reading's importance as a method for thinking about intersectionality and feminist enquiry more broadly.

Close reading methodology

Before exploring close reading's relevance in recent contemporary feminist scholarship, I will briefly introduce the concept and an account of its history. Thinking about close reading as a *method* might seem alien to readers with a background in the arts and humanities. As English and gender studies scholar Gabriele Griffin notes, a 'learning by doing' approach has been a common research premise in English for decades, with methodological statements and justifications beyond a chosen theoretical lens often not being necessary in an English education (Griffin 2005, 2). Once one has learnt the necessary literary terminology and the descriptors of language, rhythm, form, and structure, close reading can become somewhat intuitive. For those with other disciplinary backgrounds, close reading and approaches associated with English studies may not chime as a method at all, since they tend to be deemed inherently 'less systematic' than approaches which traditionally have been preferred, for example, in the social sciences (Brookman and Horn 2016).

Putting disciplinary expectations aside, relevant to both this book's focus on intersectional feminism and methods is the fact that close reading has a highly gendered and classed history that has sought to define and programmatise analytical reading as a serious methodological endeavour. As English scholar and educator Ben Knights explains, the rise of close reading was aligned with the establishment of English as a subject area as it travelled from popular education initiatives and campaigns for mass literacy and literary appreciation into the framework of the (undeniably more exclusive)

178 Sophia Kier-Byfield

university. Central to this endeavour was encouraging learners to read for detail and technique as vehicles for communicating effect and meaning, rather than historical or biographical information. For example, educator R. G. Moulton's mode of 'inductive criticism' sought to educate students in the late nineteenth century to conduct 'close observation of the textual subject matter, rather than learning up external knowledge' (Knights 2017, 32). This approach to critical reading was further developed and promoted by critics such as I. A. Richards, F. R. Leavis, and Q. D. Leavis in the 1920s and 1930s (and later by the New Critics in the US): they sought the 'establishment of a professionalised form of reading' that could 'supervise and regulate what had conventionally been seen as female cognitive styles (emotional empathy, identification, communicative nurture) and subject matters (subjectivity, relationships, romance, the family)' (Knights 2017, 44). Thus, a 'central task of the new subject "English" and its programme of arduous reading was to ward off the regression into a life of wish-fulfilment and social conformity understood to be fostered by the addictive habit of reading commercial bestsellers' (Knights 2017, 44). This was also particularly important in an emerging discipline that was based upon the analysis of works of art that awaken a felt response: 'there was a perceived need to draw clear boundaries and impose rigorous structures' (Knights 2017, 44). These early forms of institutionalised close reading were engineered towards locating a unity or coherence in the textual object, which could be distracted from if too much of the self and one's conditions were brought to bear on the process of critical response.[1]

This history of close reading highlights a gendered and classed anxiety at the heart of reading methods. Rhetorical and pedagogical moves were made to obtain a hierarchy of moral and practical earnestness to confirm the subject's position and relinquish connections to the popular, the feminine, and the emotional. This in turn protected and supported the position and views of the privileged, White thinkers at the centre of knowledge production, a specific identity position which is often masked by claims to neutrality and morality. There exists here a challenge towards the perceived egalitarian potential and capacity of close reading performed without context. For instance, as north American literary critic Jane Gallop has argued, deconstextualisd close reading has an ongoing potential as an accessible approach that does not require students to already have the historical, theoretical, and/or archival knowledge that has come to dominate critical reading strategies in more recent decades (2007). The latter is represented by UK-based theatre and performance specialist Helen Nicholson's definition of close reading as being able to 'illuminate moments of experience by placing them in the context of other cultural, artistic or social practices' (Nicholson 2017, 184). As such, reading without contextual knowledge could house potential freedom for readers who have not had a formal education. However, considering how the denial of context has also been an attempt at the removal of subjectivity and purportedly fanciful 'feminine' sentiments from close reading certainly complicates any claims to accessibility.

The anxieties of the role of the self in close reading continue to be palpable in definitions of the method. Consider US literary critic Elaine Showalter's proposal that close reading is 'a deliberate attempt to *detach ourselves* from the magical power of story-telling and pay attention to language, imagery, allusion, intertextuality, syntax and form', which is therefore also 'a form of defamiliarisation we use in order to *break through our habitual and casual* reading practices' (Showalter 2002, 98, emphasis mine). In reality, close reading may do all or none of these things, and more importantly, it might be one's very attachment to a text in a casual moment of reading that moves one to interrogate it more deeply. A binary understanding of reading strategies emerges here: one is perhaps uncritical and too influenced by desire, whilst the other is at a remove from the self and therefore apparently able to resist the allure of attachment.

Reclaiming situated close reading for intersectional feminist scholarship that acknowledges and explores it as an embodied practice is imperative, and this chapter argues that one can acknowledge and even apply one's full self and circumstances to an act of critical reading. The life of the reader, be that manifest in relationships, interests, or experiences, plays a role in drawing one's attention to parts of a text and dwelling there. In the remainder of this chapter, I want to show how the methodological and epistemological hang-ups about close reading's relationship to subjectivity and logic can help me make sense of what is going on with reading methods in recent theoretical research about the narratives and arguments in texts about feminism and intersectionality. This in turn opens up pathways for thinking about how the method can be applied and reimagined across multiple disciplinary locations. Thus, thinking about close reading becomes a way of thinking about the complexities of doing intersectional research.

Reading feminist stories

The fragmentary influences of identity and context in the process of critical reading are at the heart of close reading's pedagogical history and are an ongoing issue for the method's legitimacy and potential. Querying the role of close reading for contemporary, intersectional feminist scholarship is also relevant due to developments in the field that have centred on modes of textual production and interpretation. In recent years, feminist scholars have started to look more carefully at what Nash calls 'the politics of reading' in feminist theory, rather than in fiction: there has been an 'introspective turn' that considers not just the lived dynamics of feminism in academic spaces of production, but also how those dynamics and circumstances are told and relayed as feminist stories in the texts that substantiate the printed matter of the field (Nash 2019, 12). A key text in charting this turn was *Why Stories Matter*, by UK-based interdisciplinary gender studies scholar Clare Hemmings. The book demonstrates how 'the story of [feminist theory's] past is consistently told as a series of interlocking narratives of progress, loss, and return that oversimplify this complex history and position feminist subjects as needing to inhabit a theoretical and political cutting edge in the present' (Hemmings 2011, 3). Although these narratives are distinct, according to Hemmings, they often overlap and all rely on the idea that feminism's development is divided into clear decades or waves that simplify events and the messy nature of social change.

It was in reading and re-reading Hemmings's work that I first became alert to the potential of close reading for understanding how feminist attachments to stories in theory function. Having a background in literary studies, close reading felt like an obvious signifier for what was going on in her book. When looking at Hemmings's own description of method in more detail, she states that she is preoccupied with 'the *amenability* of our own stories, narrative constructs, and grammatical forms to discursive uses of gender and feminism', as well as the 'techniques of each story' (Hemmings 2011, 2). Instead of close reading, Hemmings calls her analysis 'discursive' and a form of 'close attention', but in turn she is also reluctant to call her categories of stories 'discourses', focusing on 'narrative' and 'patterning rather than content or context' (Hemmings 2011, 17, 229). By the latter, Hemmings is referring to her choice to select for analysis anonymised passages from articles that give an historical overview of feminism's development. She then shows the repetition of these narratives across multiple examples, rather than situating the extracts in the articles they are from and exploring their inner workings as a whole.

As just noted, 'close reading' is not a term that enters into the lexicon of the book's methodology. Hemmings works from a social sciences positionality within the academy where 'close reading' is not a methodological disciplinary norm. There are further key differences to note: Hemmings chooses texts from a specific range of journals within a certain time period, compiling a categorised corpus of story types and addressing breadth across multiple examples rather than prying into fewer passages or texts as usually happens with close reading. Her approach has more in common with discourse analysis, and yet she is hesitant to use that specific signifier as well, occupying a hybrid position within and across reading approaches. However, it is undeniable that close reading is taking place within the book's analysis, albeit in a manner unacknowledged as such, as within the selected examples close reading for argument and detail must take place. Consider also how Hemmings grapples with the role of the subjective in her work: she reflexively notes that having a framework for selection based on journal issues or years does not avoid the interplay of subjectivity entirely. She states that 'tracking my own affect is instructive, in that [...] "admirable neutrality" is of course impossible to sustain' (Hemmings 2011, 25–26). Neutrality is particularly difficult to maintain in the analysis of 'loss narratives', as she is a part of the growth of the 'professional feminist' in the university who has supposedly led to the demise of activist feminisms in the examples she has collected (Hemmings 2011, 25–26). Hemmings's awareness of her position is useful here for thinking through the tensions in close reading that I outlined earlier. Creating formulae for analysing textual phenomena does not undo the fact that the reader is implicated in the subject matter that they are looking at. Arguably, Hemmings's experience of the academy, women's studies growth within it, and her personal understanding of these stories bolster her ability to both identify and deconstruct them. As I will go on to argue, this reality of close reading should not just be acknowledged as fact but embraced as potential and capacity for the method.

It is upon Hemming's framework of feminist narratives that Nash builds by creating a taxonomy of ways in which intersectional originalism, or the repeated argument in the work of other scholars for returning to supposedly more essential and pure versions of intersectionality, operate. These are the assessment of correctness in examples of intersectional theory and research; attempts to save intersectionality from critique; and a tendency to overlook the role of institutional equality, diversity and inclusion (EDI) agendas in the popularity of intersectionality (Nash 2019, 63–69). However, in Nash's book *Black Feminism Reimagined*, close reading is more than a latent method. Rather, Nash names it explicitly as a practice, which she then identifies and critiques in the work of intersectional originalists who encourage deep engagement with a supposedly more accurate form of intersectionality, for example via the work of Crenshaw. As she states, originalism:

> operates as a methodological tool and as a political strategy. As a method, it insists on close reading as a practice and the primary way of accessing and unleashing intersectionality's 'true' meanings. It suggests that intersectionality's critics are plagued by misreadings of the analytic and argues that close(r) reading is required to bring us nearer to intersectionality's truths.
>
> *(Nash 2019, 61)*

Analysing a number of examples from commemorative journal issues about intersectionality, she demonstrates how scholars implore their readers to engage in close readings to restore intersectionality with its original promise of intellectual and political rigour. As an example, Nash quotes Vivian May, who argues that 'even if cited, earlier intersectionality texts may not be given *nuanced* reading but treated *casually* or deemed theoretically underwhelming' (Nash 2019, 63, emphasis mine). Consider here the potential correlation

182 Sophia Kier-Byfield

with Showalter's discrepancy between detached/nuanced and casual/careless readings that I discussed earlier. Another example for Nash comes from Anna Carastathis, who asks if intersectionality is 'appropriated without deep engagement with Crenshaw's work, and used in ways that distort and even invert the meaning of the concept?' (Nash 2019, 60). The suggestion here is that the concept has an inherent, organised meaning, and a purity that can be accessed through certain faithful applications or spoilt by poor use.

Critiques of originalism have indeed been articulated in other ways. For example, British sociologist Heidi Safia Mirza gently suggests that earlier works by 'Combahee River Collective, Angela Davis, Audre Lorde and Patricia Hill Collins' are 'rearticulated' by Crenshaw in her papers that 'developed' the concept of intersectionality (2013, 6). Patricia Hill Collins herself has also questioned origin stories, particularly the notion of Crenshaw 'coining' the term, and how that moment of origin is returned to and repeated in ways that restrict the types of stories that are told about Crenshaw's expansive body of work (2019, 123–124). Also relevant to this chapter is that in *Intersectionality as Critical Social Theory*, Hill Collins also employs close reading as an approach to analysis (2019, 201). Although she does not problematise close reading as a term per se, her book is animated with reflections on the politics of reading strategies. She notes the relationality between the chapters in her book and texts from different traditions (2019, 6, 13), observes different disciplinary reading approaches and how these traditions influence knowledge production and the emphases of pieces of work (2019, 111, 243), and encourages readers to come to the book with a personal direction for reading the material (2019, 326). These observations further exemplify the central position of reading, be it of theory, phenomena, or texts, in intersectional work.

So, despite the fact that originalism is acknowledged and explored in various ways, there are two primary facets and risks of originalism outlined by Nash that I want to draw attention to specifically here. First is the preoccupation with returning to and rearticulating the initial meaning of originary texts. In other words, Nash suggests in her analysis that originalists argue for keeping the concept as closely aligned as possible with its early form to ensure its political prospects in the future. Nash contends that rather than saving intersectionality from critique by engaging repeatedly with early texts, this approach restricts the growth of intersectionality as an analytical approach and world-building concept. Second, originalism involves the tendency for certain types of reading practices to be associated with a greater capacity for identifying 'truth' than others: this reading must be careful, nuanced, and concerned with more clearly defining the intentions and meanings of origin texts. Combined, the argument in favour of the close reading of original texts is potent, especially in a climate where there is such insistence on the presence of intersectionality to make any feminist activity worthwhile and even morally viable. In contrast, Nash's critique of this trend has strong philosophical implications. As she states, her work 'emphatically interrogates moments where care, love, and affection mask a pernicious possessiveness, a refusal to let intersectionality move and transform in unexpected and perhaps challenging ways' (Nash 2019, 80). This position can be further understood ontologically: the ability for the concept to exist must be premised on the potential for adaptation and change; without variation and growth there is stasis and stagnancy. Critique and questioning are therefore aligned with the health and vitality of a concept that has a diverse and active life in intellectual debate.

Whilst I agree with Nash's observations that recurring and closer readings should not be associated with accessing greater truth about a concept, questions remain about the capacities of close reading as a method for critical feminist theory. These questions are particularly relevant for the type of research that is occupied with the textual manifestations of feminism, and how it is argued for, documented, disseminated, and institutionalised as a part of academic life and its knowledge economies, of which the writing and reading of printed matter play a central part. Following Nash's line of argument, association with the method of close reading might be put aside due to its apparent obsession with the meanings to be relocated in originary texts. Although this may very well not be intentional, there is a danger here, I suggest, that the method of close reading is closed down in the same way that Nash argues intersectionality to be through such an attachment to origins. As noted earlier in the discussion of Hemmings, allusions to and routes around close reading thus draw attention to tensions between feminist research methods and approaches that warrant further thinking.

The originalist form of close reading that is identified and critiqued by Nash has interesting comparisons and differences with the tensions in close reading's methodological history and application that I outlined earlier. As noted, early approaches 'suggested that close reading would distinguish good literature from bad, thus uncovering literature that has timeless qualities because it speaks to the universal concerns of human nature' (Nicholson 2017, 183). Furthermore, as Knights describes, 'traditional literary criticism (like its American cousin, "New Criticism") was drawn to the text as an organic whole' (Knights 2017, 6). Clear parallels can be drawn here to the impetus of intersectional originalism, its allegiance to texts such as Crenshaw's, and the insistence that there are more truthful, virtuous, and sensical versions of intersectionality to be found through the right reading practices. In contrast, though, is the fact that originalist readings are preoccupied with the intention of the author as a means of locating and understanding organised meanings of intersectionality.

However, it is important to remember that close reading is not necessarily invested in finding the singular meaning of a text, in locating an organised

184 Sophia Kier-Byfield

response, or in correlating textual phenomena with authorial intent. Close reading can be understood differently. Consider for example how US literary scholar Elizabeth Freeman defines close reading as to 'linger, to dally, to take pleasure in tarrying, and to hold out that these activities allow us to look both hard and askance at the norm' (Freeman 2010, xvii). The reduced anxiety about meaning and the potential for pleasure suggested here returns the method to the subjective and its key role in drawing readers to that which they want to study and how they want to study it. Close reading can be affective as well as effective, and scholarly, pleasing, and critical; it can be an embodied practice that explores what is moving in texts, and acknowledges that what is moving might change over time and place depending on the purpose of a reading.

Furthermore, it is interesting to note that whilst Nash observes the limited employment of close reading by other scholars, her own method is not concretely defined beyond alluding to the work of Hemmings. To enact her own critique, Nash states that she 'carefully studies' intersectionality and it is obvious that she engages in a form of cautious textual analysis as she quotes and pries apart the arguments of her chosen originalists (Nash 2019, 2). Crucial here is that she states that '*all* readings are interpretations, whether they imagine themselves as such or not' (Nash 2019, 69). It can therefore be suggested that she too is conducting a close reading, although it is not named as such, to enable the enactment of her arguments about how close reading is specifically employed by intersectional originalists. Close reading is thus inevitable, and it is performed in a way that shows marks of the subject who is identifying and pursuing just one of many ways of reading.

Close reading: a feminist pedagogy

In addition to considering the applications of close reading to published texts, I want to discuss how close reading can be expanded beyond the analysis of theoretical or argument-based texts that are already in circulation to think about feminist practice. In my research on feminist pedagogy, I have reflected on teaching and learning settings and interactions that convey the complexities of the political terms and principles that arise in feminist pedagogical theory. This reflective work followed my close readings of a range of academic and non-academic texts about feminism and feminist pedagogy, across which I located and analysed textual tendencies involving four common words and their associated ideas: 'origin/al', 'resistance', 'collective', and 'alternative'. In doing so, I also sought, like Hemmings and Nash, to create a catalogue of rhetorical choices that repeatedly legitimise and uncritically support theorisations and articulations of feminist issues. I subsequently understood reflection as an exercise of producing writing about experience that could add further nuance to established and repeated stories, tropes, and principles, in this case about feminist pedagogy specifically. Doing so was driven by an impulse to accountability, as remaining attached to only prinicples and the stories about feminism that they support restricts the ability of feminists to understand their implicated positions within power dynamics in teaching and learning contexts. There was also a strong anti-origin imperative in this process, as the stories about feminist pedagogy's development that I was encountering were laced with temporally-driven claims about the pull of the past in relation to the present and future of the practice. I wanted to write about moments where feminist pedagogical principles were brought into the play of teaching and learning, but when those principles (originating in historical feminist work, in the field's norms, or indeed in one's own feminist origin story and its attachments) could not withstand the unpredictability of lived interaction, or where practice illuminated contradiction or complexity. Intersectionality becomes key here in terms of thinking about how power and privilege are articulated, experienced, and challenged in lived exchanges.

Questions therefore arose as to if and how close reading was a method that could be applied to empirical data about teaching and learning experiences and practices. As American theorists of feminist pedagogy Margo Culley and Catherine Portuges note, 'teacher and student alike bring "texts" of their own to the classroom which shape the transactions within it' (Culley and Portuges 1985, 2). Particularly relevant here is the designation of experience as text: this understanding situates the reading of experience not as separate from the close reading of published texts, but as inherently connected. In my research, I was already exploring a different approach to text selection than that of, for example, Hemmings and Nash: rather than look at texts about feminist pedagogy only from a certain period or series of journals, I was looking in a web-like manner across academia, journalism, and fiction, and looking at the textual dynamics that co-create feminist pedagogy across a broader cross-section of culture. Thus, not only do I suggest that different text types can be brought together through this expansive application of close reading, but so too can disciplinary perspectives and practices. Scholars of teaching and learning who have been exploring close reading as a means of understanding pedagogical topics have argued that rather than separating humanities and social sciences methods, they should be brought closer together for the benefit of learning across different approaches to textual enquiry (Brookman and Horn 2016, 251). The notion of close reading therefore also becomes representative of the closeness between texts as well as the perspective one applies to the material as a reader.

Including reflective, experiential work based on practice is particularly important for thinking about feminism within the frameworks of intersectionality, as it is in interaction with other bodies and voices that privilege and power manifest in complex and cross-cutting ways. Analysing classroom experience enabled not only a multifaceted understanding of conditions, influences, and behaviours in the pedagogical encounter, but also resulted in a rounded representation of the non-feminist other as far more than just negative, unenlightened, rude, or oppressed/oppressive. Theorising is, of course, a practice, but thinking about feminist pedagogy also required insights into classrooms and other learning spaces and the interactions and relationships that form there. In this sense, intersectionality becomes a practice – something that one is involved in doing rather than just analysing, reading, writing, or talking about. Close reading that takes experience as its text, rather than just instrumentally reflecting for improvement, has important implications for thinking about the positionality of researchers and how we show up as politicised subjects, bound by disciplinary norms, and with varying degrees of privilege and disadvantage in our writing and in our actions beyond the text (Loads et al. 2020). As noted earlier, close readings, just like any other type of reading, are always inherently incomplete. Likewise, reading and writing experience does not access the truth of an event or encounter, or indeed account for all of the ways it was experienced by those involved, but by embracing close reading partiality is placed at the heart of enquiry rather than as a caveat.

Conclusion

This chapter has been concerned with demonstrating that expansive close reading is a productive approach for intersectional gender studies research. I have demonstrated that despite not being named explicitly, close reading has been central to several important findings in the field about how feminist debates unfold, spread, and gain legitimacy in an interdisciplinary subject area that continues to rely heavily on knowledge production in the written form. I have also demonstrated how tensions around subjectivity, cohesion, and authenticity in close reading reappear in contemporary work about feminist texts. Subsequently, I have argued for the acknowledgement of close reading as a method and have demonstrated what further options for enquiry and thinking can be pursued by embracing close reading as a capacious interpretative practice, adaptable to different types of texts and experiences. Whilst certainly not a fool-proof method, close reading and its potential for criticality is especially important for concepts such as intersectionality which are now so commonplace that they are frequently taken for granted and dropped into claims about accountable practice without accompanying evidence. Close reading, in the non-originalist, non-harmonious sense, necessitates questioning rather than seeking out and anchoring to the supposed truths and comforts of concepts.

Finally, I would like to consider Nash's observations about intersectionality. She argues that terms such as intersectionality need to be continually re-assessed and explored in ways that are aware of the academic conditions in which they are produced. Intersectionality and its success stories need to be treated not just as the product of something *'intrinsic* to the analytic' and its essential capabilities, but also 'as reflective of a set of structural changes' in teaching and learning in higher education, where equality, diversity, and inclusion (EDI) have become far more visible strategic priorities (Nash 2019, 67). Conducting close readings of both the printed literature and the experiences of existing and operating in these spaces with an eye for ambiguities, intricacies, conflicts, and contradictions that struggle against our expectations of feminist practice are, I suggest, a means of holding our sacred terminologies and principles to account. It can be a method for new and experienced scholars alike to keep learning how to read and re-read feminisms.

Note

1 For more on the history of close reading as a pedagogical mechanism developed and consolidated at Cambridge, and the tensions between interpretation, subjectivity, and material conditions, see Samuel Solomon, *Lyric Pedagogy and Marxist Criticism: Social Reproduction and the Institutions of Poetry* (2017).

References

Bass, Randy, and Sherry Lee Linkon. 2018. "On the Evidence of Theory: Close Reading as a Disciplinary Model for Writing about Teaching and Learning." *Arts and Humanities in Higher Education* 7, no. 3 (October): 245–61. https://doi.org /10.1177/1474022208094410.

Brookman, Helen, and Julia Horn. 2016. "Closeness and Distance: Using Close Reading as a Method of Educational Enquiry in English Studies." *Arts and Humanities in Higher Education* 15, no. 2 (April): 248–65. https://doi.org/10 .1177/1474022216636517.

Culley, Margo, and Catherine Portuges. 1985. *Gendered Subjects: The Dynamics of Feminist Teaching*. Routledge and Kegan Paul.

Espinosa, Andelina Sánchez, and Jasmina Lukić. 2011. "Feminist Perspectives on Close Reading." In *Theories and Methodologies in Postgraduate Feminist Research: Researching Differently*, edited by Rosemarie Buikema, Gabriele Griffin, and Nina Lykke, 105–118. London: Routledge.

Freeman, Elizabeth. 2010. *Time Binds: Queer Temporalities, Queer Histories*. Durham: Duke University Press.

Gallop, Jane. 2007. "The Historicization of Literary Studies and the Fate of Close Reading." *Profession*: 181–86.

Griffin, Gabriele. 2005. *Research Methods for English Studies*. Edinburgh: Edinburgh University Press.

Hemmings, Clare. 2011. *Why Stories Matter: The Political Grammar of Feminist Theory*. Durham: Duke University Press.

Hill Collins, Patricia. 2019. *Intersectionality as Critical Social Theory*. Durham: Duke University Press.

Knights, Ben. 2017. *Pedagogic Criticism: Reconfiguring University English Studies*. London: Palgrave Macmillan.

Loads, Daphne, Hazel Marzetti, and Velda McCune. 2020. "'Don't Hold Me Back': Using Poetic Inquiry to Explore University Educators' Experiences of

Professional Development through the Scholarship of Teaching and Learning." *Arts and Humanities in Higher Education* 19, no. 4 (October): 337–53. https://doi.org/10.1177/1474022219846621.

Martin, Jane Roland. 2003. 'Feminism.' In *A Companion to the Philosophy of Education*, edited by Randall Curren, 192–203. Hoboken: Blackwell Publishing.

Mirza, Heidi Safia. 2013. "'A second skin': Embodied Intersectionality, Transnationalism and Narratives of Identity and Belonging Among Muslim Women in Britain." *Women's Studies International Forum* 36: 5–15. http://dx.doi.org/10.1016/j.wsif.2012.10.012.

Nash, Jennifer. 2019. *Black Feminism Reimagined: After Intersectionality.* Durham: Duke University Press.

Nicholson, Helen. 2017. "Close Reading." *Research in Drama Education: The Journal of Applied Theatre and Performance* 22, no. 2 (April): 183–85. https://doi.org/10.1080/13569783.2017.1309738.

O'Loughlin, Rebecca and Elaine Fulton. 2014. "Enquiry into Teaching and Learning in the Humanities.' In *Teaching and Learning in Higher Education: Disciplinary Approaches to Educational Enquiry*, edited by Elizabeth Cleaver, Maxine Lintern and Mike McLinden, 178–194. London: SAGE.

Showalter, Elaine. 2002. *Teaching Literature.* London: Wiley-Blackwell, 2002.

Smith, Barbara Herrnstein. 2016. "What Was 'Close Reading'?: A Century of Method in Literary Studies." *The Minnesota Review* 87 (November): 57–75. https://doi.org/10.1215/00265667-3630844.

Solomon, Samuel. 2019. *Lyric Pedagogy and Marxist-Feminsim: Social Reproduction and the Institutions of Poetry.* London: Bloomsbury.

Stang, Sarah. 2022. "Too Close, Too Intimate, and Too Vulnerable: Close Reading Methodology and the Future of Feminist Game Studies." *Critical Studies in Media Communication* 39, no. 3 (May): 230–38. https://doi.org/10.1080/15295036.2022.2080851

12

CULTIVATING A 'FEMINIST REFLEXIVE SENSIBILITY' IN SOCIAL RESEARCH

A re-evaluation of reflexivity and intersectionality in the neoliberal academy

Karen Lumsden

This chapter focuses on reflexivity and intersectionality in feminist research methods. It reconsiders and reevaluates how we can practice reflexivity as feminists in the current neoliberal higher education context in the UK. This context consists of the already well mapped out marketisation of higher education, adoption of new public management principles, audit culture, and the resultant 'micro-traumas' (Crastnopol 2015) which we may experience in our professional and personal lives, as our own values and the expectations of the neoliberal academy clash or are misaligned (Ball 2016). These developments have also resulted in, and entail, a 'speeding-up' of academic work, increased use of performance indicators, and a focus on instrumental or 'impactful' research (Lumsden 2023). They present challenges for the feminist researcher whose work often proceeds at a slower pace, is reflexive, and focuses on co-production and collaborative endeavours with participants, collaborators, and colleagues.

In this context of fast research, there is also a risk of the adoption of a positivist style of reflexivity which 'ticks the boxes' and follows certain trends (Lumsden 2019), instead of a feminist reflexive sensibility which I call for in this chapter. This sensibility can extend from our research and self to our co-formed relationships with others (whether participants, public/s, colleagues, students, and so on), the disciplinary fields we are working with/in (and often across), and also the higher education and university contexts we are working in. I argue for the extension of reflexivity (from a focus only on research relationships) into domains otherwise neglected in public accounts, and a shift from reflexivity as an individualised quality of the researcher (used to judge peers and to naval-gaze), to a collaborative, reflexive sensibility which is (ethically) mindful of the wider contexts shaping knowledge(s),

DOI: 10.4324/9781003399575-13

This chapter has been made available under a CC-BY-NC-ND license.

experience(s), the knower/knowing, and their creation, production, construction, negotiation, and contestation (Lumsden 2019). Reflexivity is valuable in feminist research because it draws attention to the researcher as a part of the world being studied. By being reflexive we acknowledge that we cannot be separated from our biographies. Crucially, a mindful feminist reflexive sensibility and approach seeks to avoid the pitfalls of a positivist-version-of-reflexivity emerging in predictable reflexive accounts which focus on the latest reflexive trend and the risk of reflexive endeavours being (re) absorbed by the neoliberal university.

The chapter also demonstrates how reflexivity should involve intersectionality (Collins and Bilge 2020) as a means of addressing contemporary forms of inequality and social justice issues in relation to intersecting social structures and identities. As the United States of America (US) Professor of Sociology Patricia Hill Collins writes: 'One way of conceptualising intersectionality is to see it as a methodology for decolonizing knowledge' (2019, 144). This discussion is situated within calls to decolonise the academy, and the decolonisation of social and feminist research methods and methodologies (Archibald et al. 2019, Kovach 2009, Smith 2012). The neoliberal academy is largely characteristic of the Global North and this forms the basis from which I am writing about the conditions of a feminist reflexive sensibility.

The chapter proceeds as follows: first, I provide the context for our consideration of reflexivity and the development of a feminist reflexive sensibility by outlining the main mechanisms of, and developments in, the neoliberal academy, such as: the privileging of 'fast' research, a focus on productivity and performance, and the impact this can have on the feminist reflexive researcher. I explore how these pressures squeeze the space available for reflexive, feminist, and intersectional research. I also consider the impact of this on our academic selves. I then outline and problematise debates concerning the shift to 'slower' forms of academic labour. I question who has the time, space, resources, and opportunities to adopt and carve out a slower approach to scholarship. The second section provides an overview and definition of reflexivity in feminist research. The third section connects reflexivity to intersectionality in feminist research and calls to decolonise methods, research, and knowledge. The fourth section outlines strategies for cultivating a feminist reflexive sensibility. It draws attention to the risk of reflexivity being co-opted into, or reabsorbed by, the neoliberal academy.

The neoliberal academy and its harms: micro-traumas and disciplinary regimes

The institutional and interpersonal pressures and harms which are created and perpetuated by the neoliberal academy and all its machinations have been extensively documented. Scholars have reflected on the impact of these pressures on their personal and academic identities and sense of self, for example in autoethnographic work (see Andrew 2019, Lumsden 2023, Moriarty 2020, Sparkes 2021). This includes experiences of 'imposter syndrome' in higher education and at different career stages (Addison et al. 2022). British sociologist Maddie Breeze reminds us that although 'imposter syndrome' is ordinary, it is not felt equally and the effect does not carry the same meaning across 'discipline, career stage, contract type, and intersections of class, gender, race and ethnicity, sexuality, disability, and factors such as caring responsibilities or first generation in higher education' (2018, 192). For example, in academia, women are often treated as '"less than" men, assumed to be administrators, infantilized for their views or commonly assumed to be students (thereby not being recognized as "real" academics)' and this 'has a personal impact on one's experience of the work environment' (Shipley 2018, 27–28).

As the quest for 'excellence' and 'outstanding' conduct, and a 'never quite good enough' performance culture continues in universities at pace, privatised feelings of imposter syndrome will be further exacerbated. Tools such as performance development reviews have become 'part of the fabric of disciplinary power' and for the academic 'there is always room for improvement' (Tomkins 2020, 62). As the US cultural theorist Lauren Berlant notes, sometimes the thing which we desire is actually an 'obstacle to our flourishing' – which she refers to as 'cruel optimism' (2011, 1). The 'cruel optimism' of academia is that the goal posts are constantly shifting: we are playing a game in which we continually try to attain/reach success. We can never win this game or reach the finish line. In the university machine, we are imperfect academic subjects, constantly in need of more moulding, shaping, and disciplining (Lumsden 2023).

A competitive environment has been ushered into academia (Back 2016), in which academics are pitted against one another, and are either winners or losers, depending on how well they navigate the system. The merit system and audit culture which define the game are, on the one hand, based on, created by, and situated within, masculinist institutional structures and ideologies, and anything outside of this is therefore 'other', including the work of those who occupy feminine, raced, working-class, and/or disabled subject positions, and are therefore disadvantaged in this system (Gill 2018). This is evident in the 'bravado of the capacities it incites: competition, individualism, self-promotion' (Grant and Elizabeth 2015, 291). On the other hand, academic audit culture has also been associated with feminisation: 'requiring diligent, conforming box-ticking and record-keeping, audit centres the subject of the "good girl"' (Grant and Elizabeth 2015, 291). The 'ideal academic has become a "technopreneur", a scientific researcher with business acumen who produces academic capitalism' (Thornton 2013, 127). These shifts result in a privileging of fast research or scholarship, which should have clear and demonstrable impacts on society.

192 Karen Lumsden

The implications are that slower, more reflective, longer-term research projects and scholarship are squeezed out. In their book, *The Slow Professor*, Canadian scholars of English, Maggie Berg and Barbara Seeber, point out that 'time sickness' is 'pervasive among academics and fostered by the corporate university' (2016, 53). It is detrimental for scholars as it emphasises instrumentalism and marketability, and impacts on subjects who require adequate time for thinking, writing (often solo), and reflecting. Instead, journal papers should be 'churned out', ready to be judged and evaluated by peers, for instance via the UK's Research Excellence Framework (REF). The difficulty faced by scholars who wish to challenge fast academia is highlighted by the British sociologist and feminist cultural theorist Rosalind Gill (2018, 99), who asks:

> when all the structures of our institutions reward the exact opposite, how can we move this from an individual to a collective strategy and also address the social justice agenda?... some and not others are better placed to adopt slowness as a mode of resistance and can do so with fewer penalties.

Those of us who are working in particular disciplines (i.e. the humanities and social sciences) and/or are doing research of a particular nature (i.e. feminist, participatory, and/or reflexive) will be unequally impacted by these pressures, as I have experienced to varying extents over the last decade, and felt in terms of pressure to shift to, or 'do', a form of research which conflicts with my values. I have reflected on the gendered and emotional dynamics of research relationships in my doctoral ethnography of boy racer culture (i.e. the largely male-dominated car modification scene in Scotland) (see Lumsden 2009, Lumsden and Winter 2014) and the pressure to engage in enterprise and 'impact' oriented work in sociological research on policing and the creation of police-academic partnerships in England (Lumsden and Goode 2018). With regards to the latter example, I highlighted the power and privilege associated with the evidence-based movement in policing and the related definitions of legitimate forms of knowledge (and research) and questions of academic freedom. The examples demonstrate both the benefits and the risks that a reflexive approach can present and the possibilities that participatory approaches can offer to academics and police. The often uncomfortable way in which we might publicly reflect on and share our accounts of 'doing' research or public engagement with groups deemed to be 'powerful', such as the police, tells us a great deal about the mechanisms by which reflexivity operates in a disciplinary sense in, for example, sociology and criminology, those settings in which researcher privilege is evident, and those instances in which we may feel more comfortable sharing our reflexive accounts of social groups (such as those in more powerless positions).

'Feminist reflexive sensibility' **193**

Reflexivity therefore risks reproducing the power imbalances and privilege which it aims to address (Lumsden 2013).

In addition, academia as currently structured and politicised can harm those who do not want to feel that they are part of a 'service-user industry that is synonymous with pleasing customers/students – and in some institutions, colleagues – at any cost' (Moriarty and Ashmore 2020, 108). These harms are often inflicted as 'micro-traumas' (Crastnopol 2015), built up over time, thus often leading to increased stress, anxiety, burnout, disengagement and disillusionment with academic life. Margaret Crastnopol, a US scholar of psychiatry, psychoanalysis, and psychology, refers to 'micro-trauma' as a 'psychic bruising that builds imperceptibly over time, little by little eroding a person's sense of self-worth and well-being' (2015, 4). We can be left with fragments of our previous selves once we have experienced and/or 'gone through' the system, which often necessitates a reimagining of who we are, what academia means to us, how it aligns (or not) with our own values, and also how we can navigate our way through (read: survive) an academic career and the pressures this entails. Research and/or becoming an academic involve our whole self/ves, and make us vulnerable via the emotional investment in our practice/s. It is often suggested that 'To be an academic is to live academia'(Chubb et al. 2017, 556). Therefore, academics can be left feeling 'disempowered' (Herrman 2007). The neoliberal governance of the university has 'systematically dismantle[d] the will to critique, thus potentially shifting the very nature of what the university is' (Davies and Bansel 2010, 4).

Employment within the sector is also changing. In recent years, greater numbers of early career researchers have turned their backs on an academic career (Hazell 2022). The 'alt-academia' trend has spread as younger scholars and post-docs seek an alternative. In 2020, the British autoethnographer and creative writer Jess Moriarty (2020) highlighted that forty per cent of academics in the UK were thinking of other employment. This takes place in the context of the 'great resignation' post Covid-19, and the 'quiet quitting' trend, in which workers refuse to work 'above and beyond' their contracted hours. Furthermore, recent years have seen continued strike action by many UK academics who are members of the University and College Union (UCU) in relation to pensions and the 'four fights' dispute, the latter of which concerns workload, casualisation, pay, and equality (UCU 2022).

But what about those who remain? The implications of the above trends in the neoliberal academy include a potential 'squeezing out' of slower, contemplative, and reflexive scholarship. Reflexivity requires the passage of time and does not only involve reflecting on what is happening 'in the moment'. As Canadian writer and social scientist Andrea Doucet argues, there is a temporal ('before, during and after') 'quality of reflexivity in research ... that become[s] apparent only with the passage of time' (2008, 83). Scholars drawing attention to how we resist the 'speeding up' of labour in universities have largely argued for a 'slower' form of scholarship (Berg and Seeber 2016). However, the notions of 'slowing down' or 'speeding up' our academic work disproportionately impacts some groups more than others. 'Speeding up' disproportionately impacts graduate students, who typically have precarious/limited access to research funding and research assistance and face increasingly competitive entry to full-time research positions. In other ways, a strategy of 'slowing down' may not be available to early career researchers and scholars, and to those who are mid-career, who face pressure to publish outputs on an annual basis as part of performance development review culture. In this stage of life, many are juggling academic work with the pressures of family life and childcare. Middle-aged and older academics may also have to care for parents. Those academics in permanent posts and especially those in senior positions may have more space and opportunities to 'slow down' their work. But for the vast majority, this is a privilege they may not have. It also depends on the institutional context and how valued research is or how much time is given to it. Two institutions with similar audit cultures but with different time allotted for research will create different kinds of impetus to speed up or opportunities to slow down. Hence, below, I wish to consider the implications that the strictures of university life have for those of us practising feminist and reflexive work. I will conceptualise reflexivity as a process extending beyond the researcher to include co-formed relationships with others and disciplinary audiences.

Reflexivity and feminism in social research

Reflexivity is a burgeoning field in social research, influenced by feminist postmodern, post-structural, and postcolonial sensibilities (Doucet 2008). Being 'reflexive' involves 'thoughtful self-aware analysis of the intersubjective dynamics between researcher and the researched' while reflexivity necessitates 'critical self-reflection of the ways in which researchers' social background, assumptions, positionality and behaviour impact on the research process. It demands acknowledgement of how researchers (co)construct their research findings' (Finlay and Gough 2003, ix). In *Beyond Methodology*, US women's studies scholars Margaret Fonow and Judith Cook (1991, 13) define reflexivity as the tendency of feminists to reflect on, examine critically, and explore analytically the nature of the research process. In line with feminist research more generally, they view reflexivity as a source of insight and as a means of consciousness-raising:

> The process of reflection is seen as 'enlightening' due to women's oppressed position that enables a view from 'bottom-up' and stems from

women's capacity to deal with inequality through intimate knowledge of their oppressors.

Qualitative researchers using critical, feminist, race-based, or post-structural theories routinely use reflexivity 'as a methodological tool to better represent, legitimize, or call into question their data' (Pillow 2003, 176). Reflexivity under feminism is about investigating the power embedded in one's own research and about doing research 'differently'; the latter of which arises from the ethical and political problems and questions raised by feminists about traditional research methods (Lumsden 2019). There is an array of means through, and places in which, reflexivity can be employed in feminist research. British feminist psychologist Sue Wilkinson argues that at its simplest reflexivity involves 'disciplined self-reflection' (1988, 493). She distinguishes between three forms of reflexivity. First, 'personal reflexivity', which focuses on the researcher's own identity where research becomes 'an expression of personal interests and values' (1988, 494) and is thus an essential aspect of the feminist research paradigm. This form of reflexivity recognises the reciprocal relationship between life experiences and research. Second, Wilkinson proposes that 'functional reflexivity' (1988, 494) involves reflection on the nature of the research enterprise including the choice of method and the construction of knowledge in order to reveal assumptions, values, and biases. Third, she suggests that 'disciplinary reflexivity' (1988, 495) focuses on the form and development of a discipline or sub-discipline. This includes, for instance, how the traditional paradigm of psychology has operated to exclude women and stall development of a feminist psychology.

Reflexivity is also shaped by university and higher education contexts. British sociologists Tim May and Beth Perry (2011, 11–12) argue that the conditions of knowledge production in universities can 'act as inhibitors to reflexivity which requires a supportive context in which to work, as opposed to a celebration of exceptionality through an overblown individualism'. Corporatization has not only prioritised certain areas of research above others but has infiltrated the ways in which all of us, across the disciplines, conduct our research and the way we think about research. The push towards the easily quantifiable and marketable rushes us into 'findings' and is at odds with the spirit of open inquiry and social critique (Berg and Seeber 2016).

Reflexivity in this sense risks being adopted as a disciplinary mechanism for the policing of social scientific research and researchers. It risks being wrapped up with/in the individual identity of the researcher, while failing to recognise the wider disciplinary, institutional, and political context(s) in which reflexivity or being reflexive takes place, and in which knowledge is constructed, situated, and (re)negotiated. It risks the production of a tick-box list of which aspects of identity should be reflected on, or of 'steps' for students/researchers to follow in order to be reflexive, as if reflexivity

196 Karen Lumsden

is something which can be done 'correctly' or 'incorrectly'. We need to acknowledge that there will be aspects of our performance as a researcher that we cannot access or research and that 'eludes the logic of the self-present subject' (Lather 1993, 685).

Intersectionality and 'decolonial reflexivity'

Recent years have also seen the surfacing of work in methods and ethics which focus on the counter-colonial voices of Indigenous peoples (Collins 2009; Russell-Mundine 2012), the importance of 'intersectionality' in research (Rice et al. 2019), and attempts to 'decolonise' methods and methodologies (Smith 2012). The focus on equality, diversity, and inclusion (EDI) has also been taken up at institutional levels. Intersectionality allows us to investigate how:

> intersecting power relations influence social relations across diverse societies as well as individual experiences in everyday life. As an analytic tool, intersectionality views categories of race, class, gender, sexuality, nation, ability, ethnicity and age – among others – as interrelated and mutually shaping one another. Intersectionality is a way of understanding and explaining complexity in the world, in people, and in human experiences.
> *(Collins and Bilge 2020,2).*

For Patricia Hill Collins, intersectionality can be conceptualised 'as a methodology for decolonizing knowledge' (2019, 144). Indigenous researchers have been heavily influenced by a feminist research paradigm and have paved the way for the creation of 'a new Indigenous research paradigm that is critical, liberationist and recognises social, political and historical contexts and that aims to decolonise and reframe research' (Russell-Mundine 2012, 86). As a result, those attempting counter-colonial research cannot rely on a 'first person' application of reflexivity to situate knowledge. Instead, there is a requirement for researchers:

> to engage with reflexive evaluation of collective and negotiated design, data collection and data analysis to consider the interpersonal and collective dynamics during the research process, and any effects that the research may potentially have into the future. Additional political and relational layers of reflexivity are essential for a researcher to critically evaluate empowerment and participation in a counter-colonial context.
> *(Nicholls 2009, 118)*

According to Australian scholar Ruth Nicholls (2009, 117), those attempting counter-colonial research cannot rely on a singular application of reflexivity to situate knowledge. This means that we need 'additional political and relational layers of reflexivity' in order to 'critically evaluate empowerment and participation by working "the spaces between" through reflection about collaboration' (ibid). Gabrielle Russell-Mundine, a cultural scholar in Australia, questions whether reflexivity enables non-Indigenous researchers to contribute to the decolonising and reframing of research (2012, 1). They caution that reflexivity will only lead to reframing and decolonising research if it 'addresses deeper issues such as interrogating the systems of the dominant White culture' (ibid).

'Decolonial reflexivity' has been described as a 'strategy for refining academic decolonisation' (Moosavi 2023, 137). It involves decolonial scholars:

> drawing upon theoretical discussions about academic decolonization to introspectively locate the inadequacies, limitations, and contradictions within our own efforts at academic decolonisation, particularly in relation to the potential for us to inadvertently perpetuate coloniality rather than dismantle it.
>
> *(Moosavi 2023, 138–39)*

The British sociologist Leon Moosavi argues that academics who wish to decolonise must continually consider the theoretical complexities that are generated by our attempts at academic decolonisation (2023, 139). Universities and academics also need to engage in greater reflexivity about the way in which they may inadvertently promote racism and coloniality. In this sense, reflexivity for Moosavi is a 'methodological tool' which provides a form of autoethnographic exploration of a scholar's work which is theoretically informed. He argues that decolonising must be viewed as a 'journey', and academics must ensure that 'these activities do not become mundane or stagnate, ensuring continued efforts to refresh' (2023, 139).

Cultivating a feminist reflexive sensibility

After interpretivism and the postmodern turn in social research methods, the question remained of how to 'deal with the fact of reflexivity, how to strategize about it for certain theoretical and intellectual interests' (Marcus 1993, 394). The US anthropologist George E. Marcus (1993, 392) argued for the crafting of 'reflexive, messy text[s]' in which we are aware of our own narrative apparatuses. In order to continue this conversation – about what it means to be reflexive – the US gender studies scholar Wanda Pillow (2003, 188) argues for 'reflexivities of discomfort' or 'interrupted reflexivity', in which we render the 'knowing' of ourselves and subjects as 'uncomfortable and uncontainable'. This sits in contrast to a view of qualitative research as neat and step-by step, following a 'box-ticking' approach to research design, data collection, and the writing-up of findings.

Andrea Doucet (2008) shares a concern with the reduction of reflexivity to a 'box-ticking' exercise and urges readers to include their disciplinary communities within their reflexive practice. She highlights the need to shift 'dominant understandings of reflexivity from a self-centered exercise to consider other critical relationships that can matter in how we come to know and write about others' (2008, 74). She uses the metaphor of 'three gossamer walls' to 'illustrate the thin and tenuous lines that exist in research relationships' which include 'relations between: researcher and self (including the ghosts that haunt us), researcher and respondents, and researchers and their readers/audiences' (ibid):

> The metaphor of gossamer walls, which combines the sheerness of gossamer and the solidity of walls, provides for a creative way of thinking about the ambiguous solidity and fluidity of reflexivity. These 'walls,' which shift constantly depending on who is on the other side, represent varied degrees of transparency and obscurity, connection and separation, proximity and distance, and moments of closure and openness in the relations that constitute research and knowing.
>
> *(ibid)*

Here, the idea of methodological 'hauntings' helps to account for the ways that as 'knowing subjects' we must acknowledge there are different 'degrees of reflexivity' (Mauthner and Doucet 2003) which only become apparent with the passage of time. As the sociologist Avery Gordon notes, haunting is 'the domain of turmoil and trouble, that moment (of however long duration) when things are not in their assigned places, when the cracks and rigging are exposed ... when disturbed feelings cannot be put away' (2008, xvi). Therefore, reflexivity is not merely sectioned-off as part of the temporal start-to-finish of a research project, or part of a neatly distinct 'writing-up' stage as we 'reflect' back, but is a process extending well beyond our inquiries. As Doucet notes, 'ghosts are part of our research process too and when they appear they become part of the researcher-self' (2008, 83). This conceptualisation of reflexivity highlights issues of transparency in knowledge production, such as the notion of an 'audit trail' as a means of 'reflexive methodological accounting' (Seale 1999) (also highlighted above). Doucet argues that we cannot claim to have access to 'knowing subjects', only their narratives (ibid). Finally, for Doucet, the 'spatial quality of reflexivity' further highlights 'differing sets of close and more distant relations' (ibid).

There is a need for an ethics of care and collaboration in feminist research, in order to repair our (broken) identities and contest the damages done by/via the managerialised and masculinised neoliberal academy. As Nicholls argues, a 'collective-reflexivity' attempts to 'articulate not only contextual change of action outcomes from the research (such as the procedural accounts of evaluation and output in the form of "lessons learned") but extends into a domain of "catalytic validity"' (2009, 124). Barbara Grant, a higher education scholar in New Zealand, suggests one means of addressing the toxic and harmful structures and practices of neoliberal academia is via the concept of 'a thousand tiny universities'. On the ground level we can challenge these forces which are out of our control by taking perspectives from within our smaller 'tiny' worlds and effecting change wherever we can (Pfaendner 2018). Grant also approaches the need to ascertain an academy identity from a 'mourning after' standpoint that values an unsettled identity, arguing that this gives us the 'possibility for a less defensive, even more productive, basis for relations with ourselves as academic developers and with the colleagues alongside whom we work' (Grant 2007, 35). British sociologist Les Back calls for 'generosity' in academia, not just as a matter of 'being nice to others', but also as a 'survival strategy' or 'a prophylactic against the corrosive aspects of intellectual cruelty' which are part of the neoliberal university (2016, 114).

British sociologist of education Stephen Ball (2016) argues that we need to change the conversation and that instead of worrying where education is going, we need to either change, or refuse, our part in neoliberalism. According to Rosalind Gill (2018), the neoliberal university produces 'inner migrants'. This is 'a specific form of alienation from oneself in which the ability to hold a double consciousness – i.e. refusing to take on the university's way of seeing you and holding onto a separate/independent sense of one's own worth and value – is both essential, difficult, and agonizingly painful' (Gill 2018, 98). Moriarty (2022, 4) argues for the 'rewilding' of academia which she says will 'provide a potential antidote to neoliberalism, helping those scholars who feel wounded by its effects to adopt different approaches to pedagogy and research that will help them to feel nourished and replenished'. She highlights autoethnography as one methodology by which to 'restore ourselves and work' (ibid).

I suggest that a feminist reflexivity sensibility offers further solutions and strategies for surviving and thriving in the university, and for aligning our personal and professional values with 'how' we do our research. A feminist reflexive sensibility is decolonial and intersectional, and permits exploration of the 'personal', 'functional', and 'disciplinary' forms of reflexivity highlighted by Wilkinson (1988, 494–95). It is also a 'collective reflexivity', as it acknowledges the inherent power and inequalities which reflexivity risks (re)producing, in terms of 'who' practices it, 'when' they practice it, and 'how' it is practised. Equally, it includes recognition of spaces in which a feminist reflexive sensibility is resisted or challenged. This feminist reflexive sensibility extends beyond the research process or project to consider the university and research structures themselves, disciplinary regimes, and the wider political economy driving and shaping university research and knowledge construction. It spirals backandforth, through-across-and-beyond (post) research project, study, or inquiry in acknowledging hauntings and ghosts which whisper insights, questions, doubts to us in those reflexive moments (see also Doucet 2008). It acknowledges the biographical nuances shaping where we have been, where we currently stand, and where we wish to go with our research endeavours and journeys.

We also need to acknowledge the spaces in which feminist scholars and researchers are able to, or permitted to, be reflexive. The notion of being able to 'slow down' our work will be varyingly experienced by researchers at different stages of their careers. As Mauthner and Doucet (2003, 415) reflect: 'The security of a job, and a position within academia, also undoubtedly make it easier to admit and articulate the confusions and tensions we felt and how these manifested themselves in our research'. In addition, they make the point (see also May and Perry 2017, Lumsden 2019) that 'intense methodological and epistemological musing on reflexivity can run counter to the aims and time lines of the institutional organizations that fund research projects' (ibid). Thus, there is a requirement for collective responsibility and pushing back against individualism in relation to training in reflexivity, to 'being' reflexive (i.e. inhabiting and embodying reflexivity), and the 'doing' or practising of reflexivity, not as a characteristic of 'research' itself, but as a means of also engaging with, navigating through, and shaping the character and sensibilities of universities, researchers, and crucially, how 'research' is conceived structurally and institutionally in universities.

Perhaps, also, this involves a politics of 'refusal' rather than 'resistance', as Ball (2016) highlights. Or, at least, a stubbornness against institutional efforts to co-opt our feminist and reflexive research and inquiries into the fast-paced, tick-box mentality and ethos of the neoliberal university. For example, although there have been some material gains from the Athena Swan (AS) gender equality initiative in UK universities, management scholars Emily Yarrow and Karen Johnston (2022, 757) draw attention to the ways in which it can also serve 'as an effective tool for institutional reputation gains and (extended) virtue signaling'. They call this 'institutional peacocking'. Therefore, we must be sensitive to the risk of co-option of reflexivity, intersectionality, and decolonialisation into neoliberal university agendas.

Instead, a feminist reflexive sensibility offers us a (hopeful!) means of (re-) aligning our personal and professional values and commitments with the ways in which we research, teach, and collaborate both within and outside the academy, reminding us of why we chose (or fell into) this career in the first place. Our 'reflexivities of discomfort' (Pillow 2003, 187) inside and outside the academy help us to 'speak back' to the profession and challenge masculinist organisational culture/s and ways of knowing and researching.

Conclusion

In this chapter, I conceptualised reflexivity as a process extending beyond the researcher to include co-formed relationships with others, disciplinary audiences, and the strictures of the neoliberal university, proposing that we cultivate a feminist reflexive sensibility both personally and collectively. The challenges posed by a neoliberal higher education context impact on us personally and professionally, often running counter to our own values. I shared my concern with the reduction of reflexivity to a 'box-ticking' exercise (Doucet 2008; Lumsden 2019) and urged readers to include their disciplinary communities within their reflexive practice. The cultivation of a feminist reflexive sensibility can help to facilitate a personal, but more crucially, a collective response to the pressures we face from the neoliberal university. Importantly, this involves recognition that power and privilege are also inherent in the space we have available for reflexivity and the production of feminist and intersectional research and writings. I further considered the growing body of work connecting reflexivity with decolonisation of methods and methodology (Kovach 2009, Smith 2012) and how reflexivity helps to address intersectionality (Collins and Bilge 2022) in our research and contemporary forms of inequality and social justice issues in relation to intersecting social structures and identities. The development of a feminist reflexive sensitivity also requires full engagement with decolonial knowledge and critiques of social and feminist research methods, methodologies, traditions, and ways of 'knowing', by applying an intersectional and 'decolonizing lens' (Kovach 2009, 77) to our reflexive work.

References

Addison, Michelle, Maddie Breeze, and Yvette Taylor, eds. 2022. The Palgrave Handbook of Imposter Syndrome in Higher Education. Basingstoke: Palgrave Macmillan.

Andrew, Martin. 2019. "Double Negative: When the Neoliberal Meets the Toxic." In *Resisting Neoliberalism in Higher Education: Volume 1. Seeing through the Cracks*, edited by Dorothy Bottell and Catherine Manathunga, 59–81. Basingstoke: Palgrave Macmillan.

Archibald, Jo-ann, Q'um Q'um Xiiem, Lee-Morgan, Jenny Bol Jun and De Santolo, Jason eds. 2019. *Decolonizing Research: Indigenous Storywork as Methodology*. London: Zed Books.

Back, Les. 2016. *Academic Diary: Or Why Higher Education Still Matters*. London: Goldsmiths Press.

Ball, Stephen J. 2016. "Subjectivity as a Site of Struggle: Refusing Neoliberalism?" *British Journal of Sociology of Education* 37, no. 8: 1129–1146. https://doi.org /10.1080/01425692.2015.1044072

Berg, Maggie, and Barbara Seeber. 2016. *The Slow Professor: Challenging the Culture of Speed in the Academy*. Toronto: University of Toronto Press.

Berlant, Lauren. 2011. *Cruel Optimism*. Durham: Duke University Press.

Breeze, Maddie. 2018. "Imposter Syndrome as a Public Feeling." In *Feeling Academic in the Neoliberal University: Flights, Fights and Failures*, edited by Yvette Taylor and Kinneret Lahad, 191–219. Basingstoke: Palgrave Macmillan.

Chubb, Jennifer, Richard Watermeyer and Paul Wakeling. 2017. "Fear and Loathing in the Academy? The Role of Emotion in Response to an Impact Agenda in the UK and Australia." *Higher Education Research & Development* 36, no. 3: 555–568. https://doi.org/10.1080/07294360.2017.1288709

Collins, Patricia Hill. 2009. *Intersectionality as Critical Social Theory*. Durham, NC: Duke University Press.

Collins, Patricia Hill and Sirma Bilge. 2020. *Intersectionality*. Second Edition. Cambridge: Polity Press.

Crastnopol, Margaret. 2015. *Micro-Trauma: A Psychoanalytic Understanding of Cumulative Psychic Injury*. London: Routledge.

Davies, Bronwyn and Peter Bansel. 2010. "Governmentality and Academic Work: Shaping the Hearts and Minds of Academic Workers." *Journal of Curriculum Theorizing* 26, no. 3. https://journal.jctonline.org/index.php/jct/article/view/250

Doucet, Andrea. 2008 "'From Her Side of the Gossamer Wall(s)': Reflexivity and Relational Knowing." *Qualitative Sociology* 31: 73–87. https://doi.org/10.1007/s11133-007-9090-9

Finlay, Linda and Brendan Gough, eds. 2003. *Reflexivity: A Practical Guide for Researchers in Health and Social Sciences*. London: Blackwell.

Fonow, Mary M. and Judith A. Cook, eds. 1991. *Beyond Methodology: Feminist Scholarship as Lived Research*. Bloomington: Indiana University Press.

Gill, Rosalind. 2018. "What Would Les Back Do? If Generosity Could Save Us." *International Journal of Politics, Culture and Society* 31: 95–101. https://doi.org/10.1007/s10767-017-9263-9

Gordon, Avery F. 2008. *Ghostly Matters: Hauntings and the Sociological Imagination*. Minneapolis: University of Minnesota Press.

Grant, Barbara M. 2007. "The Mourning After: Academic Development in a Time of Doubt." *International Journal for Academic Development* 12, no. 1: 35–43. https://doi.org/10.1080/13601440701217303

Grant, Barbara and Vivienne Elizabeth. 2015. "Unpredictable Feelings: Academic Women Under Research Audit." *British Education Research Journal* 41, no. 2: 287–302. https://doi.org/10.1002/berj.3145

Hazell, Will. 2022. "UK Universities Facing 'Staff Exodus' Because of Demoralised Academics, University and College Union Says." *i*, 25 March 2022. https://inews.co.uk/news/education/uk-universities-staff-exodus-demoralised-academics-union-1537996

Herrman, Andrew, ed. 2007. *Organizational Autoethnographies*. Milton: Taylor and Francis.

Kovach, Margaret. 2009. *Indigenous Methodologies: Characteristics, Conversations and Contexts*. Toronto: University of Toronto Press.

Lather, Patti. 1993. "Fertile Obsession: Validity after Poststructuralism." *Sociological Quarterly* 34, no. 4: 673–693. https://doi.org/10.1111/j.1533-8525.1993.tb00112.x

Lumsden, Karen. 2009. "'Don't Ask a Woman to Do Another Woman's Job: Gendered Interactions and the Emotional Ethnographer." *Sociology* 43, no. 3: 497–513. https://doi.org/10.1177/0038038509103205

Lumsden, Karen. 2013. "'You Are What You Research': Researcher Partisanship and the Sociology of the Underdog." *Qualitative Research* 13, no. 1: 3–18. https://doi.org/10.1177/1468794112439012

Lumsden, Karen. 2019. *Reflexivity: Theory, Method and Practice*. London: Routledge.

Lumsden, Karen. 2023. "Reflections and Confessions on the Making of a Performative Autoethnography: University Professional Development Reviews and the Academic Self." In *Crafting Autoethnography: Processes and Practices of Making Self and Culture*, edited by Jackie Goode, Karen Lumsden and Jan Bradford, Chapter 9. London: Routledge.

Lumsden, Karen and Aaron Winter, eds. 2014. *Reflexivity in Criminological Research: Experiences with the Powerful and the Powerless*. Basingstoke: Palgrave Macmillan.

Lumsden, Karen and Jackie Goode, 2018. "Public Criminology, Reflexivity and the Enterprise University: Experiences of Research, Knowledge Transfer Work and Co-option with Police Forces." *Theoretical Criminology* 22, no. 2: 243–257. https://doi.org/10.1177/1362480616689299

Marcus, George. 1993. "What Comes (Just) After 'Post'? The Case of Ethnography." In *The Landscape of Qualitative Research: Theories and Issues*, edited by Norman Denzin and Yvonne Lincoln, 383–406. Thousand Oaks, CA: Sage.

Mauthner, Natasha S. and Andrea Doucet. 2003. "Reflexive Accounts and Accounts of Reflexivity in Qualitative Data Analysis." *Sociology* 37, no. 3: 413–431. https://doi.org/10.1177/00380385030373002

May, Tim and Beth Perry. 2017. *Social Research and Reflexivity*. London: Sage.

Moosavi, Leon. 2023. "Turning the Decolonial Gaze towards Ourselves: Decolonising the Curriculum and 'Decolonial Reflexivity' in Sociology and Social Theory." *Sociology* 57, no. 1: 137–156. https://doi.org/10.1177/00380385221096037

Moriarty, Jess, ed. 2020. *Autoethnographies From the Neoliberal Academy: Rewilding, Writing and Resistance in Higher Education*. London: Routledge.

Moriarty, Jess and Nicola Ashmore. 2020. "Rise Up: Women Sharing Personal and Shared Stories to Resist and Heal." In *Autoethnographies From the Neoliberal Academy: Rewilding, Writing and Resistance in Higher Education*, edited by Jess Moriarty, 104–119. London: Routledge.

Nicholls, Ruth. 2009. "Research and Indigenous Participation: Critical Reflexive Methods." *International Journal of Social Research Methodology* 12, no. 2: 117–126. https://doi.org/10.1080/13645570902727698

Pfaendner, Bettina. 2018. "A Thousand Tiny Universities – My Impression From HERDSA." 24 July 2018. Accessed May, 25 2019. https://teche.mq.edu.au/2018/07/a-thousand-tiny-universities-my-impressions-from-herdsa/

Pillow, Wanda. 2003. "Confession, Catharsis or Cure? Rethinking the Uses of Reflexivity as Methodological Power in Qualitative Research." *International Journal of Qualitative Studies in Education* 16: 175–196. https://doi.org/10.1080/0951839032000060635

Rice, Carla, Elisabeth Harrison and May Friedman. 2019. "Doing Justice to Intersectionality in Research." *Cultural Studies <> Critical Methodologies* 19, no. 6: 409–420. https://doi.org/10.1177/1532708619829779

Russell-Mundine, Gabrielle. 2012. "Reflexivity in Indigenous Research: Reframing and Decolonising Research?" *Journal of Hospitality and Tourism Management* 19: 1–6. https://doi.org/10.1017/jht.2012.8

Seale, Clive. 1999. *The Quality of Qualitative Research*. London: Sage.

Shipley, Heather. 2018. "Failure to Launch? Feminist Endeavours as a Partial Academic." In *Feeling Academic in the Neoliberal University*, edited by Yvette Taylor and Kinneret Lahad, 17–32. Basingstoke: Palgrave Macmillan.

Smith, Linda Tuhiwai. 2012. *Decolonizing Methodologies: Research and Indigenous Peoples*. Second Edition. Dunedin: Zed Books.

Sparkes, Andrew. 2021. "Making a Spectacle of Oneself in the Academy Using the H-Index: From Becoming an Artificial Person to Laughing at Absurdities." *Qualitative Inquiry* 27, no. 8–9: 1027–1039. https://doi.org/10.1177/10778004211003519

Thornton, Margaret. 2013. "The Mirage of Merit: Reconstituting the 'Ideal Academic'." *Australian Feminist Studies* 28, no. 76: 127–143. https://doi.org/10.1080/08164649.2013.789584

Tomkins, Leah. 2020. "Autoethnography Through the Prism of Foucault's Care of the Self." In *The Routledge International Handbook of Organizational Autoethnography*, edited by Andrew Herrmann, 54–68. London: Routledge.

UCU. 2022. "Four Fights: What Are We Fighting For?" https://www.ucu.org.uk/media/11874/Four-fights-what-are-we-fighting-for/pdf/4_fights_for.pdf

Wilkinson, Sue. 1988. "The Role of Reflexivity in Feminist Psychology." *International Forum of Women's Studies* 11, no. 5: 493–502. https://doi.org/10.1016/0277-5395(88)90024-6

Yarrow, Emily and Karen Johnston. 2023. "Athena SWAN: 'Institutional Peacocking' in the Neoliberal University." *Gender, Work & Organization*. Online First. https://doi.org/10.1111/gwao.12941

13

LOCATION, CONTRADICTION, AMBIVALENCE

Feminist methodologies within and beyond the university

Olive Demar

The norms of the university construct it as an intellectual space, a cloistered domain of ideas and thinking. I am curious about what happens to feminist research when we refuse to think about our work as purely academic and split off from our emotional and political lives. How can we negotiate between what an institution wants us to do and other aspects of our feminist research? Research often designates activities that help academics to secure or sustain positions within colleges and universities. Research generally implies publishing books with university presses or articles in academic journals. Perhaps what feminists put on their CVs and in their tenure dossiers constitutes only a segment of their research as feminists. A feminist can do her academic work, and she also undertakes other kinds of research – her emotional work, her political work. Some types of writing we do to build up our publishing records to land a teaching job, and other types we do to make sense of our experiences in the world, to augment struggles within institutions, and to support movements on the ground. The pressure of the job market can push feminists to focus on their scholarly work and churn out publications for academic audiences. These institutional pressures to accumulate markers of intellectual achievement, status, and prestige may pull feminists away from other parts of themselves.

Feminists can approach research not simply as an academic exercise, but also as a means to support social movements and to integrate multiple parts of ourselves. The university is a site for us to do our work and also a context that takes us away from our work. How do we continue our feminist research within, and perhaps in spite of, the university? Drawn from lineages of feminist thought, I introduce a set of methodological guidelines that apply to our research in the full sense of the term, that is, our forms of study

DOI: 10.4324/9781003399575-14

This chapter has been made available under a CC-BY-NC-ND license.

within and beyond an academic job. Useful across disciplinary contexts, these invitations address various phases of the research process: how to take up the work, how to pick a topic, what interpretative questions to ask, how to relate to the subject of study. These guidelines can support bringing together within ourselves different forms of feminism.

Feminists have generated a robust literature, both disciplinary and interdisciplinary, on questions of methodology (Hesse-Biber 2012). My task here is not to write about a novel or new methodology, but to celebrate the qualities that I appreciate most within feminist work. The feminist methodologies that we need now might be ones gifted to us by previous generations of researchers, waiting to be picked up and put to use. I identify here the methodological insights that I have found helpful, grounding, and clarifying in my own research. I write to stay in connection with feminist lineages of thought and praxis. Many have asked these questions: how do I go about my research? How can it support feminist struggles? How do I bring together my academic self with my political commitments and my emotional experience? Remembering the history of others who have asked these questions can be a support in grappling with them in the present. Political scientist Jacqui True frames acknowledging our intellectual debts as core to feminist methodology: 'I was taught continually to recognize the contributions of others, to notice them as if in conversation with them, and to cite them. This is a feminist practice' (Ackerly and True 2020, 107). Paying homage to the feminists that have come before me, this chapter introduces four methodological suggestions that can apply to a wide range of feminist projects: 1) starting from one's experience, 2) learning to take in the whole of others' experiences as well as your own, 3) staying aware of the institutional context, and 4) developing emotional reflexivity within the research process.

I come to these methodological questions from the humanities and the specificity of my social location. I write from the position of being a White, cis-gendered, able-bodied woman; a US citizen born to parents from the professional–managerial class. I write also as an adjunct who has precariously pieced together teaching gigs at multiple institutions for the past seven years. While destabilising and painful, my experiences as an adjunct have been humbling and have helped me to see the university – and myself – with clearer eyes. They have taught me the limits of identifying with an institutional role and the importance of understanding one's capacities outside of what a job will recognise. Some of the most important learning for me has taken place in non-academic contexts; these experiences have provoked me to rethink my approach to academic writing.

Through the duration of my time within institutions of higher education, I have felt the consequences of splitting apart the intellectual, emotional, and political aspects of feminist work. In an experience that I imagine will resonate with others, I have felt a sense of alienation at conferences when the papers (including my own) seem emotionally shut down and/or far removed from the vitality of social movements. I have struggled with my varied motivations as a researcher, juggling my desire for a salaried academic job with a yearning to show up for social struggles in meaningful ways. Rather than escaping these tensions, we can think through and be with them more intimately. This chapter moves between different pronouns – I, you, we, they – as a way of leaving open and unresolved the relationship between us, writer, and reader.

Starting from one's experience

Deciding on a subject of study is the first step of the research process and presents a challenging set of questions. Where should you place your eyes and attention? What will you devote yourself to researching? How will you formulate the questions that will drive your inquiry? While primary, these questions are not neutral or easy to answer. These decisions can have weight and consequences for you personally as well as for the communities you wish to engage. The selection of subject matter can shed light on our priorities, values, and wounds.

In a poem titled, 'Transcendental Etude', Adrienne Rich writes, 'No one ever told us we had to study our lives, make of our lives a study' (1978, 73). This line points to a guiding principle for feminist researchers: start from where you are. Start from your own body. Use the feelings and sensations within your body as a place to begin asking questions. These feelings will help guide you to the wider social processes that deserve attention and analysis. They will help you choose subject matter that has stakes for you and for those who may share some aspect of your social location. Whatever might be there – exhaustion, grief, anger, loneliness, humiliation, hunger – can illuminate what experiences have been significant; experiences that may indicate how the wider tensions and antagonisms of the social world have emerged within your life. Attuning to one's emotional experience can be an important dimension of understanding one's political experience.

If we find ourselves not at the beginning of a research project but in the thick of one, we can reflect on what motivated us to do this research. Why this of all things? What does this mean to me? What am I trying to work out through this project? While the reasons may seem private or idiosyncratic, framing the motivations guiding a particular inquiry can help readers understand the stakes of the project. I appreciate research where you can sense the living, breathing person in the writing; projects that are deeply felt and grounded in experience.

A number of texts on feminist methods have discussed the principle of starting from experience. Rhetorical scholar Patricia Bizzell notes how feminist methods push against the assumed impersonality and distance of academic writing by 'bringing the person of the researcher, her body, her emotions, and dare one say, her soul, into the work' (2000, 16). Sociologists Mary Margaret Fonow and Judith A. Cook identify studying the situation at hand as a key tendency in feminist work: 'Once a researcher finds herself in a particular situation and recognizes the research potential in her surroundings, she may decide to make a study of it' (1991, 12). Education scholars Sara Carpenter and Shahrzad Mojab write of the forms of critical consciousness that can emerge from attempting to make sense of one's daily life. Connecting personal experience to wider social structures, they encourage feminists 'to marshal the subjective experience of patriarchy as a way of seeing into larger social relations in order to understand where and how both subjective and objective forms of consciousness arise' (2017, 63). Sociologist Joey Sprague similarly suggests contextualising research in relation to lived experience: 'We should ask ourselves questions about the connection between our personal biographies and material interests and the questions we pursue and the arguments we find compelling throughout the lifetime of each project' (2005, 189). Invoking the need for an intersectional lens, Sprague does caution against projects that are too narrowly self-focused, asking 'how can scholars who are relatively privileged be aware of and perhaps counteract the impact of that privilege on what seems interesting and important to them?' (2005, 181). Balancing these two poles, feminists can choose topics that are intimately connected to one's own experiences while also holding questions up for honest scrutiny.

The 'starting from one's experience' principle bears the feminist influences of standpoint methodology, *'theory in the flesh'* (Moraga and Anzaldúa 1983), and consciousness-raising. As developed by Dorothy Smith, Patricia Hill Collins, Nancy Hartsock, and many others, standpoint methodology illuminates the role of lived experience in shaping and producing knowledge (Harding 2004). As opposed to what Hartsock calls the 'abstract masculinity' (1998, 118) attained by distancing oneself from the conditions of daily life, standpoint theorists highlight how particular insights emerge from one's social location within a set of structural antagonisms. Similarly, Cherríe Moraga and Gloria Anzaldúa, the editors of *This Bridge Called My Back*, describe the process of thinking through the contradictions emerging in one's life: 'A theory in the flesh means one where the physical realities of our lives – our skin color, the land or concrete we grew up on, our sexual longings – all fuse to create a politic born out of necessity' (1983, 23). This resonates with the consciousness-raising methodologies that feminists have employed to harness the power of sharing experiences. Consciousness-raising groups performed the feminist work of naming and making connections between what had felt like individual problems. Marjorie L. DeVault and Glenda Gross frame consciousness-raising as a process of lateral interviewing – women 'were "interviewing" themselves and others like them and then working together to make sense of experiences' (2012, 210). These influences demonstrate how feminist research often has a personal urgency, stemming from a need to make heads or tails of some experience.

Thinking and writing from experience proves, however, to be a difficult undertaking. In Alice Echols's history of feminism in the United States from 1967 through 1975, she describes some of the early women's liberation groups as having a tendency to avoid personal discussions and to do abstract theorising, as in the case of the Westside Group of Chicago (whose membership included Shulamith Firestone and Jo Freeman) (1989, 68). Echols's excerpts from her interviews with Freeman indicate the challenges the group had in delving into their experiences and making connections between the personal and the structural. Decades later, feminist theorist Sara Ahmed makes a similar observation: 'If anything, I think it is easier to do more abstract and general theoretical work' (2016, 9). Staying in the register of abstracted theory avoids the messiness and vulnerability of speaking to the specificity of our own lives.

While not a facile task, integrating the personal in our writing deepens the research. As two stunning examples of writing that works through the author's experience, I point to June Jordan's 'Report from the Bahamas, 1982' (2003) and Sara Ahmed's *Living a Feminist Life* (2016). In narrating a set of encounters that she has on spring holiday in the Caribbean and back on campus at her teaching job, Jordan thinks through how her experience intersects and diverges with other women and how solidarities can develop across forms of difference. Similarly, taking up concrete experiences she has within the university, Ahmed's book reflects on 'how we generate feminist theory by living a feminist life. Life can be our work. We work in our life' (2016, 89). Published 34 years apart, these two texts bring the specificity of the authors' life experiences into conceptualisations of feminist politics, illuminating how daily life can inform one's work.

Learning to take in the whole of others' experiences as well as your own

While intersectionality has become a widely accepted framework, working with the concept methodologically is not straightforward. Research projects can bring up difficult questions regarding representation, reciprocity, and accountability. Intersectionality – analysis that takes up the relationships between difference and sameness – invites us to think along multiple axes at once. We are both similar and different from our subjects and objects of analysis. As we write about particular topics and people, our research can allow in difference and also find ways to join across differentiated experiences. While engaged in abstract analysis about the intersections of gender and other social determinants, we interact with the specific people in front of us and negotiate what feminist and psychotherapist Gail Lewis calls 'the micro and macro-social in the here-and-now of the inter-subjective encounter' (2013, 218). We can learn to take in the fullness of whomever we come into contact with through our research – people we may interview, those whose documents we pour over in archives, those with whom we collaborate. Encounters with others often come with misunderstandings and unnoticed assumptions. We can work with the parts of others' experiences that are easy to name and those that may be more difficult to see. Depending on their social location, feminist researchers may be attuned to particular gendered experiences but may miss dynamics surrounding class, race, nationality, language, ability, and so forth. Sorting out our own visions and suppositions from what someone else actually means takes careful attention. Taking in the ways that others think can deepen and shift our sense of the research inquiry.

Intersectional methodologies require researchers to keep alive the tensions within feminist thought and organising. Philosopher Elizabeth Spelman identifies what she calls 'the paradox at the heart of feminism', which she articulates as 'how we weigh what we have in common against what differentiates us' (1988, 3–4). Rather than resolve or avoid it, we must keep company with the dilemma of how to hold both compatibility and opposition. Audre Lorde offers these words about finding commonality despite differences: 'I do not want you to ignore my identity, nor do I want you to make it an insurmountable barrier between our sharing of strengths' (2009, 58). Solidarity between feminists is possible, but it must also be accompanied by a recognition of the gulfs and antagonisms between those trying to work together. Within each research project, feminists must contend with differentiated experiences while also finding ways to join with others.

Intersectional methods invite us to increase our tolerance for sitting with contradictions. It is tempting to want to find a resolution to these tensions; to make cleaner distinctions between friends and enemies. A methodological commitment to intersectionality requires us to take in the tensions within our research and the ambivalence that we feel towards our subjects and ourselves. Sociologist Judith Stacey provides an example of addressing in her writing the dilemmas that arise in relating to her informants during fieldwork (1988). Calling her own position into question, Stacey brings a humility to the task of representing both self and others. At each stage of the research process, feminists can reflect on the relational dynamics that surround the project and the quandaries that have emerged within it. Staying with these contradictions and the experiential complexity of the process will strengthen one's analysis. Feminists must dwell with these contradictions in our research, as they cannot be resolved through writing.

Staying aware of the institutional context

Those of us who work in higher education find ourselves within an immediate organisational context that exerts considerable pressure on how we go about our research and what forms it will take. Academics are ensconced within institutional structures that mediate the thinking and writing we do. Feminists have much to learn by investigating the immediate conditions surrounding our writing. Who generates these texts, by what means, and for whom? A set of material conditions shape academic research: university policies, funding sources, organisational dynamics, relationships, and so forth. Scholarly writing often obscures these conditions, as Tracey Potts and Janet Price observe: 'Academic discourse in general isn't very good at acknowledging the materiality of its own production, the resources and labour that enable its existence ... Only on the acknowledgements page – split off from the main body of the text' (1995, 102). Understanding this institutional and economic context can illuminate its pressure on our work.

Feminist methodologies invite researchers to grapple with the institutional context and what it does to one's thinking. In relation to the university, feminists can ask: what is this place? Where am I? Academic prose can make claims about feminism and resistance, and yet, another set of politics dwells underneath the sequence of paragraphs on the page. Whatever the content might be, the quest for salaried employment, professional status, and institutional recognition drives academic writing. A publishing record functions to make the author legible to the university as a particular type of worker, one who will receive better pay and more job security than other groups of workers. Feminists can keep this aspect of their research in mind. Academic writing has its pleasures and its limits. Staying present to the institutional context of research can help feminists address the immediate tensions and struggles of the university, rather than bracketing them and staying in the realm of abstract theorisation.

A number of feminists are clear-eyed about what it means to write within an academic context. Reflecting on the constraints of academia for African-American women intellectuals, Patricia Hill Collins observes 'the pressure to separate thought from action – particularly political activism – that typically accompanies training in standard academic disciplines' (2000, 41). Long-time organiser Selma James sharply illuminates the gap between academic writing and social movements: 'Most research doesn't aim to forge weapons for women's struggle' (2012, 199). Within a conference setting, James asks feminist academics a set of probing questions: 'What are we doing here? Are we rubber-stamping here? Are we becoming, while professing to principle, even radicalism, a kind of camouflage for what may be going on here?' (2012, 209). Chandra Talpade Mohanty advocates for a critical interrogation of the forces that shape academic fields and disciplinary contexts: 'The fact that area studies in U.S. academic settings were federally funded and conceived as having a political project in the service of U.S. geopolitical interests suggests the need to examine the contemporary interests of these fields, especially as they relate to the logic of global capitalism' (2003, 520). Collins, James, and Mohanty invite feminists to grapple with both the university's normative standards and the material interests underpinning research funding.

As an example of a feminist text that puts these questions front and centre, I point to *Unsettling Relations: The University as a Site of Feminist Struggles*, a book appearing in 1992 co-authored by Himani Bannerji, Linda Carty, Kari Dehli, Susan Heald, and Kate McKenna. Writing from different locations within the university (as graduate students, part-time teachers, lecturers on limited contracts, and assistant professors – all without tenure), these five women each contributed their own essay and collaborated on the book's introduction which excavates 'how social relations and practices of domination and oppression – and at times of struggle and empowerment – are being produced and reproduced in academia' (1992, 6). They seek 'to question academic feminists' positions in and identifications with those relations' and to do so through self-examination as well as collective reflection across the race and class differences amongst them (1992, 6). While published 30 ago, I find this book refreshingly honest about the dynamics and vulnerabilities of academic life. Demonstrating the power of collaborative writing, Bannerji, Carty, Dehli, Heald, and McKenna provide an example of what it means to think through how to be accountable to other feminists within the university and to social movements outside of it.

Following their lead, feminist researchers can distinguish what earns one institutional recognition from what supports movements for justice and liberation. Sociologist Maria Mies differentiates between research that is connected to feminist struggles and research that is published 'in the hope of perhaps still being able to find a place in the increasingly scarcer flesh-pots in the academic house of men' (1991, 82). Academic life proffers a ladder to climb, and we must not mistake professional ascension for feminist praxis. As Ahmed states succinctly, 'a feminist life is not so linear' (2016, 173). Our jobs – academic or otherwise – will not liberate us. Academia can engender the psychosocial habits of disciplining students and colleagues, rather than supporting or joining with them. From whatever role we have within the university, we can learn to see our institutional context clearly and find ways to develop lateral power with others.

Developing emotional reflexivity within the research process

Beyond honing one's clarity of thought and ability to stick with a multi-step endeavour, feminist research can also cultivate emotional literacy.

Feminists have embraced practices of reflexivity, or the careful examination of one's own methods and methodologies. As part of this willingness to study and question oneself, feminists can use emotional reflexivity to become more intimately connected with how our experiences and wounds shape the intellectual work that we do. While both Marxist feminism and Hochschildian sociology have taken up questions of emotional labour, I am thinking here about insights drawn from psychoanalytic practices. Compelling research often stems from one's ability to be emotionally present both to oneself and one's subject. Writers can make themselves available to the emotional contours and psychic ambiance of their subject matter. This emotional attunement can allow one to more fully take in the evidence under examination. Emotions come up in the research process, and feminists can take these emotions seriously, as they often point towards vital insights.

A number of methodological writings by feminists have discussed the importance of emotional reflexivity. Fonow and Cook frame an attention to the emotional dimension of research as a central component of feminist methodologies (1991, 9–11). Sociologist Gayle Letherby urges feminists to 'value reflexivity and emotion as a source of insight as well as an essential part of research' (2003, 73). She encourages writing in the first person as a means to recognise the individual author's subjectivity within the research process. Nancy Naples illustrates the role of emotions in the context of fieldwork: 'Emotions are always present in personal interactions in ethnographic work. Here the feminist perspective is useful in reminding us that emotions can form an important basis for understanding and analysis' (2003, 63). Jo Reger encourages feminist researchers to keep track of one's emotions when examining evidence, asking ourselves, 'What have I been thinking and feeling as I worked today?' (2020, 99). In contrast to bloodless, professionalised writing, these practices of reflexivity use the emotional contours of the research to develop richer connections to one's subjects and readers.

When working on a research project, a scholar faces the question of how to relate to an object of study. Does one love the object of inquiry or hate it? Does one wish to hold it up or tear it down? The writing process has both conscious and unconscious dimensions. A researcher may have well-formulated arguments for particular positions or reasons to denounce a certain text, *and* this scholar may also be up to something unconsciously through these criticisms. Moments of denunciation can carry unconscious processes of projection, as critiques can offer a way to split off unsavoury dimensions of oneself. Writers can project unwanted parts of themselves onto their subject matter, using the writing to externalise what is challenging to incorporate into one's self-understanding. Feminist methods can help us integrate disowned parts of our experience, rather than ascribe them to our subject matter.

214 Olive Demar

Indicating the exigency of this type of reflection, Audre Lorde and Gloria Anzaldúa provide two striking invitations for feminists to cultivate emotional reflexivity. In a keynote she delivered in 1981 to the National Women's Studies Association titled, 'The Uses of Anger: Women Responding to Racism', Lorde writes of the impulse for feminists to see themselves as oppressed and ignore the ways they might be holding other groups down:

> What woman here is so enamored of her own oppression that she cannot see her heelprint upon another woman's face? What woman's terms of oppression have become precious and necessary to her as a ticket into the fold of the righteous, away from the cold winds of self-scrutiny?
>
> *(2007, 132)*

In a similar gesture to Lorde's beckoning of cold winds, Anzaldúa invites gringos in the United States to examine what they may be projecting onto Latinx peoples:

> We need you to accept the fact that Chicanos are different, to acknowledge your rejection and negation of us... We need you to make public restitution: to say that, to compensate for your own sense of defectiveness, you strive for power over us, you erase our history and our experience because it makes you feel guilty – you'd rather forget your brutish acts. To say you've split yourself from minority groups, that you disown us, that your dual consciousness splits off parts of yourself, transferring the 'negative' parts onto us.
>
> *(1987, 85–86)*

Anzaldúa's text resonates with what psychoanalysts would refer to as taking back the projection. Owning the brutality of White supremacy and national borders becomes a means to integrate these projected qualities. From wherever one is located, feminists can continue to struggle with themselves and clearly see their role within wider structural antagonisms.

Rather than writing hit pieces, feminists can ascertain how they too are implicated in the dynamics under scrutiny. The writing process becomes an opportunity to understand how one is also a part of and immersed in one's object of analysis. This mode contrasts with a conception of scholarly writing rooted in the attempt to beat one's opponents through unassailable argumentation. Instead, researchers can implicate both themselves and their readers within the objects of critique, whether that is a set of material relations, a strategic impasse, a cultural logic, or a habit of mind. Avoiding the gesture of the take-down or the vogue condemnation, feminists can offer themselves up for scrutiny as much as any external object. The frame of analysis can include the roles of the writer and reader, illustrating how all are involved in the questions posed by the research inquiry. In an interactive process, scholars can think with their subjects, rather than over or about them. Inhabiting this stance allows the researcher to understand what debts, both intellectual and emotional, they owe to their subjects. These gestures help produce writing that has an emotional honesty and humility, alongside intellectual rigour.

Gail Lewis offers an example of this type of psychosocial reflection. She returned to a project she had done 15 years prior, writing a text that dissects the rage and vengeance she felt during a research interview and how this affect shaped her selection and interpretation of data. She describes how she 'was unable to make sense of and work with the powerful emotional experience of that research encounter' (2013, 215). In hindsight, Lewis discerns that her earlier study was 'a form of psychic defense against this pain but turned into a form of concealed hitting back' (2013, 212). She poignantly observes how 'researchers can unexpectedly encounter our emotional and long-felt demons in the course of a day's (research) work' (2013, 221). While writing about the past, Lewis engages in a potent form of emotional reflexivity in the present of this text. She demonstrates how researchers can make use of the intersubjective register before, during, and after a research project.

The need for emotional candour and reflexivity becomes apparent when examining how people relate to each other within academic and organising spaces. Interpersonal dynamics within higher education and social movements can be fraught. A feminist academic may write thoughtful analyses of gender and politics and yet may be cruel to her students and colleagues. An activist group can spend more time tearing each other down than finding solidarity. Working with others in institutional or movement spaces requires self-reflection and an emotional openness to learning about oneself and others.

Developing one's emotional literacy involves learning to take in a full range of affect. Rather than splitting off or projecting out our challenging emotions, we can increase our tolerance for ambivalence. We can dwell with the ambivalences that emerge within our work – our inevitably mixed feelings about our research, disciplinary context, and institutional location. A scholar can feel simultaneously authorised by an institution as well as hemmed in and caged by it. We can learn to hold multiple and divergent feelings, as for example, in the desire to be both in and out of the university at the same time. Working with this ambivalence – acknowledging difficulty and frustration alongside hope and vitality – will strengthen the thinking and writing we are doing.

Emotionally reflexive writing allows in tenderness and antagonism, love and fury. Feminists can infuse our writing with humility and gentleness as well as an unrelenting revolutionary spirit. Scholarship requires developing the calm necessary for the slow, meticulous work of research – looking

216 Olive Demar

carefully at documents, getting the correct citation, re-writing a sentence several times. This grounded poise is not easy to come by, developing only with the ability to surface and contain challenging affects. I have noticed that my years within colleges and universities have cultivated my intellectual competencies while leaving my emotional and interpersonal capacities underdeveloped. The research process can provide a site for us to learn emotionally as well as intellectually.

Methodological implications

These methodological reflections point us towards three key implications. First, when choosing a research project, feminists can move away from the question of what is 'interesting'. Scholars love to be interested. We have research and teaching interests; we have fields and sub-fields that spark our interest. These academic interests can sometimes have little to do with another set of interests – the material relations that shape our lives. Reading through research interests on departmental websites sometimes strikes me as reflective of an obliviousness to the material struggles and ecological conditions that surround us. While I have learnt immensely from the research process, I sometimes wonder if my historical studies are largely irrelevant to the wider world. In my editorial work, I have witnessed many authors have difficulty specifying why they have taken up a particular study and why it matters to a larger readership. Much academic writing does not need to be written. We can challenge the conflation of critical inquiry with institutional liberal arts, as critical reflection about the world does not belong to higher education and can be found within social movements, unions, and community centres. Maria Mies questions the circumscription of women's studies to research institutes and universities and calls for a link between praxis and research, arguing that 'contemplative, uninvolved "spectator knowledge" must be replaced by *active participation in actions, movements, and struggles* for women's emancipation' (1983, 124). In distinction to academics who are content with disinterested intellectual contemplation, those that gather around feminism have some political hopes; some motivating agenda beyond scholarship for scholarship's sake. While the social sciences have developed practices of militant co-research, the use of these frameworks in the humanities is less common. We can ask ourselves: what does my analysis of this cultural text do besides furthering my CV and/or tenure dossier? Does my inquiry support any community or group in their struggle for liberation and justice? Rather than consider what a project offers to a specific discipline, we can consider what kind of research inquiry helps us sort out how to live and fight in this particular historical moment. Feminists in the university can bring a discerning eye to the relationship between what we do for an employer and for wider forms of social struggle.

Secondly, we can honour the key role played by experiential learning in developing our capacities as researchers and feminists. While the university prizes and commodifies the delivery of didactic teaching, the classroom is not where we will learn our most important lessons. Potent forms of learning tend to be experiential – the learning that comes from the experience of trying something. As we fumble through it, the process of doing research sharpens our skills as thinkers and writers. Writing expansively about the research process, Mies sketches out the number of forms feminist knowledge can take, including:

> practical, everyday knowledge, political knowledge and political 'skills', self-recognition (insight into one's own strengths and weaknesses), critical knowledge (the ability to critique ideologies, to demystify)... social knowledge (the ability to relate to others, to recognize social conditions and develop social relationships with 'others'...)
>
> *(1991, 77)*

We can value these forms of knowledge-from-below alongside the authorised knowledge of the academy.

Resisting the gravitational pull within academic writing towards individualism and careerism, feminist methods can teach us to ground our work within relational processes. Rather than dissociating from social life, we can approach research as something we do with and for others. Instead of framing our arguments as solo-authored contributions, we can make our relational worlds visible within our writing. Feminists can approach research as an act of devotion to the movements and relationships that inform our thinking. In this way, we aim our research beyond the assignments that the university gives us and the patriarchal social relations of this hellbent world.

Acknowledgements

This chapter is dedicated to Joellen Meglin, who subtly instilled in me a more feminist approach to research, and to Irena Smoluchowski, who helped me sort out my relationship to the university among other things.

References

Ackerly, Brooke A., and Jacqui True. 2020. *Doing Feminist Research in Political and Social Science.* London: Red Globe Press.
Ahmed, Sara. 2016. *Living a Feminist Life.* Durham: Duke University Press.
Anzaldúa, Gloria. 1987. *Borderlands/La Frontera: The New Mestiza.* San Francisco: Aunt Lute Books.
Bannerji, Himani, Linda Carty, Kari Dehli, Susan Heald, and Kate McKenna. 1992. *Unsettling Relations: The University as a Site of Feminist Struggles.* Boston: South End Press.

Bizzell, Patricia. 2000. "Feminist Methods of Research in the History of Rhetoric: What Difference Do They Make?" *Rhetoric Society Quarterly* 30 (4): 5–17.

Carpenter, Sara, and Shahrzad Mojab. 2017. *Revolutionary Learning: Marxism, Feminism and Knowledge.* London: Pluto Press.

Collins, Patricia Hill. 2000. *Black Feminist Thought: Knowledge, Consciousness, and the Politics of Empowerment.* New York: Routledge.

DeVault, Marjorie L., and Glenda Gross. 2012. "Feminist Qualitative Interviewing: Experience, Talk, and Knowledge." In *Handbook of Feminist Research: Theory and Praxis*, edited by Sharlene Nagy Hesse-Biber, Second Edition, 206–36. Thousand Oaks: SAGE Publications.

Echols, Alice. 1989. *Daring to Be Bad: Radical Feminism in America, 1967–1975.* Minneapolis: University of Minnesota Press.

Fonow, Mary Margaret, and Judith A. Cook, eds. 1991. *Beyond Methodology: Feminist Scholarship as Lived Research.* Bloomington: Indiana University Press.

Harding, Sandra G., ed. 2004. *The Feminist Standpoint Theory Reader: Intellectual and Political Controversies.* New York: Routledge.

Hartsock, Nancy C. M. 1998. *The Feminist Standpoint Revisited, And Other Essays.* Boulder: Westview Press.

Hesse-Biber, Sharlene Nagy, ed. 2012. "Feminist Research: Exploring, Interrogating, and Transforming the Interconnections of Epistemology, Methodology, and Method." In *Handbook of Feminist Research: Theory and Praxis*, Second Edition, 2–26. Thousand Oaks: SAGE Publications.

James, Selma. 2012. *Sex, Race and Class—The Perspective of Winning: A Selection of Writings 1952–2011.* Oakland: PM Press.

Jordan, June. 2003. "Report from the Bahamas, 1982." *Meridians* 3 (2): 6–16. https://doi.org/10.1215/15366936-3.2.6.

Letherby, Gayle. 2003. *Feminist Research in Theory and Practice.* Philadelphia: Open University Press.

Lewis, Gail. 2013. "Animating Hatreds: Research Encounters, Organizational Secrets, Emotional Truths." In *Secrecy and Silence in the Research Process: Feminist Reflections*, edited by Roisin Ryan-Flood and Rosalind Gill, 211–27. New York: Routledge.

Lorde, Audre. 2007. *Sister Outsider: Essays and Speeches.* Berkeley: Crossing Press.

Lorde, Audre. 2009. "I Am Your Sister: Black Women Organizing Across Sexualities." In *I Am Your Sister: Collected and Unpublished Writings of Audre Lorde*, edited by Rudolph P. Byrd, Johnnetta Betsch Cole, and Beverly Guy-Sheftall, 57–63. New York: Oxford University Press.

Mies, Maria. 1983. "Towards a Methodology for Feminist Research." In *Theories of Women's Studies*, edited by Gloria Bowles and Renate Duelli Klein, 117–39. Boston: Routledge.

Mies, Maria. 1991. "Women's Research or Feminist Research? The Debate Surrounding Feminist Science and Methodology." In *Beyond Methodology: Feminist Scholarship as Lived Research*, edited by Mary Margaret Fonow and Judith A. Cook, 60–84. Bloomington: Indiana University Press.

Mohanty, Chandra Talpade. 2003. "'Under Western Eyes' Revisited: Feminist Solidarity through Anticapitalist Struggles." *Signs: Journal of Women in Culture and Society* 28 (2): 499–535. https://doi.org/10.1086/342914.

Moraga, Cherríe, and Gloria Anzaldúa, eds. 1983. *This Bridge Called My Back: Writings by Radical Women of Color.* New York: Kitchen Table, Women of Color Press.

Naples, Nancy A. 2003. *Feminism and Method: Ethnography, Discourse Analysis, and Activist Research.* New York: Routledge.

Potts, Tracey, and Janet Price. 1995. "'Out of the Blood and Spirit of Our Lives': The Place of the Body in Academic Feminism." In *Feminist Academics: Creative Agents for Change*, edited by Louise Morley and Val Walsh, 102–15. New York: Taylor & Francis.

Reger, Jo. 2020. "What's So Feminist about Archival Research?" In *Feminist Research in Practice*, edited by Maura Kelly and Barbara Gurr, 97–100. Lanham: Rowman & Littlefield.

Rich, Adrienne. 1978. "Transcendental Etude." In *The Dream of a Common Language: Poems 1974–1977*. New York: W. W. Norton & Company.

Spelman, Elizabeth V. 1988. *Inessential Woman: Problems of Exclusion in Feminist Thought*. Boston: Beacon Press.

Sprague, Joey. 2005. *Feminist Methodologies for Critical Researchers: Bridging Differences*. Lanham: Rowman & Littlefield.

Stacey, Judith. 1988. "Can There Be a Feminist Ethnography?" *Women's Studies International Forum* 11 (1): 21–27. https://doi.org/10.1016/0277-5395(88)90004-0.

INDEX

abangan 53
able-bodied 123
Abrams, M. H. 89, 90, 151
abstract masculinity 208
academic audit culture 191, 194
academic history 147
academic prose 211
Ackerly, Brooke 163, 171
Acquired Sex and Intersex Status
  (ASIS) bill 31
Ahmed, Saifuddin 168
Ahmed, Sara 89, 91,209, 212
Ali, Kazim 83
Allen-Collinson, Jacquelyn 133
alt-academia 193
American Historical Association
  147, 155
American legal system 6
American Political Science Association
  (APSA) 160, 161
Andreassen, Rikke 104
Androgen Insensitivity Syndrome
  (AIS) 35
Anglophone world-literature 119
Anzaldúa, Gloria 208, 214
archival empathy 146
archival fetishism 147
archival work 11
Arthur, Stone 89
Athena Swan (AS) 200
audit trail 198
Australian Capital Territory 42

autoethnodrama 32
autoethnography 99, 100, 129,
  132–134, 199

Back, Les 199
Ball, Stephen 199
Ball, Stephen J. 200
becoming strongwoman, case study
  129–131; auto/ethnographic
  approach 131–132; embodiment
  135–136; embracing emotion 133–
  135; empowerment debate 138–140;
  strongwoman identity 136–138
Berbary, Lisbeth 32
Berg, Anne-Jorunn 102, 103
Berg, Maggie 192
Berlant, Lauren 191
Bhabha, Homi 17
Bilge, Sirma 4, 6
Bilski, Gwynne 88
Bissell, David 70
Bizzell, Patricia 207
Black Feminism Reimagined (Nash) 181
Black Lives Matter 16
Black/Trans* Studies approach 31
Bochner, Arthur 134
bodily empowerment 138
Bookerscape 114
'box-ticking' exercise 198, 201
Braidotti, Rosi 52
Breeze, Maddie 130, 191
Brenner, Johanna 118

222 Index

Bright Felon (Ali) 83
British Labour Party 151
British Transport Police (BTP) 9, 66, 73
Buckley, Michelle 67
Bunsell, Tanya 130, 138
Burke, Tarana 49
business process outsourcing 117, 124

call-centre fiction 117
Carastathis, Anna 182
Carby, Hazel 5–6
Carpenter, Sara 208
Carr, E. H. 147
Carter, Erica 100
Caswell, Michelle 146
Cifor, Marika 146
City Challenge programme 23
close reading 176, 177, 186; feminist
    pedagogy 184–186; methodology
    177–179; reading feminist stories
    179–184
Cob, Ellen Pinkos 48
collaboration 8, 10, 86, 95
collective memory work 105
collective-reflexivity 199
colonial discourse 49
composite characters 37–38
consciousness-raising process 208
Cook, Judith A. 194, 208, 213
Cooke, Jennifer 1, 10
Cooke, Miriam 52
Copp, Martha 133
Corfield, Penny 149
corporatization 195
Crastnopol, Margaret 193
Crawford, June 100, 101
creative methods 9; casting 38–41;
    composite characters 37–38;
    ethnodrama and ethics 32–35;
    ethnodrama as prefigurative acts 41–
    42; queer methodological approach
    30–31; setting the scene 31
Crenshaw, Kimberlé W. 4, 6–8, 21, 30,
    131, 161, 176, 181–183
crime prevention 73
critical feminist theory 183
critical reading 178, 179
Crossley, Nick 136
cruel optimism 191
Culley, Margo 185

Danish care leavers 108
Davidoff, Leonore 149

Davie, Grace 53
Davin, Anna 1485
Davis, Angela 26
Deckard, Sharae 116, 118, 119
decolonial reflexivity 197
decolonisation 169, 171
DeGeneres, Ellen 33
Delgado, Daryll 115, 125
Depo-Provera 19, 152
DeVault, Marjorie L. 208
Dever, Maryanne 152
Dharma Wanita 55
disciplinary reflexivity 195
Djoyoprawiro, Sulami 57
Dolan, Kathleen 167
Doorn-Harder, Nelly van 55
double colonisation 125
Doucet, Andrea 193, 198, 200
Dungy, Camille 84
Duterte, Rodrigo 125
Dworkin, Shari L. 135, 139

Echols, Alice 209
ecological writing 79–96
eco-poetry 82, 83
Edensor, Tim 68
Electronic Information and
    Transactions (ITE Law) 50
Ellis, Carolyn 134
Elthaway, Mona 51
embodied intersectionality: Black
    feminist activism, post-colonial
    racist order 16–20; buzzword to
    20–23; intersectional feminist
    methodologies and methods 25–27;
    Muslim women's agency and
    resistance 23–25; quilting feminist
    life 13–16
emotional reflexivity 213, 214
empowerment 138, 139
Enloe, Cynthia 151
equality, diversity and inclusion (EDI)
    20, 181, 187, 196
ethnodrama 29, 32–35; Narrator 37; as
    prefigurative acts 41–42
ethnography 26, 129, 132
evidence-based policing (EBP) 72
experience writing 105

familial care 123
female bodybuilding 138, 139
*Female Sexualization: A Collective
    Work of Memory* (Carter) 100

Index **223**

femininity rules 139
feminist curiosity 151
feminist historiography 145, 148
feminist history 146–148, 154–156
feminist methodologies 148, 151, 152, 154, 206; developing emotional reflexivity within research process 212–216; learning about oneself and others 209–210; methodological implications 216–217; starting from one's experience principle 207–209; staying aware of institutional context 211–212
'Feminist Methodologies Symposium' 106
feminist reflexive sensibility 189; cultivation 197–200; intersectionality and decolonial reflexivity 196–197; neoliberal academy and its harms 190–194; in social research 194–196
feminist solidarity 154
feminist standpoint theory 64, 69
feminist survey research: decolonizing survey research 169–171; feminist epistemologies 165–169; intersectional approach 164–165; limitations and possibilities 163–164
fiction 9, 48, 114
fictional organisations 33
Filipino fiction 117, 118
Filipino literature 117, 120
Finding a Voice (Wilson) 14
Fonow, Mary Margaret 194, 208, 213
Frankland, Emma 39
Freeman, Elizabeth 184
Freeman, Jo 209
friendship 133
functional reflexivity 195

Gallop, Jane 176
Gay and Lesbian Alliance Against Defamation (GLAAD) 36
Gendered Lives Research Group 1
gender history 145, 147
Gender Recognition Act 2004 (GRA) 31, 42
Gender Recognition Reform (Scotland) Bill (GRR) 31, 42
gender reversal techniques 106
genocide in Indonesia 58
geography 27
'Georgia Safe Schools Coalition' 104

Gill, Rosalind 191
glass ceiling 135, 139, 140
Global Anglophone writing 119
Global North 152, 168, 169, 171, 190
Global South 48–49, 52, 58, 114, 151, 168, 171
Goffman, Erving 136
Goode, Jackie 106, 107, 109, 110
Gordon, Avery 198
Gouweloos, Julie 41
Grant, Barbara 199
'greater Romantic lyric' 89
Griffin, Gabriele 177
Gross, Glenda 208
gross domestic product (GDP) 117
The Ground Aslant (Tarlo) 81

Hall, Catherine 147, 149, 154, 156
Hall, Rebecca Jane 118
Halsaa, Beatrice 52
Hancock, Ange-Marie 4, 5, 161, 165, 166
Haraway, Donna 65, 69
Harding, Sandra 64
Hart, Judith 153
Hartsock, Nancy 208
Haug, Frigga 99, 100, 111
Hemmings, Clare 180–181, 183, 184
Heryanto, Ariel 56, 57
heterosexual desirability 139
Hidden From History (Rowbotham) 149
Highmore, Ben 67
Hill Collins, Patricia 3, 4, 6, 7, 134, 161, 182, 190, 196, 211
Hinden, Rita 151
historical method 146–147
historicism 146
hooks, bell 5, 27, 154
Houlden, Kate 118
Humphrey, Harvey 9

imposter syndrome 191
independent social reality 64
Indian Register 169
Indonesian Communist Party (PKI) 54
inductive criticism 178
Institute for Advanced Studies in the Humanities (IASH) 84, 86
Institute of Fiscal Studies (IFS) 16
'The Institute Project on Decoloniality 2021–2024' 85
institutional peacocking 200
International Booker Prize 114
international relations (IR) 151

224 Index

intersectional feminism 47, 49, 145, 146, 177
intersectionality 4–9, 64, 131, 161–166, 176, 181–183, 185–187, 196, 209
Intersectionality as Critical Social Theory (Hill Collins) 182
intersectional methods 210
intersectional originalism 181, 183

James, Selma 211
Jensen, Stine Grønbæk 108, 109
Johnson, Amber 134, 137
Johnson, Corey 104
Johnston, Karen 200
Jordan, June 209
Jordan-Zachery, Julia S. 164
Jose, Adelaimar Arias 115, 122, 125

Kapil, Bhanu 88
Kipfer, Stefan 67
Kleinman, Sherryl 133
Knights, Ben 177, 183
knowledge 64, 71, 134
Kristiansen, Elsa 140

landscape poetry 10, 81, 82
Laslett, Barbara 118
'Lavender Menace' 36
'Lavender Scare' 36
Ledbury Poetry Critics Programme 85
Lefebvre, Henri 63, 67–68
Letherby, Gayle 213
Lewis, Gail 209, 215
Lewis, Sian 9
LGBTI community 39, 40
LGBTI organisations 33
Lohman, Kirsty 41
London Underground network 10, 63–66, 68–71, 73, 74
'looking glass self' 136
Lorde, Audre 210, 214
Loukaitou-Sideris, Anastasia 65

Madrid-Morales, Dani 168
male gaze 135
Marching, Soe Tjen 9
Marcus, George E. 197
marginalisation 32
Marte-Wood, Alden Sajor 117
Marxist theory 118
masculine 136, 138
Mason-Bish, Hannah 65
Mauthner, Natasha S. 200

May, Tim 195
May, Vivian 181
McCall, Leslie 165, 166
McGrath, Ann 149
memory work 10, 98, 110; as collaborative research method 102–105; at international feminist research conference 106–110; intersectional feminist pedagogy 105–106; origins and developments 98–100; in practice 100–102
#MeToo movement in Indonesia 9, 47, 50–53, 58; atheist woman 57–58; publicity boost of White celebrities 49–50; secularism *versus* Islam 53–56; struggles of women survivors before #MeToo 56–57
micro-traumas 189, 193
Mienczakowski, Jim 32
Mies, Maria 212, 216, 217
mimic men *see* Bhabha, Homi
Mirza, Heidi Safia 182
modern Euro-America 155
Mohanty, Chandra Talpade 211
Mojab, Shahrzad 208
Mojares, Resil B. 115
Moosavi, Leon 197
Moraga, Cherríe 208
Moriarty, Jess 193, 199
Morrison, Toni 23
Mosedale, Sarah 138
Moulton, R. G. 178
Mulvey, Laura 135
Mutia Eusebio, Jen 115
Myong, Lene 104

Najmabadi, Afsaneh 155
Nan Shepherd Prize 85
Naples, Nancy 213
Nash, Catherine 30
Nash, Jennifer 176, 177, 179, 181–186
National Front 16
National Women's Studies Association 214
neoliberalism 199
Neumann, Birgit 119
neutrality 178, 171
New Cross Massacre 16
Newman, Hannah 10
New Ohio Review 89, 92
New Order 54, 57
Nicholls, Ruth 196, 198
Nicholson, Helen 178

Index **225**

Nisa, Eva 51, 52
non-white/lacking 104
Norway 103, 130
Notting Hill Carnival 16
Nuffield Foundation 26
Nuril, Baiq 50, 51
Nyhagen, Line 52, 105, 106, 109, 110, 111n2

O'Brien, Diana Z. 164
Ohio Women's Rights Convention in 1851 4, 20
Orchids XOXO 32, 35
Organisation of Women of African and Asian Descent (OWAAD) 5, 16, 18
originalism 181, 182
Our Time is a Garden 84, 85
Owens, Patricia 151
Owton, Helen 133

paradigm shift 7
Parents, Families and Friends of Lesbians and Gays (PFLAG) 36
Parry, Benita 116
Pawestri, Tunggal 48
peaceful demonstration 168
Pearce, Ruth 41
Pedersen, Susan 147, 155
Pengkhianatan G30S/PKI 55
performance-enhancing drug (PED) 140
Perry, Beth 195
personal experience 9
personal reflexivity 195
Peterson, Kirsten Holst 125
Philippine National Book Award 115
Philippine reproductive fiction 117
Philippines 114–115; capitalist world-system 115–119; literary production 115–119; reading of short stories 122–125; short story and women writers 119–122
Pillow, Wanda 197
Pirmohamed, Alycia 8, 10
political engagement 168
political knowledge 167
political science 10, 160–162; research 163, 164, 166; scholarship 160
political scientists 151, 160–162
political thought 151
Portuges, Catherine 185
Potts, Tracey 211
Price, Janet 211

Racial inequality 25, 26
Ramazanoğlu, Caroline 3, 30
Ranke, Leopold von 146
Real Health Experience (RHE) 32–35
Real Life Experience (RLE) 33, 35
recursive process 102
reflection process 194–195
reflexivity 190, 192–195, 201
Reger, Jo 213
'Rehearsing Life' (Jose) 115, 122, 124, 125
Reid-Musson, Emily 67
Research Excellence Framework (REF) 192
rhythmanalysis 63, 64, 67, 68
Rich, Adrienne 207
Riley, Charlotte 10, 11
Riley, Denise 147, 150
Rippl, Gabriele 119
Robinson, Emily 153
Robinson, Victoria 130
Rodriguez, Robyn Magalit 117
Roen, Katrina 30
Rose, Richard 151
Rowbotham, Sheila 149
Royal Historical Society (RHS) 153, 155, 156
Russell-Mundine, Gabrielle 197
Rutherford, Anna 125

Saldaña, Johnny 32
'Salve' (Delgado) 115, 122, 124
santri 53
#sayajuga 48
Scotland 42, 85, 153
Scott, Joan Wallach 147, 150
Scottish BPOC Writers Network 86
'Scree' project 87–93, 95
secularism 52, 58
Seeber, Barbara 192
self-reflexivity 137
sexual harassment on public transport 63; feminist epistemologies 64–66; London Underground 67–69; police's situatedness and rhythms 71–73; research context and method 66–67; rhythmanalysis 67–69; women's situatedness and rhythms 69–71
Shapiro, Stephen 116, 119
Shilling, Chris 130
Showalter, Elaine 179, 182

226 Index

Sing, Anneliese 104
Sisjord, Mari 140
situated knowledges 65, 73, 74
slowing down strategy 194
The Slow Professor (Berg and Seeber) 192
Smith, Brett 133
Smith, Tuhiwai Linda 3–4
social reproduction 118
Sojourner Truth 20
Southall Black Sisters 5
Spare Rib magazine 152
Sparkes, Andrew 133
speeding up 189, 194
Spelman, Elizabeth 210
Spender, Dale 152
Sprague, Joey 208
Stacey, Judith 210
standpoint methodology 208
standpoint theory 63, 65, 69
Stanley, Liz 65
Stauffer, Katelyn E. 164
Strange Encounters (Ahmed) 89
Strauss, Kendra 67
strength athletics 130
The Sun Magazine 84

Tamboukou, Maria 68
Tanyag, Maria 117
Tarlo, Harriet 81, 82
technopreneur 191
'Theory Revolt' collective 147
This Bridge Called My Back (Anzaldúa and Moraga) 208
Thomlinson, Natalie 148
Thorpe, Holly 67
Tillmann-Healy, Lisa 133
time sickness 192
Tosh, John 149
Tower Hamlets 23, 24, 26
traditional literary criticism 183
'Transcendental Étude' (Rich) 207
Transport for London (TfL) 66
triple oppression 5
True, Jacqui 163, 206
Truth, Sojourner 4, 150
Turner Syndrome 35

UK-based Warwick Research Collective (WReC) 116
UN International Women's conference 152
United Kingdom (UK) 6, 18, 19, 29, 31, 41–43, 63, 85, 129, 145, 149, 189, 193
United Nation's (UN) Fourth World Conference on Women 5
United States (US) 4, 20, 119, 138, 149, 160, 167, 209, 214
University and College Union (UCU) 193
UN's World Conference Against Racism 5
urban cyclical time 68

The Vertical Interrogation of Strangers (Kapil) 89

Walby, Sylvia 64
Walkowitz, Rebecca 119
Wallerstein, Immanuel 116, 118
Weinstein, Harvey 49
Welch, Susan 161
Welsh, Sandy 65
Westside Group of Chicago 209
Widerberg, Karin 105
Widodo, Joko 56
Wilkinson, Sue 195, 199
Wilson, Amrit 14
Wilton, Demi 10
women's empowerment 138
women's history 145, 149, 150, 154
women's liberation movement (WLM) 145, 148
Wood, Dominic 72
World Professional Association for Transgender Health (WPATH) 34
World Values Surveys 168

Yarrow, Emily 200
Young, Hannah 150
Young, Iris Marion 135

Zempi, Irene 65

Printed in the United States
by Baker & Taylor Publisher Services